AN INVINCIBLE SUMMER

AN INVINCIBLE SUMMER
FEMALE DIASPORAN AUTHORS

TOMMIE LEE JACKSON

Africa World Press, Inc.

P.O. Box 1892
Trenton, NJ 08607

P.O. Box 18
Asmara, ERITREA

Africa World Press, Inc.

P.O. Box 1892
Trenton, NJ 08607

P.O. Box 48
Asmara, ERITREA

Cover design: Ashraful Haque
Book design: Wanjiku Ngugi

Library of Congress Cataloging-in-Publication Data

Jackson, Tommie Lee.
    An invincible summer: female diasporan authors / by Tommie Lee Jackson.
        p. cm.
    Includes Bibliographical references and index.
    ISBN 0-86543-823-4 -- ISBN 0-86543-824-2 (pbk.)
        1. American literature--Afro-American authors--History and criticism.
    2. American literature--Women authors--History and criticism 3. Caribbean
    literature (English)--Black authors--History and criticism. 4. Caribbean
    literature (English)--Women authors--History and criticism. 5. Caribbean
    literature (English) African influences. 6. Women and literature--English
    speaking countries. 7. American literature--African influences. 8. English
    literature--African influences. 9. Women and literature--United States. 10.
    Abandoned children in literature. 11. Loss (Psychology) in literature. 12.
    Betrayal in literature. I. Title.

PS153.N5 J39 2000
810.9'9287'08996073--dc21   99-059962

PERMISSIONS

as follows: *Le Malentendu Suivi de Caligula* (Paris: Gallimard, 1944); *L'Etat de Siège* (Paris: Gallimard, 1948); *Les Justes* (Paris: Gallimard, 1950.) Reprinted by permission of Knopf.

Extracts from *The Rebel: An Essay on Man in Revolt,* by Albert Camus. Trans. Anthony Bower. (New York: Alfred A. Knopf, 1956.) Copyright © 1956 Knopf. Originally published in French as *L'Homme Révolté* (Paris: Gallimard, 1951.) Reprinted by permission of Knopf.

Extracts from *Jonah's Gourd Vine,* by Zora Neale Hurston. (New York: HarperCollins, 1934.) Copyright © 1934 Zora Neale Hurston. Copyright renewed © 1962 John C. Hurston. Reprinted by permission of HarperCollins.

An early version of "Orphanage in Simone Schwarz-Bart's *The Bridge of Beyond* and Alice Walker's *The Third Life of Grange Copeland"* appeared in the fall, 1996, issue of *The Griot.* I am grateful to the Editor of *The Griot,* Andrew Baskin, for permission to reprint the material.

To Kofi Ulysses

CONTENTS

ACKNOWLEDGMENTS

I thank the following professional colleagues who read and commented on one or more draft chapters, thus improving my eyeview of the manuscript: Professors Andrew Baskin, Berea College; Lillian Corti, University of Alaska at Fairbanks; and Nike Lawal, St. Cloud State University.

I thank as well the students at St. Cloud State University who have enrolled in my classes over the years; my dialogue with the students has contributed to my deeper understanding of Diasporic literature.

I thank the Editorial Department of Africa World Press; their careful perusal of the manuscript improved its accuracy.

Finally, I thank my beloved son Kofi Ulysses Bofah; his being is a source of great joy.

INTRODUCTION

The reference by Alice Walker to Bessie Head in *The Temple of My Familiar* as a chronicler of her people's history, "It is only because Bessie Head sits there in the desert, in her little hut, writing, that we have knowledge of a way of life that flowed for thousands of years, which would otherwise be missing from human record" (178), and her identification by Walker in *In Search of Our Mothers' Gardens* of influential works, such as Buchi Emecheta's *Second-Class Citizen* and Bessie Head's *Maru,* attest to her familiarity with the literature of a wide range of African women authors. Not only has Walker identified elsewhere Bessie Head, in addition to Camara Laye and Ayi Kwei Armah, as among her "favorite uncelebrated foreign writers" (Eilersen 289), but she has proclaimed the vision of Bessie Head "trustworthy, her wisdom there to lean on, to borrow from, and to remember" (qtd. in Eilersen 167).

Albeit Walker does not mention Mariama Bâ's novel *So Long a Letter* in her collection of critical essays *In Search of Our Mothers' Gardens,* her Pulitzer Prize-winning novel *The Color Purple,* in its epistolary style, bears a striking resemblance to Bâ's *So Long a Letter.* Indeed, Gay Alden Wilentz in her recently published dissertation, *Binding Cultures: Black Women Writers in Africa and the Diaspora (1992),* contends that the unvarnished style of Celie's letters, which are written in dialect, and Celie's recently-acquired literacy give to *The Color Purple* the quality of the spoken word, or orature. Moreover, Wilentz asserts that the infusion by Alice Walker, Toni Morrison, and Paule Marshall of folktales and legends into their literature and their use of family stories as the basis for their novels further align them with African women authors Ama Ata Aidoo, Flora Nwapa, and Efua Sutherland whose works commonly feature folktales that teach compliance with African traditions and socialize youth to their respective communities (5-10).

Wilentz's recently published dissertation represents ground-breaking research in that it is one of a limited number of critical resources that analyze comparative influences among female African American and African authors. Another valuable resource is the work by Karla F.C. Holloway, *Moorings and Metaphors: Figures of Culture and Gender in Black Women's Literature* (Rutgers UP, 1992), whose publication, along with Wilentz's book, led Scott Heller in his 3 June 1992 article for the *Chronicle of Higher Education* to declare an "explosion of interest in Afro-American writers [that] has broadened to take in the works of black writing in Africa and the Caribbean" (A 8).

SIGNIFICANCE

The acknowledgement by some female African American authors, such as Alice Walker and Toni Morrison, of the influence of African literature on their craft attests to the need for more comparative research on female African and African American authors. In a 1983 interview with Kay Bonetti, Toni Morrison spoke of having "no technical models for the kind of writing [she] wanted to do," writing which would have an "artlessness and non-book quality," until she discovered works by African authors that were "loose, unstructured, and sounded like someone was telling a story." Philip Page in his work *Dangerous Freedom: Fusion and Fragmentation in Toni Morrison's Novels* contends that the circularity of *Beloved* is reflective of the African storytelling tradition that relies upon digressions and repetitiveness for newness of effect (142). Furthermore, the scarcity of criticism on African women authors suggests that more critical attention needs to be paid to these authors. Carole Boyce Davies had the following to say about the scant treatment of works by Black women authors from other parts of the world, writers such as Merle Collins, Joan Riley, Beryl Gilroy, Grace Nichols, and others:

> [T]he work of Black women writing in Britain has to be significantly addressed. For here is a whole dynamic of Black women's writing which matches in intensity the output of Black women writing in the United States yet is not considered part of the ongoing discussions of this field unless a critic herself, as did Hazel Carby or Rhonda Cobham,

migrates from Europe to the US. . . . Writings by writers
like Merle Collins, Joan Riley, Beryl Gilroy, Grace Nichols
get little exposure in the US. (33)

The study *An Invincible Summer: Female Diasporan Authors*
serves a two-fold purpose: first, it contributes to the small, but
growing, body of comparative research on African American, African, and Caribbean authors; and, second, it augments in general
the feminist criticism on Black women authors.

BACKGROUND

Katherine Frank in her article "Feminist Criticism and the African
Novel" has eschewed the "question-begging stylistic approach" to
feminist criticism wherein the author largely rails against the ste-
reotypical portrayals of the female characters. Classifying the ste-
reotypical approach as "dead-ended" because the critic concen-
trates on the "inferior literary works or on the flawed aspects of
successful ones" (37), Frank proposes instead an archetypal approach to feminist criticism. One example cited of the archetypal
approach to feminist criticism is Sandra M. Gilbert and Susan
Gubar's *The Madwoman in the Attic: The Woman Writer and the
Nineteenth-Century Literary Imagination* (38). Gilbert and Gubar
identify images of enclosure, as well as an obsession with madness, suicide, ghosts, and doubles—states of being which mirror
the suppression of their own lives and their desire for escape—as
common to female authors of the nineteenth century. Gilbert and
Gubar write in the Preface to *The Madwoman in the Attic:*

> Both in life and in art, we saw, the artists we studied were
> literally and figuratively confined. Enclosed in the archi-
> tecture of an overwhelmingly male-dominated society, these
> literary women were also, inevitably, trapped in the spe-
> cifically literary constructs of what Gertrude Stein was to
> call "patriarchal poetry." For not only did a nineteenth cen-
> tury woman writer have to inhabit ancestral mansions (or
> cottages) owned and built by men, she was also constricted
> and restricted by the Palaces of Art and Houses of Fiction
> male writers authored. We decided, therefore, that the strik-
> ing coherence we noticed in literature by women could be
> explained by a common, female impulse to struggle free

from social and literary confinement through strategic re-
definitions of self, art, and society. (xi-xii)

According to Katherine Frank, archetypal criticism has a dual function: it imparts to readers the authors' "vision of what it means to
be a woman in a particular environment" and it gives readers "insight into a writer's artistic gifts—the way in which she transforms
experience into art by creating telling and effective symbols, images, and metaphors for her vision" (39).

There is evidence that critics have heeded the call by Frank for
African criticism that is both descriptive and valuative. Florence
Stratton's article "The Shallow Grave: Archetypes of Female Experience in African Fiction" is one example. Stratton argues that
the prevalence of the images of enclosure and escape in the fiction
of writers such as Mariama Bâ, Buchi Emecheta, Bessie Head,
Rebeka Njau, Flora Nwapa, and Grace Ogot is suggestive of "the
possibility of there being a female literary tradition that transcends
all cultural boundaries" (97). On Rama's confinement in Mariama
Bâ's *So Long a Letter* after the death of her husband Modou Fall,
Stratton writes:

> Ramatoulaye writes her letter during the four months and
> ten days of secluded mourning prescribed by Islam for wid-
> ows. In this Islamic practice, Bâ found her archetypal im-
> age of female experience. . . . Ramatoulaye's physical con-
> finement during this period of mourning in the house she
> once shared with Modou replicates her psychological con-
> finement in a debilitating stereotypical view of a woman's
> role. (114)

In addition to images of enclosure and escape, one might identify
another image replicated in the fiction of some African American,
African, and Caribbean authors, namely, that of abandonment, a
state of being descriptive of the socio-historical and existential dimensions of literature of the Diaspora.

INSPIRATION
The inspiration for the study is Mbye B. Cham's article "Contemporary Society and the Female Imagination: A Study of the Novels

of Mariama Bâ" wherein Cham analyzed the theme of abandonment in the literature of Mariama Bâ. Although Cham recognized the existence of the theme in other literature by African American and African women authors, he stopped short of a treatment of its development in the literature, considering such a comprehensive analysis beyond the scope of his article: "In detailing the nature and implications of this universal feminine cry on the African soil, both [of Mariama Bâ's] novels explore at the same time a dominant issue whose persistent recurrence in recent years in the works of African and Afro-American female writers, in particular, is somewhat disproportionate to the volume and quality of its treatment in the critical literature" (89).

Cham had defined abandonment in his article as "a social disease. . . , the cumulative result of a process that could be referred to as the gradual opening and enlargement of the emotional/sexual circle that originally binds two partners (a husband and a wife) to introduce and accommodate a third partner (a second wife) in a manner so devious and deceptive that a new process is set in motion" (92). For the purposes of this study, abandonment not only becomes a metaphor for female oppression, but for the diasporic condition of blacks, the condition of the elderly, as well as for man's existential condition in an indifferent universe. The study therefore extends Cham's analysis; that is, it examines the thematic links in selected works by female African American, African, and Caribbean authors.

METHODOLOGY

An examination of the aforementioned literary works not only shows the cross fertilization of fictional content among female African American, African, and Caribbean authors, as evidenced in chapter three in a discussion of Hurston's *Jonah's Gourd Vine,* but likewise with French existentialist thought. Since the literature of a people is inextricably linked to their culture and history, as Wilentz has noted in her work, an interdisciplinary approach is warranted in a study of fiction: "Moreover, the task of exploring works of cultures suppressed by the dominant culture needs an interdisciplinary approach to criticism, an examination of the literature's historicity and social significance, attention to its oral/folkloric inheritance, and an understanding of the writer's commitment to reflect and often reform the culture that the literature represents" (xiii).

THE TITLE OF THE WORK

The title "An Invincible Summer" is taken from the essay "Return to Tipasa," by Albert Camus. Camus had returned to the rain-drenched Algiers, "the city of summer," at the age of forty in order to experience again the beauty of his Algerian homeland. He had returned, however, during the month of December, and the city was besieged with rain: "But the summer city herself had been emptied of her laughter and offered me only bent and shiny backs" (195). A reprieve from the rain had come nonetheless, and Camus was able to re-visit Tipasa, where he saw again the mountain Chenoua that bordered the bay of Tipasa and the ruins at Tipasa, located a few feet from the sea. There amidst the ruins at Tipasa, Camus re-discovered his harbor; also, in the middle of winter, he "discovered that there was in me an invincible summer" (202).

Camus's sojourn to Tipasa is analogous to the reprieve of Sisyphus from his rock. Encapsulated in the mythic hero Sisyphus is the existentialist ethic of the exigency of grace in the face of futile suffering. Because of his defiance of the gods, Sisyphus was condemned for perpetuity to roll a boulder up a steep hill, only to have it roll down again once he had reached the summit. However, Camus imagines Sisyphus happy during his descent. To be sure, it has been "that breathing space" during his descent that has produced the consciousness, namely, that "There is no sun without shadow" (123), that has made him transcendent of his rock (*Myth* 121).

The female Diasporan authors surveyed in this study—Mariama Bâ, Simone Schwarz-Bart, Buchi Emecheta, Beryl Gilroy, Zora Neale Hurston, Paule Marshall, Toni Morrison, and Alice Walker—are linked both by their collective use of the trope abandonment in their literature, symbolic of the diasporic condition of blacks, and by their existentialist depiction of characters who, in contrast with the bad faith of others before the void, are endowed with that "special grace" in the face of futile suffering.

WORKS CITED

Camus, Albert. *The Myth of Sisyphus and Other Essays.* Trans. Justin O'Brien. New York: Knopf, 1955. Originally published in French as *Le Mythe de Sisyphe* (Paris: Gallimard, 1942).

————. "Return to Tipasa." *The Myth of Sisyphus and Other Essays.* 195-204.

Cham, Mbye B. "Contemporary Society and the Female Imagination: A Study of the Novels of Mariama Bâ." In *Women in African Literature Today* 15. Ed. Eldred Durosimi Jones. Trenton: Africa World Press, 1987.

Davies, Carole Boyce. *Black Women, Writing and Identity: Migrations of the Subject.* London and New York: Routledge. 1994.

Eilersen, Gillian Stead. *Bessie Head Thunder Behind Her Ears: Her Life and Writing.* Portsmouth, NH: Heinemann, 1996.

Frank, Katherine."Feminist Criticism and the African Novel." *African Literature Today* 14 (1984): 34-48.

Gilbert, Sandra M.,and Susan Gubar. *The Madwoman in the Attic: The Woman Writer and the Nineteenth-Century Literary Imagination.* New Haven: Yale UP, 1979.

Heller, Scott. "Africa Diaspora Studies: Reconceptualizing Experiences of Blacks Worldwide." *Chronicle of Higher Education* 3 June 1992, sec. A: 7-8.

Holloway, Karla F.C. *Moorings & Metaphors: Figures of Culture and Gender in Black Women's Literature.* New Brunswick, New Jersey: Rutgers UP, 1992.

Morrison, Toni. Interview by Kay Bonetti. Columbia, Mo.: American Prose Library, 1983.

Page, Philip. *Dangerous Freedom: Fusion and Fragmentation in Toni Morrison's Novels.* Jackson: U of Mississippi P. 1995.

Stratton, Florence. "The Shallow Grave: Archetypes of Female Experience in African Fiction." *Emerging Perspectives on Buchi Emecheta.* Ed. Marie Umeh. Trenton: Africa World Press, 1966. 95-124. Originally published in *Research in African Literatures* 19, no. 1 (summer 1988): 143-69.

Walker, Alice. "From an Interview." In *In Search of Our Mothers' Gardens.* New York: Harcourt, 1983. 244-72.

————. *The Temple of My Familiar.* New York: Washington Square Press, 1989.

Wilentz, Gay Alden. *Binding Cultures: Black Women Writers in Africa and the Diaspora.* Bloomington: Indiana UP, 1992.

Chapter 1

THE ORIGINS OF THE DIVESTITURE TROPE IN SELECTED LITERATURE OF THE AFRICAN DIASPORA

In his work *History of the People of Trinidad and Tobago,* Eric Williams estimates that during the eighteenth and nineteenth centuries, at least 50,000,000 African slaves were exported to the Caribbean, Brazil, and the United States (30). The exports were to facilitate development in the New World. In the Caribbean, the exports were to replace the decimated group of Amerindian labourers, caused by slave trading among West Indian islands and massacres resultant from their revolt against Spanish conquest and Church sanctions (23-25), and to assist in the development of cash crops such as cocoa, sugar cane, cotton and indigo:

> In 1618, with the first report of the discovery of cocoa, the warning note was sounded that Trinidad would go the way of other West Indian islands. It was suggested that in order to develop the cocoa industry, 300 'pieces of slaves' should be sent to Trinidad, of whom two-thirds should be men and one-third women. (27)

The origins and fates of those who were brought to the new territories in the United States and who settled in the West Indies were similar. The Africans were sundered from their families and tribes in order to facilitate subjugation and to promote division. Eric Williams writes: "Deliberately divided to break up not only families but also tribes in order that they might more easily be ruled, the absence of a common language and the mixing up of different customs and cultural traits were further obstacles in their way" (37).

Due to this shared history, images abound in African American and West Indian literature of disinheritance and the ramifications of that disinheritance. In the article "How 'Bigger' Was Born," Richard Wright relates the genesis of his character Bigger Thomas: "Bigger is a product of a dislocated society; he is a dispossessed and disinherited man; he is all of this, and he lives amid the greatest possible plenty on earth and he is looking and feeling for a way out" (xx).

The abolition of slavery in the United States, which was coincident with the Emancipation Proclamation, issued on 1 January 1863, did not lead immediately to enfranchisement, as sixteen years later, in the aftermath of the Reconstruction era, Benjamin Brawley could write that "By 1879 conditions in the South had changed so much that Negroes were denied political recognition, were charged exorbitant prices by many merchants, were forced to pay excessive rents, and generally kept down in every possible way" (129).

By the same token, the emancipation of slaves in the West Indies did not lead to substantial improvement of their lot. Eric Williams notes that the Trinidadians, although declared free on 1 August 1833, had the dubious distinction of being "half slave, half free" (88); full emancipation was deferred until 1 August 1838. In the interim, Trinidadians had to work the plantations of their former masters as apprentices without any hope of themselves obtaining land given the decree that "it would be most injurious to the interest of the colony to dispose of any area smaller than 320 acres" (87). Williams concludes that

> It was the attempt to maintain the fictions in the British West Indies to prevent Negro land ownership, and to perpetuate the plantation economy by governmental action, the attempt in other words to interfere with the normal laws of supply and demand in the labour market and to prescribe the status of men who were in the same breath being called free, that gave rise to all the social troubles of the 19th century in the West Indies. (88-89)

Dissatisfaction with conditions in the Southern United States—

"mechanization of agriculture, general economic depression, reduction of cotton acreage, the depredation of the boll weevil and floods, and discriminatory agricultural programs" (Davis and Donaldson 53)—as well as the post-war boom which created a demand for labor in the Northern states, led to an exodus of approximately 500,000 blacks during 1915-18 (Brawley 171). George A. Davis and Fred Donaldson in their work *Blacks in the United States: A Geographic Perspective* refer to 1915 as the year of "the great migration": "It was this great migration that marked a significant change in the distribution of Blacks in the United States. Most, if not all, of this increase in the northern, urban black population originated in the rural areas of the South" (31). The major destinations of the black migrants were the gateway and the industrial cities of the North—Chicago, Detroit, St. Louis, and Kansas City (Davis and Donaldson 33). This massive "out-migration" produced in the North severe housing shortages as well as racial strife. Brawley writes that "In Pittsburgh and Philadelphia congestion in housing conditions became so great as to demand immediate attention. In more than one place moreover there were outbreaks in which lives were lost" (172). According to George A. Davis and O. Fred Donaldson, the North had its own brand of racism and "Negro jobs":

> There were two types of policy [in the North] with regard to the hiring of Blacks: one was to hire Blacks in menial positions, the other was to employ no Blacks at all. The vast majority of black men worked as porters, janitors, teamsters, chauffeurs, elevator operators, longshoremen, waiters, and in other service and general laborer jobs. Black women continued as domestics. (89-90)

It is one of the "Negro jobs" as chauffeur that the twenty-year-old Bigger Thomas takes in *Native Son*, a novel set in Chicago during the 1940s. A migrant from Mississippi, violence has been one factor that has driven the family of four North. Bigger reveals to Jan Erlone that his father was killed in a riot in the South (74). A high school drop out, the only jobs open to him are menial ones, and he does not have the choice of refusal. He has no choice in the matter of whether or not to take the relief job as chauffeur for the

Daltons. As his mother had put matters to him bluntly, "'If you don't take that job the relief'll cut us off. We won't have any food.' Hence, he could take the job at Dalton's and be miserable, or he could refuse it and starve. It maddened him to think that he did not have a wider choice of action" (16). Bigger's accidental murder of Mary Dalton, ironically, bestows upon him liberty, as he is now free to live out the consequences of his actions; his fate now becomes one that is freely chosen, as when he chooses the manner of his own death. Bigger refuses to negotiate a plea with Buckley, the State's Attorney, in order to escape the death penalty. An insanity plea, for instance, could lead to life imprisonment rather than death. Buckley bargains, "If you tell me everything, I'll see that you're sent to the hospital for an examination, see? If they say you're not responsible, then maybe you won't have to die . . ." (286). Cognizant of his ineluctable fate, Bigger places little hope in Max's request from the Governor for a stay of execution. Instead, he makes the decision to die as he had lived—defiantly (392): "What I killed for, I am!"

The trope of divestiture, descriptive of the disenfranchisement that in Richard Wright's novel *Native Son* leads to murder, likewise pervades James Baldwin's novel *Go Tell It on the Mountain*. John Grimes, the illegitimate son of Elizabeth Grimes, embodies the history of African Americans. Ignorant of his blood father, John Grimes has to endure the irrational hate of his step-father Gabriel Grimes cast by Baldwin in the role of the symbolic white man who makes his step-son John Grimes the scapegoat for his personal failures. Robert A. Bone has written on the archetypal portrayal of John in *Go Tell It on the Mountain:*

> Baldwin sees the Negro quite literally as the bastard child of American civilization. In Gabriel's double involvement with bastardy we have a re-enactment of the white man's historic crime. In Johnny, the innocent victim of Gabriel's hatred, we have an archetypal image of the Negro child. Obliquely, by means of an extended metaphor, Baldwin approaches the very essence of Negro experience. That essence is rejection, and its most destructive consequence is shame. (35)

The upshot of the alienation of John and, by extension, the black individual is an existential angst that Baldwin depicts vividly in Part One: The Seventh Day of *Go Tell It on the Mountain* (26).

The characterization of the white slaveholder as both master and father has its origin in a number of slave narratives. Frederick Douglass in the *Narrative of the Life of Frederick Douglass* cannot provide the particulars of his own birth; neither of his parentage. Although he knew, rather indistinctly, his mother, he writes that the identity of his father was a source of speculation:

> My father was a white man. He was admitted to be such by all I ever heard speak of my parentage. The opinion was also whispered that my master was my father; but of the correctness of this opinion, I know nothing; the means of knowing was withheld from me. (24)

The theme of bastardy, and its attendant ills, is likewise the focus of Zora Neale Hurston's first novel *Jonah's Gourd Vine,* published in 1934. John Buddy, the illegitimate son of Amy Crittenden, is described as having "uh li'l white folks color in yo' face" (2). His mulatto identity in the novel attests to the reality of blacks being "uh mingled people" (9). A former slave of Alf Pearson, Amy had given birth to John Buddy while on the Pearson plantation. John Buddy's knowledge of his parentage, however, similar to Douglass', remains a mystery, as evidenced when he is questioned by the school teacher over the Big Creek of his background:

> "What's yo' name?"
> "John."
> "John what? You got some other name besides John. . . ."
> ". . . Mama and all of 'em at home calls me John Buddy."
> "Buddy is a nickname. What's yo' papa' name?"
> John scratched his head and thought a minute. "'Deed Ah don't know, suh." (26)

John Buddy's hybridity is evidentiary of miscegenation; John Buddy's journey over the Big Creek to Notasulga (41), later to Opelika (57), back to Notasulga (65), to Sanford, Florida (103), to Eatonville (108), and, finally, to Plant City (186), evidentiary of the state of vagabondage peculiar to African Americans both during the slavery and post-slavery era.

In the 1800s the United States courts defined the slaves as chattels: "Court decisions in Virginia, Kentucky, and Florida declared the slave to be a chattel" (Moore 98). The United States Supreme Court, in a judgement written by Chief Justice Roger B. Taney, rendered in 1857 its decision on the suit brought by Dred Scott against Dr. Emerson/Sandford on grounds that his transport to federal territory north of Missouri in 1836 made him a free man. Judge Taney declared that a slave was "an ordinary article of merchandise and traffic . . . so far inferior that [he] had no rights which the white man was bound to respect" (qtd. in Finkelman 61). Given this legal definition of the slave as real estate, slaveowners could dispose of their property as they saw fit. This disposition governed trade, inheritance, or transfer as occasioned by economic or personal circumstances.

Linda Brent of *Incidents in the Life of a Slave Girl* was bequeathed to the niece of her mistress who was later entitled, under the Fugitive Slave Law of 1850, to lay claim to Linda Brent who had fled North some eight years prior, in 1842, and remand her to slavery. Linda Brent's reluctance to leave the city, upon her discovery of the arrival of Mr. and Mrs. Dodge in New York, is indicative of exhaustion caused by her life as a fugitive: "I was weary of flying from pillar to post. I had been chased during half my life, and it seemed as if the chase was never to end" (198).

Frederick Douglass in the *Narrative of the Life of Frederick Douglass* identifies himself as having served two masters: Captain Anthony and Captain Thomas Auld. The first master, Captain Anthony, was "the overseer of overseers" (31) to Colonel Edward Lloyd, Talbot County, Maryland, the latter of whom was reported to own approximately 1,000 slaves (41). His second master, by inheritance, Captain Thomas Auld, was the husband of Lucretia Auld, the daughter of Captain Anthony. Between the two masters and a sundry of relatives and other slave owners, Douglass was shuttled back and forth between Talbot County and Baltimore, Maryland, no fewer than seven times: to Baltimore, after Captain Anthony had loaned Douglass to the brother of his son-in-law Hugh Auld to care for Thomas, the son of Mr. and Mrs. Hugh Auld (52, 55); to Talbot County, for the purposes of valuation and division following the death of Captain Anthony (73); to Baltimore, after his lot had fallen to Lucretia Auld rather than her brother Andrew who "was known to us all as being a most cruel wretch,—a common drunkard, who had, by his reckless mismanagement and profligate dissipation, already wasted a large portion of his father's property" (74); to St. Michaels (119), after a quarrel had erupted between the two brothers, causing Thomas Auld to demand the return of Douglass "as a means of punishing his brother" (78); to Edward Covey a year later, to be "broken" (87); to William Freeland to work for two years as a hired hand (111); and, finally, to Baltimore for protection (127), after an escape plan by Douglass, while he was in the employ of Freeland, had been foiled. It was in Baltimore where Douglass escaped in 1838, after having spent approximately twenty years in bondage. The effects of his vagabondage are clear: a loss of familial ties and a sense of place; an inability to trust; and a lack of individuation and autonomy, as the slave is treated as no less than a pawn to be moved back and forth as economic circumstances—and sometimes caprice—warrant. Douglass has written poignantly in the *Narrative* of the trauma caused by the early separation of mother and child:

> Frequently, before the child has reached its twelfth month, its mother is taken from it, and hired out on some farm a considerable distance off, and the child is placed under the care of an old woman, too old for field labor. For what this separation is done, I do not know, unless it be to hinder the development of the child's affection toward its mother, and to blunt and destroy the natural affection of the mother for the child. This is the inevitable result. (24)

Gustavas Vassa, as he narrates in *The Life of Olaudah Equiano,* exchanged hands no fewer than twelve times before he was able to purchase his freedom in 1766 from the Quaker merchant Robert King for forty pounds sterling. Whereas homelessness for Douglass resulted in his disaffection, the same condition inspired the opposite emotion in Equiano, as Equiano relates to his masters as surrogate fathers and remains loyal to them long after his period of service has ended. Of Captain Pascal, he writes:

> My intention was to make a voyage or two, entirely to please

> these my honored patrons; but I determined that the year
> following, if it pleased God, I would see Old England once
> more, and surprise my old master, Captain Pascal, who was
> hourly in my mind; for I still loved him, notwithstanding
> his usage to me. . . . (102)

Peculiar to Equiano and former slaves, nonetheless, is a restless-
ness (122) that for Equiano may be said to have stemmed from his
vocation as a seafarer; too, from his classification as a tradeable
commodity. Thus, Equiano is a precursor to both the inhabitants
of L'Abandonnée in Simone Schwarz-Bart's *The Bridge of Beyond* and Paul D of Toni Morrison's *Beloved.*

The classification of slaves as property induced within them
feelings of powerlessness, as can be seen in Paul D of Toni
Morrison's *Beloved,* "an historical novel, framed in purpose,
thematics, and structure after the African-American slave narrative" (95 Samuels and Weems). Shackled and on the verge of being sold away from Sweet Home after an aborted attempt to escape, Paul D perceives the lot of the pugilistic cock "Mister" preferable to his own, "Mister looked so . . . free" (72). Wilfred D.
Samuels and Clenora Hudson-Weems posit in the work *Toni
Morrison* that "[their] assessment of Morrison's work is grounded
in the premise that her fictional characters are marginal (liminal)
personalities who lack social, spiritual, psychological, historical,
geographical, or genealogical place or center. Their betwixt-and-
betweenness necessarily involve them in a quest for personal and/
or communal wholeness and fulfillment" (x).

In West Indian literature, liminality is not only a condition as-
cribed to slaves as a result of their classification as property, but
also as a condition of their birth location, the latter often creating
situations that exacerbate their "betweenity." In contrast to America,
distinctions were often made among slaves in the Caribbean islands based upon their birth location. Accordingly, slaves born
during the Middle Passage, or during the voyage from Africa, were
labeled "salt-water creoles" (Higman 22). According to B.W.
Higman in his work *Slave Populations of the British Caribbean,
1807-1834,* "only the registration returns of Antigua, Montserrat,
British Honduras, and the Cayman Islands failed to distinguish
clearly between slaves born in Africa and those born in the Ameri-

cas (creoles)" (21). Furthermore, Higman contends that Creoles, rather than African-born slaves, the latter of whom were often males, were more likely to be children of West Indian whites or freed men who frequently retained Creole mistresses (383).

Higman's contention that Creoles were likely to be sired by West Indian planters is corroborated by Laura E. Ciolkowski. In her article "Navigating the *Wide Sargasso Sea*: Colonial History, English Fiction, and British Empire," Ciolkowski avers that "'In the West Indies, sexual relationships between black and coloured women and white plantocracy [were] an integral part of the social structure of the islands.' Some actually married white plantation owners and, if the law allowed it, were able to legitimize their children, ironically bastardizing the English 'race' still further in the eyes of the English community at home" (344).

Antoinette Cosway Mason of Jean Rhys' novel *Wide Sargasso Sea* is the product of a union between a plantocrat and a Martinique woman. The widowed plantocrat Cosway took as a second wife a white Creole Annette. Consequently, their daughter Antoinette, a white Creole, resides in two worlds—European and Caribbean—but belongs to neither. That is, she comes from British stock (67); however, Jamaica is the only home that she has known: "She belonged to the magic and the loveliness" (172). Her hybridity therefore makes her alien to both worlds: "I often wonder who I am and where is my country and where do I belong and why was I ever born at all" (102).

"Betweenity," which was the fate of the offspring of Africans exported as manual labourers during the eighteenth and nineteenth centuries to the West Indies and the United States, was likewise the fate of the colonized West Indian islands. Eric Williams adopts the phrase coined by "wags in British Guiana" (51) to describe Tobago's colonial past. First a territory of the British, Tobago was later claimed by France, then Holland, and, subsequently, by the Duke of Courland, ruler of a principality now known as Latvia, who laid claim to it on the basis of a grant from the King of England in 1664 (51). In the chapter "Tobago in a State of Betweenity," Williams relates Tobago's checkered colonial past:

This is how Tobago lived up [to] the end of the eighteenth

century—between Britain and France, or between France and Holland, or between Holland and Britain, now invaded by the buccaneers, now attacked by Spain, now settled by Courlanders. Holland changed the island's name and called it New Walcheren. The French changed the name of Scarborough and called it Port Louis. Betwixt and between, betwixt changes of ownership and between national flags— that was colonialism in Tobago. (51)

This "state of betweenity" is also alluded to by George Lamming in his autobiographical novel *In the Castle of My Skin.* The colonial history of Barbados is regarded as unique, largely because it had escaped the fate of a number of the islands: "Barbados or Little England was the oldest and purest of England's children, and may it always be so. The other islands had changed hands. Now they were French, now they were Spanish. But Little England remained steadfast and constant to Big England. Even to this day" (3).

Ironically, dispossession, the fate of the Caribbean islands during colonialism, was also the condition after decolonization. In *Castle,* Lamming describes the new order as no different from the old. The reins of power have been transferred from the British landowner Creighton to Mr. Slime, a Creighton villager, former village school teacher and founder of the Penny Bank and Friendly Society; however, the exploitation that has been the legacy of colonialism continues unabated, as Slime purchases the land with the funds from depositors of Penny Bank and bestows upon them the privilege of land purchase thrice over; that is, they may purchase parcels of land at $300 each at interest rates that nearly double the purchase price. The narrator 'G' overhears the calculations by the partners of Penny Bank:

> The spots were about three hundred dollars each, and I forget how much interest the purchaser would have to pay if he couldn't deliver the money cash. Someone said they would make about five hundred dollars on each spot if they got the interest they expected. The man was certain the interest would increase since the villagers couldn't pay more than three or four shillings a week. (259)

Frantz Fanon considers the retrograde nature of neo-colonialist politics not only representative of "the mutilation of the colonized people by the colonial regime" (149), which is the bane of national unity, but also symptomatic of the spiritual penury of the national bourgeoisie. He writes in *The Wretched of the Earth:*

> The national bourgeoisie of underdeveloped countries is not engaged in production, nor in invention, nor building, nor labor; it is completely canalized into activities of the intermediary type. Its innermost vocation seems to be to keep in the running and to be part of the racket. The psychology of the national bourgeoisie is that of the businessman, not that of a captain of industry; and it is only too true that the greed of the settlers and the system of embargoes set up by colonialism have hardly left them any other choice. (149-50)

In that the new leaders in underdeveloped countries are strawmen of the former colonialists, Fanon considers that the former mother country practices indirect rule, both through the national bourgeoisie that caricatures Europe and the national army that suppresses dissent (174). Importantly, the appellation "Slime" for the neo-colonialist in *In the Castle of My Skin,* who straddles both the past and the present colonialist regimes, is fitting. Jean-Paul Sartre in *Existential Psychoanalysis* has associated the viscous, or the slimy, with the "in betweenity" of the two states of being: the in-itself, which is identified with materiality, and the for-itself, which, on the other hand, is identified with potentiality (134). Hazel E. Barnes in her work *Humanistic Existentialism: The Literature of Possibility* illuminates further the aberrant nature of the viscous, which, incidentally, could be applied to Mr. Slime: "It [the slimy] represents symbolically a dreaded state in which a person wants to launch forth a free project of himself into the future but feels himself caught back by invisible chains from the past" (260).

The symbolic rape of a culture, namely, the Indian culture, is also chronicled in V.S. Naipaul's *A House for Mr. Biswas.* Mr. Biswas, an Amerindian in Trinidad, Raghu, Mr. Biswas' late father, and Adjodha, Mr. Biswas' uncle, are representative of the cultural group that has lost virtually all ties to the Mother country, India. Eric Williams estimates in his work *History of the People of Trinidad and Tobago* that "Between 1838 and 1917, no fewer than 238,000 Indians were introduced into British Guiana, 145,000 into Trinidad, 21,500 into Jamaica, 39,000 into Guadeloupe, 34,000 into Surinam, 1,550 into St. Lucia, 1,820 into St. Vincent, [and] 2,570 into Grenada" (100). The large number of immigrants was to fill the void left by the freed blacks who had turned to ventures such as trading and shopkeeping that were more profitable than sugar cultivation and those who had emigrated to the Panama Canal, Costa Rica, the United States, and Cuba (115). In the chapter "The Contributions of the Indians," Williams observes that although the number of sugar exports increased five fold between 1833 and 1896 (119), the sizable increase in sugar exports is not the major contribution of the Indians to Trinidad society and economy. Instead, it has been their creation of a class of small farmers.

The Ordinance of 17 July 1899 that consolidated governance of immigration, namely, the Indian immigrants to Trinidad, had made provision for their return at the end of their service contracts. However, inasmuch as departures outnumbered arrivals, the policy was deemed economically inefficient (114). Consequently, inducements, such as small land grants, became a means to ensure a stable labor force, but only after attempts to re-indenture the Indians had failed. Eric Williams concludes:

> Thus by a curious irony, the sugar planter who, in the seventeenth and eighteenth centuries, refused to grant land to the white indentured servant, who, after emancipation, tried to prevent the purchase of land by the former slaves, found himself obliged in the 19th century to grant land to the indentured immigrants in order to reduce the expense of immigrant labour. Indian immigration, designed to compete with the Negro landowners, ended in the establishment of a class of Indian landowners. (120)

The Tulsis of *A House for Mr. Biswas* are part of the class of Indian landowners who have settled in Trinidad at the end of their service contracts: "The Tulsis had some reputation among Hindus as a pious, conservative, landowning family" (81). They are atypical, however, in their maintenance of contact with their place of origin, use of Hindi language (200), practice of Sanatanist, Tulsi-like idol worship (383), and Hinduism. Subsequently, Hanuman

House in Arwacas is characterized by its solidity, or impregnability (86), "to the extent that it is possible" (Cudjoe 52), quite in contrast with the nomadism of the novel's anti-hero, Mr. Biswas, and the "temporariness" of the elderly gentlemen who congregate outside the Tulsi store smoking clay cheelums, reminiscing of India and vowing to return when the opportunity arose, but reluctant to leave the "familiar temporariness" (194) of Trinidad. Gordon Rohlehr, in his article "Character and Rebellion in *A House for Mr. Biswas*" finds Mr. Biswas' "nowhereness" as representative of the existential plight of modern man who cast into an alien world has to create existentially his own significance, or identity, by virtue of his actions. Rohlehr writes:

> [I]f he resembles some of the grotesques of Dickens, he has been created by a writer who has a more contemporary sense of the themes of void, loneliness, meaninglessness and absurdity, prevalent in modern European literature. Biswas' nowhereness may be something much more universal, yet, as we have seen, he is representative enough of our local predicament: a man without a past, an orphan wavering between equally dubious cultural alternatives; winning a sort of independence and returning in humiliation to the people he is still forced to fight; turning anxiety into absurdity by using humour as a weapon and an escape; trying to create an identity from the void, and sometimes unknown to himself, exercising and expressing identity in the very act of searching for it. (92-93)

The "nowhereness" of the characters surveyed in this chapter—Mr. Biswas of *A House for Mr. Biswas,* Paul D of *Beloved,* and Bigger Thomas of *Native Son*—becomes the cause sui generis of their creation. The angst that attends the challenge of self-creation and the individual responses to that anxiety are the subjects of the following chapters.

WORKS CITED

Baldwin, James. *Go Tell It on the Mountain.* New York: Dell, 1952.

Barnes, Hazel E. *Humanistic Existentialism: The Literature of Possibility.* Lincoln: U of Nebraska P, 1959.

Bone, Robert A. "James Baldwin." *James Baldwin: A Collection of Critical Essays.* Ed. Keneth Kinnamon. Englewood Cliffs, N.J.: Prentice, 1974. 28-51.

Brawley, Benjamin. *A Short History of the American Negro.* Rev. ed. New York: Macmillan, 1924.

Ciolkowski, Laura E. "Navigating the *Wide Sargasso Sea:* Colonial History, English Fiction, and British Empire." *Twentieth Century Literature* 43 (fall 1997): 339-59.

Cudjoe, Selwyn R. *V.S. Naipaul: A Materialist Reading.* Amherst: U of Massachusetts P, 1988.

Davis, George A., and O. Fred Donaldson. *Blacks in the United States: A Geographic Perspective.* Boston: Houghton, 1975.

Douglass, Frederick. *Narrative of the Life of Frederick Douglass: An American Slave.* 1845. Reprint. Ed. Benjamin Quarles. Cambridge: Harvard UP, 1960.

Fanon, Frantz. *The Wretched of the Earth.* Trans. Constance Farrington. New York: Grove Press, 1963.

Finkelman, Paul. *Dred Scott v. Sandford: A Brief History with Documents.* The Bedford Series in History and Culture. Boston: Bedford, 1997.

Higman, B.W. *Slave Populations of the British Caribbean, 1807-1834.* Baltimore: John Hopkins UP, 1984.

Hurston, Zora Neale. *Jonah's Gourd Vine.* 1934. Reprint, with a foreword by Rita Dove. New York: HarperCollins, 1990.

Jacobs, Harriet A. *Incidents in the Life of a Slave Girl.* Written by Herself. 1861. Reprint, edited and introduced by Jean Fagan Yellin. Cambridge: Harvard UP, 1987.

Lamming, George. *In the Castle of My Skin.* New York: Schocken, 1983.

Moore, Wilbert E. *American Negro Slavery and Abolition: A Sociological Study.* New York: The Third Press, 1971.

Naipaul, V.S. *A House for Mr. Biswas.* New York: Penguin, 1961.

Rhys, Jean. *Wide Sargasso Sea.* New York: Norton, 1966.

Rohlehr, Gordon. "Character and Rebellion in *A House for Mr. Biswas.*" *Critical Perspectives on V.S. Naipaul.* Ed. Robert D. Hamner. Washington, D.C.: Three Continents Press, 1977. 84-93.

Samuels, Wilfred D., and Clenora Hudson-Weems. *Toni Morrison.* New York: Twayne, 1990.

Sartre, Jean-Paul. *Existential Psychoanalysis.* Trans. Hazel E. Barnes. New York: Philosophical Library, 1953.

Vassa, Gustavus. *The Life of Olaudah Equiano.* Written by Himself. 1814. Reprinted in *The Classic Slave Narratives.* Ed. Henry Louis Gates, Jr.

New York: Mentor, 1987. 1-182.

Williams, Eric. *History of the People of Trinidad and Tobago*. New York: Frederick A. Praeger, 1962.

Wright, Richard. "How 'Bigger' Was Born." *Native Son*. New York: Harper, 1940. vii-xxxiv.

————. *Native Son*. New York: Harper, 1940.

Chapter 2

THE DIASPORA AS A TROPE FOR
THE EXISTENTIAL CONDITION

In the philosophical work *Being and Nothingness: An Essay in Phenomenological Ontology,* Jean-Paul Sartre differentiates between two types of being: the being for-itself and the being in-itself. The being in-itself is equated with objects in the world that are immutable; the being in-itself "has to be what it is" (lxv). Whereas the being in-itself is "actuality" (74), the being for-itself is potentiality. Sartre uses the trope "Diaspora" to describe the multiplicity of being that is the for-itself: "In the ancient world the profound cohesion and dispersion of the Jewish people was designated by the term 'Diaspora'. It is this word which will serve to designate the mode of being for the For-itself; it is diasporatic" (112). Contrary to the being in-itself which "has to be what it is" (lxv), the for-itself aims "to be what it is not and to not-be what it is" (113). To be sure, it is the vacuity of the for-itself that introduces nothingness into the world:

> The Being by which Nothingness arrives in the world must nihilate Nothingness in its Being, and even so it still runs the risk of establishing Nothingness as a transcendent in the very heart of immanence unless it nihilates Nothingness in its being in connection with its own being. The Being by which Nothingness arrives in the world is a being such that in its Being, the Nothingness of its Being is in question. (23)

The rear-ended pursuit that characterizes the for-itself, similar to that of the canine chasing its own tail, Sartre concretizes in *Being and Nothingness* in the example of the donkey that attempts to grasp a carrot suspended from a stick that is attached to the shaft of the cart. Each movement by the donkey sets in motion the entire apparatus that remains equidistant to the donkey that pursues it. Sartre summarizes in *Being and Nothingness:*

> Thus we run after a possible which our very running causes to appear, which is nothing but our running itself, and which thereby is by definition out of reach. We run toward ourselves and we are—due to this very fact—the being which cannot be reunited with itself. (178)

Alfred Stern in his work *Sartre: His Philosophy and Existential Psychoanalysis* criticizes Sartre for his absolutism and rejoins that the absence of causality in Nature, a premise for the absurd, neither precludes probability nor the absence of absolute necessity, relative necessity (41). For his part, Sartre notes that individuals adopt an attitude of seriousness in order to escape confrontation with the nothingness of the for-itself. In the serious mood, "more reality [is attributed] to the world than to oneself" (*Existential Psychoanalysis* 71). One's existence is thus "of the world" and assumes the consistency, the inertia, the opaqueness of the rock (*EP* 72).

André Lemordant in "The Childhood of a Leader," by Jean-Paul Sartre, is demonstrative of the attitude of seriousness. Contrary to Lucien Fleurier who questions his existence because he can never grab hold of it, André Lemordant is "a man with convictions" who is associated with solidity: "His tiny mouth, his heavy cheeks, yellow and smooth, were not made to express feelings: he was a Buddha" (237). Enthralled by the "impenetrable look" of Lemordant, Lucien joins the anti-Semitic group the camelots, with which Lemordant is involved, forges an identity founded on racist ideology, "[H]e thought I am Lucien! Somebody who can't stand Jews" (266), and in so doing becomes someone whose opinions now carry weight:

> Lucien thrust himself into this soft crowd like a steel wedge; he thought; "It's not me any more. Only yesterday I was a

big, bloated bug like the crickets in Férolles." Now Lucien felt clean and sharp as a chronometer. (264)

Demonstrative also of the attitude of seriousness similar to that of Lemordant in "Childhood of a Leader" is Dr. Rogé in Jean-Paul Sartre's *Nausea*. Possessed with a powerful build, penetrating gaze, and an imperious manner, Dr. Rogé is an intimidating "rock like" presence (69). Accordingly, he dispenses advice as quickly as he labels people. Under his scrutiny, the diminutive bistro customer who insists on being addressed by the waitress as Monsieur Achille gets tagged by Dr. Rogé a "loon" (66). The ability of Dr. Rogé both to prescribe and circumscribe bestows upon him an infallible essence:

> The doctor knew how to take him [M. Achille]! The doctor wasn't the one to let himself be hypnotized by an old madman on the verge of having his fit; one good blow, a few rough, lashing words, that's what they need. The doctor has experience. He is a professional in experience: doctors, priests, magistrates and army officers know men through and through as if they had made them. (67)

Sartre argues that individuals adopt various guises, *i.e.*, attitudes of seriousness, in an attempt to hide from themselves their superfluousness. Man's utter responsibility for the being that he is and, by extension, for humankind inasmuch as his choice of projects posits his ideal vision of humankind thus is central to the existential concept of abandonment:

> And when we speak of "abandonment" . . . we only mean to say that God does not exist, and that it is necessary to draw the consequences of his absence right to the end. . . . [I]f God does not exist, . . . man is in consequence forlorn, for he cannot find anything to depend upon either within or outside himself. (*Existentialism and Humanism* 32-34)

Abandonment is descriptive of both the metaphysical and physical condition of Cholly Breedlove in Toni Morrison's *The Bluest Eye*. Cholly and Pauline Breedlove had migrated from Alabama to Lorain, Ohio, where Cholly had found work in a steel plant. Over the years, however, his employment had become sporadic and/or non-existent, as he had deteriorated into drunkenness. It may be argued that Cholly's inertia stems from the inability to make choices. Junkheaped when he was four days old by his mother, rejected by his father, Cholly had come to feel that he was of no account and, subsequently, has lived his life governed completely by instinct: "Abandoned in a junkheap by his mother, rejected for a crap game by his father, there was nothing more to lose. He was alone with his own perceptions and appetites, and they alone interested him" (126).

Cholly's "betweenity" is conceptualized in his portrayal as a man-child. After the dismissal of Cholly by Samson Fuller, the man purported to be his father, who mistakes him for someone else, Cholly regresses into infantilism: "Finding the deepest shadow under the pier, he crouched in it, behind one of the posts. He remained knotted there in fetal position, paralyzed, his fists covering his eyes, for a long time" (124). Congruent with the conceptualization of Cholly as man-child is the viscous imagery (vomit, slime) that surrounds him, which Sartre in *Existential Psychoanalysis* identified as indicative of the state of "betweenity": "Nothing testifies more clearly to its [the slimy's] ambiguous character as a 'substance in between two states' than the slowness with which the slimy melts into itself" (134).

According to Alfred Stern in his work *Sartre: His Philosophy and Existential Psychoanalysis,* the characters in Sartre's fiction typically desire to assume the quality of an in-itself; however, he contends that their mergence into thinghood is impossible inasmuch as man, as a for-itself, continuously creates himself anew. Thus existence itself becomes defined by its "betweenity":

> But it is impossible for a man to attain this totality of thinghood symbolized by the statue, the brute and mere being-in-itself. As Kant has said, man is a citizen of two worlds, the moral world of freedom and the physical world of determinism. When Sartre says that man is partly a being-for-itself and partly a being-in-itself, this only translates Kant's dualism into another terminology. For the being-for-itself is freedom, and the being-in-itself is the deterministic world of thinghood. But Sartre added something very important to this Kantian dualism: the insight that man

is never entirely the one and never entirely the other; he has never entirely the fluidity of water and never entirely the solidity and impentrability of a stone. (196)

Paul D's "betweenity" or liminality in Toni Morrison's *Beloved* is underscored by his appellation "Paul" which Samuels and Weems in their work argue "denotes small," while his lack of a surname "impl[ies] anonymity" (125). Although Samuels and Weems identify Paul D's journey north to Delaware and eventually to Ohio as "part of his journey to physical wholeness, authentic existence, and self" (127), it may be argued that Paul D's perambulatory nature is denotative not only of the attempt of the for-itself to realize itself, but, also, of his state of vagabondage.

On the other hand, Mr. Biswas' state of vagabondage in *A House for Mr. Biswas* is explicitly evidenced in the inutile, second-hand possessions that Mr. Biswas collects at the various locations during his odyssey. When Mr. Biswas becomes a shopkeeper for the Tulsis in the Chase, he and his wife Shama assume ownership of "a large, canopy-less cast iron four poster where black enamel paint was chipped and lacklustre" (145). The bedboard, ridden with bedbugs, had been doused by Shama with kerosene; henceforth, it had emanated both the smell of kerosene and bedbugs. When Mr. Biswas purchases for $5,500 the house on Sikkim Street from the solicitor's clerk, the four poster on the moving lorry represents one of a number of second-hand goods, either by workmanship or design, that he has acquired in his forty-six years. For example, with dimensions of six feet long and nearly four feet wide, the destitute's dining table had failed in its practical function. After his resignation from his job as a reporter for the Sentinel, Mr. Biswas had accepted the job as Community Welfare Officer. With surveys to conduct, questionnaires to complete and tabulate, subsistence and allowance claims to submit, and reports to file, the destitute's dining table had been pressed into service; however, the dining table and Mr. Biswas' machinations with it, reminiscent of those of the copyist Nippers in Herman Melville's short story "Bartleby" which seem designed to thwart rather than to promote production, take on an absurdist aspect:

[Mr. Biswas] worked late into the night, squatting on a chair

> before the dining table. The table was too high; sitting on
> pillows had proved unsatisfactory; so he squatted. Some-
> times he threatened to cut down the legs of the dining table
> by half and cursed the destitute who had made it. (510)

Anxiety is a trademark of Existentialism and is derivative of the
metaphysical condition of existence, or of being-in-the-world,
which is deemed supernumerary, or *de trop*, and, hence, absurd
(Stern 31). Hence, Roquentin in *Nausea*, by Jean-Paul Sartre, concludes that "Every existing thing is born without reason, prolongs itself
out of weakness and dies by chance" (133). His reaction to the
gratuitousness of the world is nausea: "I should like to vomit" (122).

Gordon Rohlehr argues that Mr. Biswas' anxieties stem from
his uprootedness: "His [Mr. Biswas'] elaborate poses, daydreams,
assertion of self and evasion of responsibility are a result of the
cultural, social and psychological nowhereness produced by his
position as an untalented second generation Hindu in poverty-
stricken colonial Trinidad. He is appropriately an orphan" (66).
By the same token, Alvin Toffler identifies contemporary man as a
transient being. His relations with others, things, places, institutional or organizational environments have been telescoped, and it
is the high rate of turnover, or "through-put" in the life of contemporary man that leads to feelings of rootlessness. The adaptive
burden that the accelerative thrust poses for contemporary man
produces in turn the potentially devastating social illness future
shock: "New discoveries, new technologies, new social arrangements in the external world erupt into our lives in the form of increased turnover rates—shorter and shorter relational durations.
They force a faster and faster pace of daily life. They demand a
new level of adaptability. And they set the stage for that potentially devastating social illness—future shock" (181). Thus it may
be argued that the nomadism of Mr. Biswas pre-figures the condition of contemporary man.

On the other hand, Selwyn R. Cudjoe contends that the fragmentation of the psyche of Mr. Biswas is caused by the conflict
between essence and existence:

> This confrontation with himself—and the various forms of
> alienation that are generated by the society—leads Mr.

Biswas to face his society and question his place within it.
Unable to reconcile the feudal aspects of his past with the
capitalist order of the present, Mr. Biswas, in an important
moment of his life, becomes frozen between two points of
existence. (60)

Jean-Paul Sartre in the work *Existentialism and Humanism* identifies as rudimentary to existentialist thought the belief that existence precedes essence. Contrary to the artisan who produces a paper knife coincident with his conceptualization of it, man lacks an essence, or prior conception of himself. Given the absence of a supernal artisan of the world to bestow upon man his fundamental essence, man is condemned to define his own being:

Thus, there is no human nature, because there is no God to
have a conception of it. Man simply is. Not that he is
simply what he conceives himself to be, but he is what he
wills, and as he conceives himself after already existing—
as he wills to be after that leap towards existence. Man is
nothing else but that which he makes of himself. (28)

Man cannot have recourse to determinism since he alone constitutes the sum of his actions: "In life, a man commits himself, draws his own portrait and there is nothing but that portrait" (42). Sartre therefore dismisses the reproaches against the philosophy, namely, that it is too pessimistic and rejoins that "what people reproach us with is not, after all, our pessimism, but the sternness of our optimism" (42).

The being for-itself, as noted earlier, introduces nothingness into the world; the being for-itself also manifests itself as body, which is to say that the for-itself is inseparable from the senses that it contains. Sartre in *Being and Nothingness* refers to this condition that is indistinguishable from fact as "facticity" and "finitude": "In this sense *finitude* is the necessary condition of the original project of the For-itself" (303). Indicative of consciousness as body, "The for-itself exists its body as consciousness," is the sensation of nausea that Sartre has described in the novel by the same title; also, an all-enveloping fog similar to the one that Lucien Fleurier experiences in the short story "Childhood of a

Leader": "He was there, he digested, he yawned, he heard the rain tapping on the windowpanes and the white fog was unravelling in his head" (233).

Sartre equates the body with the "facticity" of the for-itself, inasmuch as the body inscribes the for-itself as past with respect to its birth and, in like manner, conditions its future projects (*BN* 304). The "facticity" of the for-itself is not only delineated by the body, but is governed likewise by the existence of the Other. Save for the Other, the individual as for-itself remains a free subjectivity, his acts inseparable from the instruments employed toward a particular end, as illustrated by the eavesdropper who is moved, by jealousy, curiosity, or vice, to spy through a keyhole:

> The door, the keyhole are at once both instruments and obstacles; they are presented as "to be handled with care;" the keyhole is given as "to be looked through close by and a little to one side," etc. Hence from this moment "I do what I have to do." No transcending view comes to confer upon my acts the character of a given on which a judgment can be brought to bear. (*BN* 235)

Only after the eavesdropper is surprised by the sound of approaching footsteps of the Other is he made cognizant of his objectivation by the Other. Sartre likens the situation to an external hemorrhage where "the world flows out of the world and I flow outside myself. The Other's look makes me be beyond my being in this world and puts me in the midst of the world which is at once this world and beyond this world" (237). Sartre also views the objectivation by the Look of the Other as analogous to slavery in that "I am no longer master of the situation":

> I am a slave to the degree that my being is dependent at the center of a freedom which is not mine and which is the very condition of my being. In so far as I am the object of values which come to qualify me without my being able to act on this qualification or even to know it, I am enslaved. (243)

Given that the aim of each for-itself is transcendence, Sartre concludes that "The essence of the relations between consciousnesses is . . . conflict" (405).

Lynn S. Chancer in her work *Sadomasochism in Everyday Life* has observed the futility of studying the phenomenon of dominance and subordination outside a larger historical context and contends that the phenomenon is steeped, accordingly, in capitalism. The capitalist and the proletariat are yoked in a symbiotic relationship of mutual dependency that does violence to them both: the proletariat requires a job to subsist qua family; the capitalist, to subsist qua capitalism:

> Capitalists 'appropriate' the surplus value produced by workers historically disenfranchised from ownership of land and forced to sell their labor in exchange for wages. A sense of powerlessness and dependency results for the worker forced to accept conditions of work set by the more authoritative capitalist. . . . Simultaneously, the capitalist's desperate need for the worker, for the proletariat's labor that allows her or him to remain in a position of power, remains obscured. (33-34)

The capitalist and proletarian each has value only in terms of utility, and Chancer contends that this commodification replicates itself in the post modern world in all aspects of our public and private life:

> What distinguishes capitalism from all social systems before it, asserted [Georg] Lukacs in paraphrasing Marx, is that nothing any longer has value in and of itself: all relations, animate and inanimate, become viewed as instrumental, commodities valued only insofar as they are useful for *another* rather than for oneself, insofar as they become thinglike and exchangeable in market terms. (34)

The commodification of Sethe as a brood sow in *Beloved* leads her to view her children as property; hence, she can do with them as she sees fit. According to Sartre, possession is a will to power; so, too, is destruction. Sartre contends in *Existential Psychoanalysis* that destruction is another form of appropriative behavior in that the object of destruction gets seized into being by memory, or by the consciousness that destroys it: "I re-create it by recreating myself; thus to destroy is to re-create by assuming oneself as solely responsible for the being of what existed for all" (101-2). Samuels and Weems contend that it is precisely the issue of parental ownership that Morrison is intent on exploring in *Beloved:*

> But whereas heretofore Morrison seemed interested in probing and in fact advocating the importance of her characters' obligation to not act in "bad faith," that is, to act with existential responsibility for self and being, by accepting the challenge of their existential freedom in a chaotic and hostile world, she focuses in *Beloved* on the possible limitations of that freedom as well. (109)

On the other hand, the commodification of the black male in some instances as an inutile object is a constant source of despair. Daryl C. Dance has written in the article "Daddy May Bring Home Bread, But He Don't Cut No Ice: The Economic Plight of the Father Figure in Black American Literature": "We all know . . . that any man who is unable to protect and provide for his family, any man denied the opportunity to compete with other men for the kinds of jobs that bring a sense of fulfillment and pride, will eventually be psychologically emasculated" (298).

Cholly's emasculation in *The Bluest Eye* had attended his first act of copulation. Surprised by two white hunters, Cholly was goaded for their voyeuristic pleasure into a performance that he no longer felt. Humiliated beyond measure, Cholly was later to direct his shame and anger at Darlene, the female who bore witness to his impotence:

> He was, in time, to discover that hatred of white men—but not now. Not in impotence but later, when the hatred would find sweet expression. For now, he hated the one who bore witness to his failure, his impotence. The one whom he had not been able to protect, to spare, to cover from the round moon glow of the flashlight. (119)

The psychological emasculation of the Trinidadian Mr. Biswas in *A House for Mr. Biswas* is symbolized in the destruction of the doll house that he had given to his daughter Savi as a Christmas gift, one that violated the established tradition of the Hanuman House of uniformity in gift-giving. To put an end to the persecution that Savi had been subjected to, "Puss-puss here. Puss-puss there" (226), as a result of this introduction of disorder into Hanuman House, Shama, the wife of Mr. Biswas, had herself destroyed the doll house. Regarding the conditioned behavior of Shama and the members of Hanuman House in their acceptance of tyranny, one critic has written: "The children in Hanuman House are taught to ridicule the non-conformist much the same way as creolized Negro slaves were used to mock new arrivals from Africa into submission" (Rohlehr 90). The destruction of the doll house thus presages the destruction of the house for Mr. Biswas at Green Vale; it constitutes as well the "symbolic murder" (Rohlehr 90) of Mr. Biswas for the "good" of Tulsidom:

> Trinidad laws do not permit the Tulsis to lynch, but they do know how to commit symbolic murder. When Biswas, ignoring the pressures which the Tulsis bring to bear on the aspiring individual, gives his daughter a doll house, he upsets the entire equilibrium of Hanuman House, and their rejoinder is to tear the doll house apart. (Rohlehr 90)

Within the Sartrean ontology, those who attempt to shirk the responsibility of inventing themselves by their assumption of prescribed social roles are said to be guilty of bad faith. On the meaning of the concept, John Killinger has written in his work *Hemingway and the Dead Gods: A Study in Existentialism:*

> Bad faith . . . is a concept common to the thinking of major existentialists, and means generally any acceptance of a way of living incognito, or of losing one's self in a larger entity, so as to slough off all personal responsibility for one's choices and actions. (37)

Seth of *A House for Mr. Biswas* is illustrative of bad faith. His ossification as oppressor is apparent in his identification with the in-itself of authoritarianism, namely, muddy bluchers (86, 94, 166, etc.). Rohlehr has aptly observed:

> Seth is almost an allegorical representation of Power. It is

> amazing, on reflection, how little we are told of Seth. Time
> and again we hear of his big military boots, see him in his
> khaki uniform, note his big hands and square fingers, and
> hear his voice. He is almost above the struggle. He con-
> trols it. But he can rule without Mrs. Tulsi no more than
> she can rule without him: for it is together that they fulfill
> the psychology of rulership. (89)

A person is in bad faith, according to Jean-Paul Sartre, if he attempts to affirm his facticity "as *being* and transcendence as *being*
facticity" (*Existential Psychoanalysis* 175-76). In the view of
Sartre, certain popular expressions, such as "He has become what
he was," contain the spirit of bad faith in that they express attitudes of "self-negation" (154): "We can see the use which bad
faith can make of these judgments which all aim at establishing
that I am not what I am" (177). Yet another kind of duplicity, or
bad faith, emerges from the alliance of one's being-for-itself with
one's being-for-others, as in the example from *Existential Psychoanalysis* of the waiter who "plays" at being a waiter in order to
convince his clientele that he is "nothing but a waiter": "He bends
forward a little too eagerly; his voice, his eyes express an interest a
little too solicitous for the order of the customer" (182). His representation of himself as only a waiter, however, is in bad faith since
he remains apart from his objectivation: "What I attempt to realize is a being-in-itself of the café waiter, as if it were not just in my
power to confer their value and their urgency upon my duties and
the rights of my position" (184).

Symptomatic of the bad faith of John Buddy of Zora Neale
Hurston's *Jonah's Gourd Vine* is his alliance of his being-for-itself
with his being-for-others, namely, his actualization of the cultural
myth of the black man as super stud. Alan Brown in his article
"'De Beast' Within: The Role of Nature in *Jonah's Gourd Vine*"
identifies sexual prowess as the means by which John Buddy defines himself:

> John is a tragic figure in the Greek sense of the term. As
> Hurston was trying to create a realistic portrait of the black
> males she was acquainted with in 1930s Florida, she real-
> ized that her tragic hero could not be afflicted with the nor-
> mal tragic flaws of Greek tragedy—pride, arrogance, or

excessive jealousy—because society would not permit these qualities to develop. Her personal observations led her to believe that the black man's route to manhood lay in the sexual conquest and exploitation of women. John's tragic flaw, therefore, lies not in some quirk of the mind, which was not allowed to develop to its full potential, but in one of the needs of his body, which, by contrast, was overly developed: John is sexually promiscuous. (79-80)

Sartre has labeled elsewhere cowards those who, such as John Buddy of *Jonah's Gourd Vine* and Seth of *A House for Mr. Biswas,* flee from their freedom: "Those who hide from this total freedom, in a guise of solemnity or with deterministic excuses, I shall call cowards" (*Existentialism and Humanism* 52). The dichotomous nature of man's being is conveyed imagistically in the chapter "Green Vale" of *A House for Mr. Biswas,* namely, in the description of the "winged ants" that represent aspiration and their antithesis, the "undertaker ants" that thwart realization:

> [T]he room was full of these ants enjoying the last minutes of their short life. Their small wings, strained by large bodies, quickly became useless, and without wings they were without defence. . . . Their enemies had already discovered them. . . ; they were the biting ants, smaller, thicker, neater, purple-black with a dull shine, moving slowly and in strict formation, as solemn and stately as undertakers. (289)

In Toni Morrison's *The Bluest Eye,* the bad faith of the Breedloves is evidenced in their internalization of the regard of the Other. In bad faith, they come to embrace the view accorded them by the Other as unworthy. Morrison writes of them in *The Bluest Eye:*

> You looked at them and wondered why they were so ugly; you looked closely and could not find the source. Then you realized that it came from conviction, their conviction. It was as though some mysterious all-knowing master had given each one a cloak of ugliness to wear, and they had each accepted it without question. (34)

The bad faith of the Breedloves, however, is not singular. Instead, it typifies that of fellow blacks in the novel who, as a result of the contempt displayed them by the Other, seek to emulate the prescribed standard of beauty, which Morrison terms "probably the most destructive [idea] in the history of human thought" (*BE* 97), and "extinguish [themselves] as pariahs" (Samuels and Weems 11). On the bad faith of Pecola, Samuels and Weems have written:

> Pecola's failure to define and accept her own perceptions denies her inherent freedom and responsibility but does not negate their existence. Because she fails to realize this responsibility, Pecola fashions a life in what Sartre called "Bad Faith and Falsehood." She remains dishonest with herself. This is the crucial point that Morrison's text reveals about Pecola: By acting in "Bad Faith," Pecola remains responsible, in the final analysis, for what happens to her. (15)

The self-negation that leads to madness is prefigured in the novel in Pecola's ponderance of the dichotomous nature of dandelions as weeds and/or flowers. By symbolic implication, Pecola struggles to determine whether she has worth beyond her own instrumentality. The disdain displayed toward her by others, however, because of her blackness, leads her to conclude that she, by implication, and they are ugly: "They *are* weeds" (43).

As shall be seen in a later chapter in this study, namely, in Simone Schwarz-Bart's *The Bridge of Beyond,* this existential angst resultant from both disinheritance and the petrification of the Other by *les lâches* that characterize the Breedloves and Mr. Biswas likewise becomes transmuted into madness.

Psychosis is also the result of Margaret Cadmore's dislocation in *Maru,* a novel by South African author Bessie Head. A Masarwa, "a term of contempt which means, obliquely, a low, filthy nation" (12), Margaret Cadmore had been orphaned and had been reared by the British woman Margaret Cadmore for whom she had been named. Mistaken for the racial group Coloured by Dikeledi, another primary school teacher, and the principal Pete, Margaret Cadmore belongs nowhere. To dramatize the "nowhereness" of Margaret, Head introduces a pair of goats with the same characteristics as Margaret, namely, they seem to belong to no one, "the owners of Sheba and the Windscreen-wiper never seemed to bother about their comings or goings or how they spent their days or what they ate" (111); their appearance makes them an anomaly, "She was big and snow white, the baby pitch black, with shiny, curly hair" (95); and Margaret and the goat Windscreen-wiper both suffer the trauma of abandonment.

The Windscreen-wiper had witnessed the slaughter of his mother and had returned "trembling from head to toe in an agony all his own" (119). In the same manner, Margaret had suffered abandonment, in the figurative sense by her mother who had died in childbirth (12) and in the literal sense by Margaret Cadmore, her adopted mother, who retired to England after having succeeded only in part in her "experiment" to "unBushman" Margaret (18). The affinity between Margaret and Windscreen-wiper could be no less clear than as evidenced in the following description of their mergence of beings:

> The previous day he had seen his mother slaughtered before his eyes. It had almost deranged his mind. His owners had tied him to a tree and that morning he had broken free of the string and run away. He darted into the safety of the room. She pushed the door shut. The remaining threads went snap, snap, snap behind her neck and she half-stumbled, half reeled to the bed and fell on it in a dead faint. (120)

Among the titles under consideration in this study—Alice Walker's *The Third Life of Grange Copeland,* Simone Schwarz-Bart's *The Bridge of Beyond,* Mariama Bâ's *So Long a Letter* and *Scarlet Song,* and Beryl Gilroy's *Frangipani House*—virtually all depict madness in relation to racial and sexual politics and reveal that the disorder is related to racial and social conditions. Each novel presents a criticism of a patriarchal political and social system for its petrification of the individual into stereotypes, which Sartre identifies as "the profound meaning of the myth of Medusa" (*Being and Nothingness* 406), and its repudiation of the free subjectivity of the individual for either capitalistic or paternalistic ends, or both. The intersection of racism and sexism is most apparent in the works of African American authors Zora Neale Hurston, Toni Morrison, and Alice Walker, in Caribbean author Simone Schwarz-Bart, and African author Buchi Emecheta, who often depict females as suffering from triple jeopardy: oppression due to race, gender, and, in some instances, poverty, and illiteracy. Marie H. Buncombe argues that the impact of race and class on gender roles can be seen in Alice Walker's *The Third Life of Grange Copeland* in Grange's instrumentalization of women in his first and second lives in order to achieve manhood:

> In his first life of grinding poverty and despair as a black sharecropper in Georgia, Grange Copeland sought refuge in the ample girth of Josie, the owner of the local whorehouse. His misguided ideas of manhood, he subsequently realized, led him to believe that his cruelty and indifference to his wife and son were the fault of an oppressive white society; his infidelities were born out of necessity for self-respect and his feeling of manliness . . . playing out the role of the despised, depraved, desperate brute . . . . [In his second life], he preyed on the old and weak in order to eat; sold drugs, liquor and black women on Harlem streets in order to survive. (422)

On the fictional objectives of Buchi Emecheta, Rose Mezu summarizes in her article "Buchi Emecheta, The Enslaved African Woman and the Creative Process": "[The] main themes of my novels are African society and family: the historical, social and political life as seen by a woman through events. I always try to show that the African male is oppressed and he too oppresses the African woman" (qtd. in Mezu, 67).

Simone de Beauvoir in her work *The Second Sex* conceives of the female as the Other incarnate for the male and hence representative within the existential ontology of the *en-soi*. The conviction of the female as Other, as argued by de Beauvoir, is contained in the creation myth, namely, in the following well-known legend of Genesis: Eve was not created in her own right, but as a help mate for Adam; too, she was not fashioned from the same clay of the earth, as was Adam, but from the flank of Adam. Hence, according to de Beauvoir, the destiny of the female was that of complement, or Other, to the Subject, the male: "She was destined by

Him for man; it was to rescue Adam from loneliness that He gave her to him, in her mate was her origin and her purpose" (131). Man's literal and figurative possession of the female, the *en-soi*, is representative therefore of the attempt of the male, the *pour-soi*, to achieve his own apotheosis, to become coincident with himself, or to become the foundation of his own being, the *en-soi-pour-soi:*

> Appearing as the Other, woman appears at the same time as an abundance of being in contrast to that existence the nothingness of which man senses in himself; the Other, being regarded as the object in the eyes of the subject, is regarded as *en soi;* therefore as a being. In woman is incarnated in positive form the lack that the existent carries in his heart, and it is in seeking to be made whole through her that man hopes to attain self-realization. (131)

Cynthia A. Davis in her article "Self, Society, and Myth in Toni Morrison's Fiction" has argued, in a manner similar to the author in her assertion that Mr. Biswas experiences angst as a result of his reification as an inutile object, that the black woman is similarly "inadequate" as object, since she is "the antithesis of American beauty" (12). As a consequence of race and gender, black women are "doubly defined as failures and outsiders [and] are natural scapegoats for those seeking symbols of displaced emotions" (12-13). The character Pecola in *The Bluest Eye* and Sula in the book by the same title may be identified, respectively, as scapegoats for the community at large in that they mirror their own shame. Davis views this proclivity to scapegoat by the community as exhibitive of Sartrean bad faith not only because it internalizes white values, but displaces onto the Other one's own shame:

> Sartre says that one way to handle the gaze of the Third [the institutionalization of the Look] is to 'ally myself to the Third so as to look at the Other who is then transformed into our object' (*BN,* p. 392). The internalization of white values is one such act. The choice of a scapegoat goes further, displacing onto the Other all that is feared in the self, and so remaining 'free.' (12)

The consequence of objectivation by the Other is a divided consciousness resultant from the rivalry between two states of being, one's existence, or one's being as a for-itself, and one's essence, or one's being-for-others. Sartre writes in *Being and Nothingness* that "To put on clothes is to hide one's object-state; it is to claim the right of seeing without being seen; that is, to be pure subject" (265). A number of the novels surveyed depict female protagonists, such as Télumée in Simone Schwarz-Bart's *The Bridge of Beyond* and Selina Boyce in Paule Marshall's *Brown Girl, Brownstones,* who are able to repulse the assaults upon their personhood and, in so doing, achieve some degree of autonomy. Hence, these two works, from the survey of works by female authors of the African diaspora, are among the most optimistic.

Before proceeding with the examination of abandonment as a trope for divestiture related to the existence of the Other and/or the givens of race, gender, and age—prohibitions to personal freedom that result in self-alienation—and the collective responses by the aforementioned female authors to these imposed limits to their personal freedom, it may be necessary to establish more clearly the links between female African American and African literature; hence, in the following chapter, the ethnographical elements of Zora Neale Hurston's *Jonah's Gourd Vine* will be explored.

Works Cited

Beauvoir, Simone de. *The Second Sex.* Trans. and ed. H.M. Parshley. New York: Knopf, 1952. Originally published in French as *Le Deuxième Sexe* (Paris: Gallimard, 1949).

Bloom, Harold, ed. *Modern Critical Views: Toni Morrison.* New York: Chelsea House, 1990.

Brown, Alan. "'De Beast' Within: The Role of Nature in *Jonah's Gourd Vine.*" *Zora in Florida.* Eds. Steve Glassman and Kathryn Lee Seidel. Orlando: U of Central Florida P, 1991. 76-85.

Buncombe, Marie H. "Androgyny As Metaphor in Alice Walker's Novels." *College Language Association Journal* 30 (1987): 419-27.

Chancer, Lynn S. *Sadomasochism in Everyday Life: The Dynamics of Power and Powerlessness.* New Brunswick: Rutgers UP, 1992.

Cudjoe, Selwyn R. *V.S. Naipaul: A Materialist Reading.* Amherst: U of Massachusetts P, 1988.

Dance, Daryl C. "Daddy May Bring Home Some Bread, But He Don't Cut No Ice: The Economic Plight of the Father Figure in Black American Literature." *Journal of Afro-American Issues* 3 & 4 (summer/

fall, 1975): 297-308.

Davis, Cynthia A. "Self, Society, and Myth in Toni Morrison's Fiction." Bloom, 7-25.

Head, Bessie. *Maru*. London: Heinemann, 1971.

Killinger, John. *Hemingway and the Dead Gods: A Study in Existentialism*. Lexington: U of Kentucky P, 1960.

Mezu, Rose U. "Buchi Emecheta: The Enslaved African Woman and the Creative Process." *The Zora Neale Hurston Forum* 8 (fall 1993): 61-85.

Morrison, Toni. *The Bluest Eye*. New York: Washington Square Press, 1970.

Naipaul, V.S. *A House for Mr. Biswas*. New York: Penguin, 1961.

Rohlehr, Gordon. "Character and Rebellion in *A House for Mr. Biswas*." *Critical Perspectives on V.S. Naipaul*. Ed. Robert D. Hamner. Washington, D.C.: Three Continents Press, 1977. 84-93.

Samuels, Wilfred D., and Clenora Hudson-Weems. *Toni Morrison*. New York: Twayne, 1990.

Sartre, Jean-Paul. *Being and Nothingness: An Essay in Phenomenological Ontology*. Trans. Hazel E. Barnes. Secaucus: Philosophical Library, 1956.

———. "Childhood of a Leader." *Intimacy and Other Stories*. Trans. Lloyd Alexander. New York: New Directions, 1948.

———. *Existentialism and Humanism*. Trans. Philip Mairet. London: Methuen, 1948.

———. *Existential Psychoanalysis*. Trans. Hazel E. Barnes. New York: Philosophical Library, 1953.

———. *Nausea*. Trans. Lloyd Alexander. New York: New Directions, 1964. Originally published in French as *La Nausée* (Paris: Gallimard, 1938).

Stern, Alfred. *Sartre: His Philosophy and Existential Psychoanalysis*. 2nd rev. and enlarged ed. New York: Delacorte, 1967.

Toffler, Alvin. *Future Shock*. New York: Random, 1970.

Chapter 3

RESONANCES OF THE AFRICAN CONTINENT IN SELECTED FICTION AND NON-FICTION BY ZORA NEALE HURSTON

In *Jonah's Gourd Vine*, Hurston's first novel, readers find vestiges of African culture, such as the symbolic washing of the bride and groom. Among some African peoples, the rite is performed the morning following the couple's union. The two wash themselves in cold water in a courtyard enclosure that is guarded by the bride's sister. The ritual act symbolizes a binding together of the couple and the beginning of a new state of matrimony; also, the beginning of productivity, or the bringing forth of new life. According to John S. Mbiti in *African Religions and Philosophy:* "Symbolically these ritual ablutions are partly the death of the former life of unproductivity, and partly the resurrection of the new life of pro-creation" (183).

As can be gleaned from a reading of *Jonah's Gourd Vine*, some of the purity of the customs has been lost; that is, they exist in an adulterated state, *e.g.*, the ritual act is performed before rather than after the union of the couple, but even so, they are recognizable: "Us goin' and bath M'haley fuh huh weddin'-night. Some uh y'all men folks grab Pomp, and give him uh washin' off" (84).

Another African custom that is retained is the burial of the umbilical cord. Pheemy functions in the role of mid-wife at the Pearson plantation, and she has been given the responsibility of performing the ancient rites of burying the umbilical cord, a sign of the child's attachment to the mother. The burial of the umbilical cord in the backyard represents the membership of the child in the larger community and, concurrently, its physical separation from the mother. Mbiti in *African Religions and Philosophy* examines the importance of this custom:

> Physically the placenta and umbilical cord symbolize the separation of the child from the mother, but this separation is not final since the two are still near each other. But the child now begins to belong to the wider circle of society. For that reason, the placenta is kept close to the house or placed in a calabash for everyone to see it. (147)

As can be gleaned from *Kaffir Boy: The True Story of a Black Youth's Coming of Age in Apartheid South Africa,* by Mark Mathabane, the burial of the afterbirth is also designed to protect the mother and child from evil. After the birth of Mathabane's third sister, Merriam, Mathabane espies midwives engaged in the secret burial:

> In keeping with tribal tradition, she [my mother] and the baby remained in seclusion for about two weeks, and for that period my father, George and I had to be housed by neighbours, for the presence of males was forbidden during seclusion. The day the baby was born, I spied, in the dead of night, midwives, under a cloak of great secrecy, digging small holes near the house. When I asked what the holes were for, I was told that "sacred things from my mother and the new child" were being buried to prevent witches from taking possession of the stuff and using it to affect the well-being of both. (91)

Reference to the ancient custom is made likewise in *Jonah's Gourd Vine* upon the arrival of John, Amy Crittenden's son, at the Pearson plantation. It immediately bestows a familial aspect upon Pheemy's relationship with John. She tells him: "Ahm yo' granny! Yo' nable string is buried under dat air chanyberry tree. 'Member so well de very day you cried" (19). When John marries Lucy Potts and Lucy gives birth to their children, Pheemy also presides over the deliveries and the burial of the umbilical cord(s). The performance of the ritual has taken on a religious mien, since one is led to believe that a failure to honor this ancient ritual is to invite disaster upon the young mother and her child (92).

In Alice Walker's *The Temple of My Familiar,* the practice of burying the afterbirth is to bring good fortune. The elder Hal relates to Suwelo, the nephew of his belated friend Rafe, the occasion of the birth of Lulu, the daughter belonging to him and Lissie:

> "When the afterbirth came—a lump of bloody, liverish-looking stuff that made me feel even woozier than I was—she wrapped it in newspaper and gave it to me to bury at the corner of the house for luck, so that we could have a houseful of babies." (107)

The burial of the umbilical cord and the afterbirth is one vestige of African custom in African American culture; another is the belief in Voodoo. African Voodoo is identified as a religion that is an inherent part of African American folklore. Barbara Speisman in her article "Voodoo as Symbol in *Jonah's Gourd Vine*" argues that given the criticism that the novel lacks structural and character development, readers may gain a better understanding of John Buddy by "conceiv[ing] of him as a voodoo doctor who turns away from God and uses voodoo to gain his power over his family and congregation" (88). She notes three symbols associated with the Voodoo faith in *Jonah's Gourd Vine:* the sermons used to inspire worshippers (Speisman 89), the serpent that represents "the unknown spirit who creates everything" (88), and the drum. According to Speisman, the drum in chapter two of *Jonah's Gourd Vine* is denotative of "the mysteries of Africa" (89): "So they danced. They called for the instrument that they had brought to America in their skins—the drum—and they played upon it" (29).

Other than referring to the drum as a symbol of "the mysteries of Africa," Barbara Speisman in her article is surprisingly reticent on the unique functions of the drum in African, African American, and Caribbean culture. According to the *Larousse Dictionary of World Folklore,* however, the drum in ancient times was used as "a means of communication, particularly over distance, by agreed signals or by mimicking the actual patterns, intervals and inflections of human speech" (152); also, as a protective measure during funerals and weddings; and as a musical instrument "to set the pace for communal dancing or folk songs" (152). The latter application hold true for *Jonah's Gourd Vine*. The communal dancing marks the end of the harvest season. Hogs, yams, and peanuts are roasted, and only (29) the drum ("Us don't want no fiddles, neither no guitars, neither no banjos. Less clap!") warrants inclusion in this communal celebration.

In Haitian culture, according to the *Funk and Wagnalls Standard Dictionary of Folklore, Mythology and Legend* (326-27), the vodum drum, often a wooden Lapp drum, is a source of devination. In an elaborate naming ceremony, the vodum drum is endowed with a soul, and custom prohibits the playing of the drum until after it has been christened. Various paintings, carvings, and attachments of various objects to the drum increase its mystical power:

> Signs and figures painted with blood or alder bark juice on the head of a type of Lapp drum were used for divination. A collection of small rings on the head were kept in motion as the drum was beaten, and according to the signs on which they came to rest the shaman made predictions. (327)

The drum in African American and Caribbean literature accretes additional meaning. For example, in *Jonah's Gourd Vine,* the drum takes on as well the aspect of resistance. Legend has it that Cuffy, when stripped of his raiments by slavers in Africa, "seized his drum and hid it in his skin under the skull bones" (29). The drum embodies his ancestry that he is intent on preserving; it also embodies the concept of resistance, since the drum was taken in defiance of the slavers who had reasoned that "He will serve us better if we bring him from Africa naked and thing-less" (29). The connection of the drum to resistance is apparent in *The Bridge of Beyond* as well. Ma Cia, for instance, champions Télumée to "Be a fine little Negress, a real drum with two sides. Let life bang and thump, but keep the underside always intact" (39).

John S. Mbiti in *African Religions and Philosophy* differentiates in his discussion of the concept of mystical power between "good magic," one of the implements of its practitioners being the drum, and "evil magic," which is linked to witchcraft, "a term used more popularly and broadly, to describe all sorts of evil employment of mystical power, generally in secret fashion" (264). "Good magic" is the form practiced by specialists such as rainmakers, diviners, or medicine-men who employ their power for the good of their community (259). On the other hand, "evil magic" is used by the practitioners to harm others. As a result of their association with death and misfortune, Mbiti identifies the practitioners of "evil magic," or sorcerers, as "the most feared and hated members of their communities" (261).

The truth of Mbiti's statement is contained in Mark Mathabane's *Kaffir Boy: The True Story of a Black Youth's Coming of Age in Apartheid South Africa.* At an early age, Mathabane had impressed upon him by his mother the danger of association with witchdoctors. Often delirious from hunger, he would resort to begging food from the neighbors in his Alexandra township. On one occasion, he was punished by his mother on her suspicion that he had accepted unsuspectingly poisoned food from voodoo doctors purported to give food to gullible victims in order to test the potency of their concoctions (99). So terrorized was Mathabane by the revelation that he had begged to be taken to a tribal doctor to have the alleged poison counteracted. So effective was the reprimand of the mother that Mathabane thereafter was to give a wide berth to strangers: "I now refused food from strangers, fearful that it might be voodooed. I even avoided standing anywhere near unfamiliar people, afraid that they might suddenly grab me and forcibly feed me voodooed food" (99).

Ironically, the mother, as Mark Mathabane reports in *Kaffir Boy in America,* had failed to heed her own advice, as she had taken into their Alexandra home a wizard and his family of five. The arrangement was to have been a temporary one; however, when the mother had asked the Mathebulas after several months to seek alternative living arrangements, the wizard, described by Mathabane as "a proud and chauvinistic man" (99), had taken offense. Mathabane learns from a letter written by family members to him in America that "From strands of my mother's hair and pieces of clothing, which he had gathered while he lived in our house, he allegedly concocted his voodoo and drove my mother mad" (99). Treatment was sought from Mark Mathabane's aunt, a powerful *isangoma,* or medicine woman. After a one-year treatment, Mathabane reports in *Kaffir Boy in America* that the sorcerer was identified, the evil magic reversed, and his mother cured. Mathabane cites illiteracy as the primary cause for the popular belief in witchcraft among Black South Africans. Lacking knowledge of causal relationships, they blame their problems—unemployment, gambling, arrests—on witchcraft. The "cures" effected by the *isangomas* he deems the result of the medicine women's knowledge of the medicinal effects of bark, leaves, and roots and the psychological relief that they provide to those seeking cures.

In light of Mbiti's classification of magic, the wizard referred to by Mathabane in this instance may be classified as a doer of "evil magic" and the medicine woman a doer of "good magic." The former classification would apply to Dangie Dewoe of *Jonah's Gourd Vine* as well, as she uses her power to drive a wedge between Lucy and John Pearson and to destroy Lucy. When Hattie visits her with a complaint of John Buddy's disinterest, Dangie Dewoe instructs her to eat the wish-beans that she provides her and to deposit the casings outside the gate that borders the Pearson home (126). Mbiti describes a myriad of methods used by sorcerers that coincide with one of those employed by Dangie Dewoe, as described above: "[T]hey dig evil medicine in the ground where the victim will pass; they put magic objects in the homes or where the victim will pass; they put magic objects in the homes or fields of their victim; or send 'death' from a distance; they might change into animals [lycanthropy] in order to attack their victims; or they place harmful medicines where the victim will come into contact with it" (262).

Dangie Dewoe in *Jonah's Gourd Vine* is named for Aunt Dangie Deveaux (pronounced Andangie Dewoe, a famed obeah woman of the Bahamas ("Hoodoo in America" 320). In the article "Hoodoo in America," Hurston recounts some of the obeah woman's exploits, which identify her unequivocally with evil. For example, legend has it that she avenged the desertion by a sailor of her granddaughter by sinking the ship *Smile* that he was believed to be aboard: "Andangie took her bottle in her mouth and bent way over till her head nearly touched the ground. She turned all of her clothes over her head and the *Smile* went to the bottom of the sea as if it had been torpedoed" (404). Hurston also notes in the same article that to "walk out of the sight of man . . . , you have to sell yourself to the devil first" (387).

Part of the stock in trade of witchdoctors, as contained in *Mules and Men, Jonah's Gourd Vine,* and the article "Hoodoo in America" are coffins, grave yard dirt ("Hoodoo in America" 388), and bitter bones. After the instruction of Dangie Dewoe to Hattie in *Jonah's Gourd Vine,* Dangie Dewoe "held de bitter bone in [her] mouf so's [Hattie] kin walk out de sight uh men" (126).

Illuminative of the function of the bitter bone and its source is *Mules and Men,* a collection of Negro folklore compiled by Hurston during various field expeditions to the South. On one expedition, Hurston was an understudy of the New Orleans hoodoo/voodoo doctor Father Watson, or "Frizzly Rooster," and it was under his tutelage that she had learned of the potency of the bitter bone on its subjects "to walk invisible. Some things must be done in deep secret, so you have to walk out of the sight of man" (207). Hurston in *Mules and Men* also describes her capture of a black cat for the bitter bone. The end product was achieved by "pass[ing] the bones of the [immolated] cat through my mouth until one tasted bitter" (208).

Dangie Dewoe, in order to part John and Lucy Pearson of *Jonah's Gourd Vine,* utters the incantation "Fight and fuss 'til you part, . . . rub[s] her hands and forehead with war powder, put the catbone in her mouth, and [lay] herself down in the red coffin facing the altar and went into the spirit" (126). Three months later, Lucy is pronounced dead. From evidence provided by Hurston in *Mules and Men,* one can draw the conclusion that Dangie Devoe has performed a "killing ceremony."

It was during a training period with Anatol Pierre, a New Orleans hoodoo doctor who laid "some feeble claim to kinship with the Marie Leveau" (196), that she witnessed a "killing ceremony" *(Mules and Men* 213) similar to the one performed by the witch doctor Dangie Dewoe in *Jonah's Gourd Vine.* A man named Muttsy Ivins, fearful of reprisals from the husband of his mistress, sought the services of Anatol Pierre: "Ah wan't him out de way—kilt, cause he swear he's gointer kill me. And since one of us got to die, Ah'd ruther it to be him than me" (198). As part of the "killing ceremony," a black cat was entombed and covered with a cloth to prevent its escape. Later entombed with the black cat for a period of one month was a black chicken that had been fed "a half glass of whiskey in which a paper had been soaked that bore the name of the person who was to die" (199). At the end of the one-month period, a six-inch coffin containing a small doll that represented the victim was carried to the grave of the cat and the chicken and buried upon the remains. The culmination of the "death ceremony" was the repose of Anatol Pierre every night for ninety days, surrounded by black burning candles, in "a black draped coffin": "Every night for ninety days Pierre slept in his holy place in a black draped coffin. And the man died" (199).

The time markers in *Jonah's Gourd Vine* are these. The sons Hezekiah and John are still away at school in Jacksonville, Florida, when Lucy becomes bedridden. Thus reader can date the onslaught of Lucy's illness around June (127). Three months later, correspondent with the period of repose by the hoodoo doctor as recorded by Hurston in *Mules and Men*, Lucy expires: "They put Lucy in a little coffin next day, the shiny coffin that held the beginning and the ending of so much. And the September woods were ravished by the village to provide tight little bouquets for the funeral" (135).

Hurston notes in *Mules and Men* that the popularity of voodooism among African Americans is symbolic of their African ties:

> New Orleans is now and has ever been the hoodoo capital of America. Great names in rites that vie with those of Hayti [sic] in deeds that keep alive the powers of Africa.
> Hoodoo, or Voodoo, . . . is burning with a flame in America, with all the intensity of a suppressed religion. It has its thousands of secret adherents. (176)

Hattie is identified in *Jonah's Gourd Vine* as one of the "thousands of secret adherents"; another is Deacon Harris who confesses to Hattie his belief in witchcraft as well as his suspicion that John Buddy's hold upon members of his flock is due to sorcery (146). Curiously enough, Hurston describes in "Hoodoo in America" the practice, as ascertained from Ruth Mason, a well-known hoodoo doctor of New Orleans, of maintaining a congregation: "Take Shia seeds, mustard seeds, nine spoons of powdered sugar. Put in deep plate. Put blue candle in plate and put Shia seeds with sugar and mustard and burn one candle every day for three days, and put it at the four corners of block and people will flock there and never notice nothing [preacher] has done" (375). Indeed, Deacon Harris implies that John Buddy is a shaman, and by invoking "Jonah's gourd vine," ("Ah'd cut down dat Jonah's gourd vine in uh minute") condemns him as a fraud in the same manner that the protective shield for Jonah was fraudulent. After its destruction, the Lord chastises Jonah for his lamentations of loss:

> "You pity the plant, for which you did not labor, nor did you make it grown, which came into being in a night, and perished in a night. And should not I pity Ninevah, that great city, in which there are more than a hundred and twenty thousand persons who do not know their right hand from their left, and also much cattle?" (Jonah 4:10-11; qtd. in Foreword, xii)

Given Lucy's role in the novel as confidante, protector of John and as intercessor between him and the congregation, she is analogous to the gourd vine. Such is clear when John describes Lucy's care-giving manner in the following protective terms (173):

> Lucy must have had good eyes. She had seen so much and told him so much it had wearied him, but she hadn't seen all this. Maybe she had, and spared him. She would. Always spreading carpets for his feet and breaking off the points of thorns. But . . . her likes were no more on this earth!

John's fall is related not only to his insouciance, but it is related too to his behavior toward Lucy when she is close to dying. Although John prides himself in not being a "woman jessie," one who "beat[s] up women and run[s] from mens" (56), the indiscriminate act toward Lucy seems to have placed upon him a curse. Lucy had pronounced that "De hidden wedge will come tuh light some day, John. Mark mah words" (129). Alice Walker corroborates the sentiment that the destruction of Hurston's male characters stems from their ill treatment of their wives. Walker has justified Tea Cake's death in Hurston's *Their Eyes Were Watching God* as punishment for Tea Cake's braggadocio which formed part of Janie's public humiliation:

> An astute reader would realize that this [the beating] is the
> real reason TeaCake is killed by Janie in the end. Or, rather,
> this is the reason Hurston **permits** Janie to kill TeaCake in
> the end. For all her "helpless" hanging on him, Janie knows
> she has been publicly humiliated, and though she acts the
> role of battered wife . . . , her developing consciousness of
> self does not stop at that point. She could hardly enjoy
> knowing her beating becomes "visions" for other women .
> . . and "dreams" for TeaCake's male friends. (*In Search of
> Our Mothers' Gardens* 305-6)

In an explanation to Carl Van Vechten of the novel's title, Hurston
had proffered: "Oh yes, the title you didn't understand (Jonah 4:6-
10). You see the prophet of God sat up under a gourd vine that had
grown up in one night. But a cut worm came along and cut it
down. Great and sudden growth. One act of malice and it is with-
ered and gone" (qtd. in Hemenway 192).

Hurston provides clues in *Jonah's Gourd Vine* that are at odds
with her stated claim that John Buddy's fall is due to his own responsibility. In fact, she suggests the opposite in the novel, namely,
that John's fall is the result of voodoo. An example is found in
chapter nineteen, where John confronts his second wife and the
town vamp Hattie with questions regarding his seven children with
Lucy, his church, and his marriage to her, since he lacks remembrance (144). The deacons of Zion Baptist Church agitate for his
removal in light of his recent behavior—his marriage to his mistress three months after Lucy's death and the report that he "drawed
uh knife" on his namesake who attempted to prevent Hattie from
taking possession of the feather bed belonging to Isis. Hattie, aware
of the enmity against her, gloats, "Dey can't move me—not wid de
help Ah got" (139), apparently in reference to the "piece of John-
de-conquer root," reported by Hurston as the most widely used
root by root-and-conjure doctors, underbraided in her hair aimed to
protect their marriage at the same time that it effectuates John
Buddy's disaster. In *Mules and Men* and in the article "High John
De Conquer," Hurston reports that the John de Conqueror roots
are the most widely used by root-and-conjure doctors (179; 262).

John De Conquer, as legend has it, is the protector of the African American race. His spirit is said to reside in the High John de

Conquer root that is used as a charm against catastrophe: "High John de Conquer went back to Africa, but he left his power here, and placed his American dwelling in the root of a certain plant. Only possess that root, and he can be summoned at any time" (452).

Further evidence of the nature of the voodoo practices, as used by Hattie Tyson to secure her marriage to John Buddy, is implicated by Hambo in his identification to John Buddy the precise method of his ruination: "John, youse in boilin' water and tuh you—look lak 'tain't no help fuh it. Dat damn 'oman you got b'lieves in all kinds uh roots and conjure. She been feedin' you outa her body fuh years" (161). Hambo's claim, "feedin' you outa her body fuh years," is meant literally, as Hurston describes in "Hoodoo in America" the voodoo practices from New Orleans and Palatica, Florida, respectively, of putting urine (372) or menstrual blood in the food of the object to secure his affection: "Take nine days—wait till you see the new moon to begin. Take one teaspoon of your own urine each day and put it in his tea or coffee or anything, and you can lead him by the nose" (372).

Hattie Tyson, after John Buddy's expression of doubt, combined with regret, over the union of the two, wonders whether "de roots jus' wore out and done turn'd back on me" (144). Attendant the cure of insanity of Mark Mathabane's mother in *Kaffir Boy in America* has been the reversal of the effects of the hoodoo upon the wizard. Mathabane's mother had opposed revenge; however, "[i]t was believed that no cure of witchcraft was complete until the black magic had reverted to the sorcerer" (100). The reversal brings tragedy to the Mathebulas, namely, the loss of two sons from murder by *tsotsis* (gangsters). Thus, the reversal of roots, in this instance, is not the result of a lack of potency, as Hattie Tyson avers, but, possibly, of retribution.

Given the propensity of the author to depict John Buddy as a victim of circumstance, as when he is described as sacrificed "on the altar of destruction" (167), the reader is inclined to disagree with Rita Dove's assertion that the narrative voice is a neutral one (xiv-xv). Hurston is clearly empathetic with John Buddy, as a reading of her autobiography *Dust Tracks on a Road* would indicate. For example, John Buddy, after his assault upon his brother-in-law Bud Potts, following Pott's seizure of their wedding bed in order to satisfy a three-dollar debt, goes scot-free. It may be argued that a warrant to settle personal scores, as executed by Potts, is deemed by the town culture as an act of cowardice or poor gamesmanship: "Decency was plumb outraged at a man taking a beating and then swearing out a warrant about it" (*Dust Tracks on a Road* 44). A similar view is expressed by one of the townspeople in *Seraph on the Suwanee* subsequent to the brawl between Jim Meserve and Hawley Pitts and the appeal by the sheriff for witnesses:

> "It was a fair fight wasn't it?" one irritated citizen blurted out at last. "What more can a man ask for than that? If Pitts had of won he would of felt that Jim was a sorry sport to have swore out a warrant against him, wouldn't he? I wouldn't go a step to testify for nothing." (93)

Hurston's biographer Hemenway, the author of *Zora Neale Hurston: A Literary Biography,* also seems to take issue with this claim of neutrality, as he argues that John Buddy fails to achieve tragic dimensions because the author sacrifices his individuality for group analysis:

> Hurston suggests that this lack of control over one's destiny is the obvious product of Afro-American history. Uprooted from his homeland, thrown into an alien culture, the African adapted as best he could to the barbaric institutions offered him by the white man. But the African heritage was never lost. (Hemenway 197)

Alan Brown goes even further and argues that

> Although Hurston's sympathies certainly lie with Lucy Pearson, whose loyalty, perseverance, and love border on the messianic, her novel is not a total indictment of Lucy's husband. In fact, she seems to have a grudging admiration for a man who will not allow himself to be the paragon of virtue that the community requires him to be. (84)

Not only are the sentiments of the author conveyed through characterization, as Brown's remarks make clear, but as well through the imagery surrounding minor characters. The character Ned Crittenden, for example, is given a name that connotes an animalistic nature. That is, he is described in terms that reveal the brutal-izing impact of slavery. He is described as "[looking] scarcely human on the floor. Almost like an alligator in jeans. His drooling blue lips and snaggled teeth were yellowed by tobacco" (8).

Jonah's Gourd Vine is an autobiographical novel. In the Intro-duction to *Critical Essays on Zora Neale Hurston,* Gloria L. Cronin observes that "In *Jonah's Gourd Vine* (1934), Hurston described the plight of her mother, her preacher father, and herself in the patriarchal Christian South" (2). The parallels between Hurston's first novel and Hurston's autobiography *Dust Tracks on a Road* are clear. Eatonville, Florida, the all-Negro village referred to in the novel is the birthplace of Hurston (*Dust Tracks on a Road* 3). John Hurston, described in *Dust Tracks on a Road* as a mulatto with "gray-green eyes and light skin" (19), married the diminutive ninety-pound Lucy Potts, the daughter of landowner Richard Potts. In *Dust Tracks on a Road,* the father was described as "two hundred pounds of bone and muscle and Mama weighed some-where in the nineties" (22); however, despite the contrast in ap-pearances, the mother was the dominant force in the marriage, namely, due to her sharp tongue.

It is Pearlie Peters' contention in *The Assertive Woman in Zora Neale Hurston's Fiction* that talk becomes a means by which the females in Hurston's fiction, folklore, and drama assert their worth (xvi). Peters also contends that their metamorphosis is pre-figured in speech, and the example is given of Lucy in *Jonah's Gourd Vine* who, after suffering many years of marital infidelity by John Buddy, becomes transfigured from an innocent child bride to an embit-tered wife (5). The faithful wife to an adulterer, according to Pe-ters, is one of a number of types of the assertive woman in Hurston's fiction, folklore, and drama. Another is the jook woman, such as Big Sweet of *Mules and Men,* who has built a reputation on both her verbal and physical pugnaciousness (31-32).

Peters argues that the antithesis of the assertive woman is the female, such as Hattie Tyson of *Jonah's Gourd Vine,* who lacks the same verbal arsenal and has to rely upon hoodoo in order to achieve her ends (20). Peters conceptualizes Tyson as an inconsequential opponent to Lucy, largely because she resorts to witchcraft to thwart her opponent:

> A woman resorting to this indirect method of self-expression is such a petty, pitiful figure when placed alongside of the assertive woman of natural and direct verbal power who survives on native wit and direct confrontation. The latter talks to bring about action and change directly; she does not need the devious mediation of hoodoo to accomplish her goals. We cannot imagine a Big Sweet, Janie or Lucy soliciting the aid of a hoodoo practitioner to do evil or to win control of a man or fight a battle with a woman adversary. The drama of word power is the assertive woman's potent weapon of self-defense. (21)

Peters' dismissal of the methods used by Hattie Tyson to secure her ends seems premature, especially since she is aided and abetted by Dangie Dewoe, the conjurer named for the legendary obeah woman Aunt Dangie Deveaux of the Bahamas and since the illness that claims Lucy's life remains a mystery, an illness that Peters matter-of-factly diagnoses as tuberculosis (123). Peters is correct, however, in noting that John Buddy is no match for Lucy "who spoke in tune with an Omnipotent God. Her assertive voice fostered his prosperous rise and predicted his most tragic fall. Throughout the novel, Lucy speaks with the voice of truth and authority in her mouth, although her marriage to John for the most part was one of misery and betrayal" (125-26).

John Buddy is subjected to a series of Lucy's "tongue lashes" in *Jonah's Gourd Vine,* one of which follows his desertion while Lucy is pregnant with their fourth child. It is during his absence that Bud Potts, Lucy's brother, takes possession of the wedding bed in order to satisfy an outstanding three-dollar debt. John Buddy's assault upon Bud that he considers a defense of his honor leads to incarceration. Lucy intercedes with Judge Alf Pearson on his behalf, but prior to his arrest for assault, she "tongue lashes" him on his irresponsibility, evoking from him the following response: "Dat piece uh red flannel she got hung 'tween her jaws is equal tuh all de fistes God ever made and man ever seen" (96).

Isis, the younger of the two daughters in *Jonah's Gourd Vine,* is the fictional surrogate for Zora Neale Hurston; the elder, for Sarah, who has been identified in her autobiography as the favorite of her father (97). On the other hand, Isis in *Jonah's Gourd Vine* is described by Lucy as "mah chile 'bove all de rest" (127). Just as Isis had inherited her mother's "spunk," the daughter Sarah had inherited her father's mildness. Hurston writes in *Dust Tracks on a Road:*

> My older sister was meek and mild. She would always get along. Why couldn't I be like her? Mama would keep right on with whatever she was doing and remark, "Zora is my youn'un, and Sarah is yours". . . . She meant by that that Sarah had a disposition like Papa's, while mine was like hers (21-22).

An example of the father's preference of Sarah is contained in Hurston's autobiography. From Hurston's *Dust Tracks on a Road,* it is learned that the school-age children, including the author herself, were sent, or returned, to Jacksonville following the mother's death to attend school; however, the first-born daughter and, also, the favored child, Sarah, was to return home to be near her father. It was Sarah's criticism of the father's premature marriage to the second wife and the step mother's jealousy of the intimate bond between father and daughter that caused the split. The new wife had ordered Sarah out of their home and had commanded that Sarah be taught a lesson as a result of her impertinence. The upshot was that Sarah soon married, went to live at Manater River, taking the baby brother Everett with her (*Dust Tracks on a Road* 97).

In *Jonah's Gourd Vine,* John's propensity to indulge the first-born daughter is suggested in the characterization of her as a "doll-baby" (93) upon her birth. In *Dust Tracks on a Road* Hurston recalls that she and the other siblings were often saved from chastisement by Sarah's involvement in their schemes:

> If the rest of us wanted to sneak jelly or preserves and get off without a licking, the thing to do was to get Sarah in on it. Papa might ignore the whipping purge that Mama was organizing until he found that Sarah was mixed up in it. Then he would lay aside the county newspaper which he was given to reading, and shout at Mama, "Dat'll do! Dat'll do, Lulu! I can't stand all dat racket around de place." (99)

Another autobiographical feature of *Jonah's Gourd Vine* is the manner of John Buddy's death, namely, by automobile accident comparable to that of Hurston's own father. Hurston in *Dust Tracks on a Road* relates a conversation with her brother following the news of their father's death: "My father had been killed in an automobile accident during my first years at Morgan, and Bob talked to me about his last days. In reality, my father was the baby of the family. With my mother gone and nobody to guide him, life had not hurt him, but it had turned him loose to hurt himself" (172).

Early reviewers of *Jonah's Gourd Vine* remarked the novel's "juicy humor" (Cronin 5) and dialect, but, according to Cronin, failed to appreciate other elements of the novel, among them its biographical dimensions:

> Hershel [sic] Brickell in the *North American Review* called John Pearson's sermon "simply magnificent," as did the *New York Age's* Mary Ovington White, who praised its magnificent phraseology. In short, the subtle ethnographic agendas, the womanist critique, and the biographical dimensions of the book were invisible to these early reviewers. (5)

The kinship of *Dust Tracks on a Road* to *Jonah's Gourd Vine* is not only in its autobiographical nature, as Hurston's recollections in both of memories of her parents' deaths would indicate, but in their ethnographical content as well.

Those familiar with Hurston's autobiography will also recognize the scenes descriptive of the mother's death. Again, rituals are performed in order to protect the living and to ease the loved one's passage into the afterlife. For instance, the draping of the mirror has genesis in African Voodooism. Mystic powers are associated with reflective surfaces, and the entrapment of the visage in reflective surfaces is viewed in African culture as tantamount to the entrapment of the soul. Barbara Speisman on these practices has written in "Voodoo as Symbol in *Jonah's Gourd Vine*":

> Lucy, who even on her deathbed opposes the primitive beliefs that surround her, begs her daughter not to let them practice their voodoo upon her. Her wish, however, is not

heeded, and John turns the mirror to the wall so that it will not reflect the face of the dead for eternity. (87-88)

Isis had been instructed by her mother to ignore these "superstitions," but their performance underscores the power of tradition, such as turning the body to face the East (132). The import of this practice has been underscored by Mbiti in *African Religions and Philosophy:* "The grave has an east-west shape, presumably capturing the 'movement' of the sun" (197). The practice has been identified in *Mules and Men* as one of the superstitions related to death in African American culture: "It is well known that church members are buried with their feet to the east so that they will rise on that last day facing the rising sun. Sinners are buried facing the opposite direction. The theory is that sunlight will do them harm rather than good" (213). Hurston's inability to carry out her mother's wishes produced grave feelings of helplessness and guilt that are evidenced, respectively, in *Jonah's Gourd Vine* (133) and *Dust Tracks on a Road.* In *Dust Tracks on a Road,* Hurston recounts her regret over her inability to fulfill her mother's last wishes, namely, that neither the pillow be removed from beneath her head nor that the clock and looking glass be covered:

> Now, I know that I could not have had my way against the world. The world we lived in required those acts. Anything else would have been sacrilege, and no nine-year-old voice was going to thwart them. My father was with the mores. He had restrained me physically from outraging the ceremonies established for the dying. If there is any consciousness after death, I hope that Mama knows that I did my best. She must know how I have suffered for my failure. (89)

In the "Hoodoo" section of *Mules and Men,* wherein Hurston describes various superstitions relating to the dead, she relates the one regarding mirrors. Inasmuch as it is believed that "the newly released spirit from the body is likely to be destructive, . . . a cloth is thrown over the face of a clock in the death chamber and the looking glass is covered over. The clock will never run again, nor will the mirror ever cast any more reflection if they are not covered so that the spirit cannot see them" (214).

The death ritual of covering mirrors, or reflective surfaces, is also practiced in the Caribbean culture: "In the room of the house of the deceased where the company met to attend the funeral, every clear or shining object was covered with white cloths, as looking glasses, pictures, etc." (Opie and Tatem 250). In Beryl Gilroy's *Frangipani House,* following the death of Miss Ginchi Thorley, her grandson Carlton "drew the blinds, turned the pictures to face the wall, and put out all her plants and flowers" (77) before making the announcement of her death. The practice is not only to protect the living from the dead, since "It is feared that the soul, projected out of the person in the shape of his reflection in the mirror, may be carried off by the ghost of the departed, which is commonly supposed to linger about the house till the burial" (*A Dictionary of Superstitions* 250), but it serves to intimate, as well, that "all .. vanity .. is over with the deceased" (250).

Finally, in *Dust Tracks on a Road,* Hurston wrote that her mother "exhorted her children at every opportunity to 'jump at de sun.' We might not land on the sun, but at least we would get off the ground" (20-21). In *Jonah's Gourd Vine,* it is apparent that John Buddy is likewise the beneficiary of Lucy's encouragement when she tells him to "Cover de ground you stand on. Jump at de sun and eben if yuh miss it, yuh can't help grabbin' holt uh de moon" (95).

Part of the craft of Hurston is her knack for transforming fact into fiction; of creating a rich tapestry founded on human experience. As Robert Hemenway has observed in his biography on Hurston, *Zora Neale Hurston: A Literary Biography:*

> Often the novel portrays John and Lucy in ways in which she [Hurston] apparently never thought of her parents, and the novel's plot does not follow exactly the family story. For example, there is more than a hint that Lucy's death is caused by the workings of a hoodoo doctor, an idea worth dramatic potential but apparently no basis in fact. (189-90)

Unique to Hurston, as befitting a folklorist, is also her fidelity not only to the mores of African, Caribbean and African American culture, but to the Black Southern dialect. One early reviewer wrote of *Jonah's Gourd Vine:* "Miss Hurston approached her task with a knowledge of Negro dialect and customs that is rare in contemporary writers. . . . Few will be able to deny Miss Hurston's accomplishments in an effective use of dialogue and traditional customs" (Felton 4-5). Another reviewer wrote upon the novel's publication in 1934: "Miss Hurston, who is a graduate of Barnard College and a student of anthropology, has made the study of Negro folklore her special province. This may very well account for the brilliantly authentic flair of her novel and for her excellent rendition of Negro dialect" (Wallace 8).

Hurston recalls idiomatic expressions that those who have grown up amidst the culture can respond to with the thrill of recognition. The words of Herschel Brickell, in a review of *Seraph on the Suwanee,* could apply easily to *Jonah's Gourd Vine:* "Anyone who grew up in the South will find him [her]self encountering on every page the familiar expressions of his [her] childhood, half forgotten, and invoking nostalgia, like a language that has been put away in the subconscious, being no longer heard nor used" (196). Hence, Hurston's work is priceless because it gives back the language, the culture, and, ultimately, the people to themselves. Walker was to recount the responses of her black Southern friends to her reading of Hurston's *Mules and Men:*

> No matter how they read the stories Zora had collected, no matter how much distance they tried to maintain between themselves, as new sophisticates, and the lives their parents and grandparents lived, no matter how they tried to remain cool toward all Zora revealed, in the end they could not hold back the smiles, the laughter, the joy over who she was showing them to be: descendants of an inventive, joyous, courageous, and outrageous people; loving drama, appreciating wit, and, most of all, relishing the pleasure of each other's loquacious and *bodacious* company. ("Zora Neale Hurston" 85)

Characteristic of the authenticity of Hurston's work are idiomatic expressions such as "rubbing one's nose in it," as respecting John's new love interest (154). "Proagin'" is another uniquely Southern expression, which, incidentally, Kirland C. Jones refers to as "a mispronunciation of probing" (27). In the context below, "proagin'," in reference to John, is synonymous to "tomcatting." Hence, the term is descriptive of John's infidelity, as seen in the following exchange between Hattie and John (142): "Is dat any way fuh you tuh do? Proagin' 'round half de night lak uh damn tom cat and den come heah, wakin' me up tuh ast uh damn fool question?"

The linguistic authenticity of the novel notwithstanding, the heavyhanded use of imagery, however, is criticized by Rita Dove in the foreword to the work.

> As a work of fiction, *Jonah's Gourd Vine* certainly has its flaws: transitions that jog, a little too much "local color." And though Hurston can hardly be blamed for wanting to infuse the text with the fieldwork she had done as an anthropologist, all too often her eloquent commentary stands full-blown and self-contained, interrupting the narrative flow. John's final sermon is a case in point, for even its masterful train imagery seems too heavy-handed a foreshadowing when the locomotive comes barreling out of the blue, a modern-day *deus ex machina*, to seal John's fate. (xiv)

The train, introduced in chapter two, encapsulates John's failing as a prisoner of the flesh. According to Claudia Tate in her discussion of *Dark Princess*, a Romance by Edward Burghardt DuBois, in her critical work *Psychoanalysis and Black Novels: Desire and the Protocols of Race*, "The pounding and pounding of iron" of the train roaring "through the night" are standard Victorian icons for sexual desire. . ." (73). John Buddy, having recently arrived from "over the creek," exults in his newly-acquired freedom and manhood which in the folk culture is equated to the number of female conquests. The train is described as a "panting monster" whose engine's sides "seemed to expand and contract like a fiery-lunged monster" (16). Susan Edwards Meisenhelder in her work *Hitting a Straight Lick with a Crooked Stick: Race and Gender in the Work of Zora Neale Hurston* argues that the train represents power, both sexual and material (47), and concludes that the values imbued in the train and adopted by John are the very ones that destroy him: "The 'damnation train' that kills him is the set of values displayed in this sermon and in the entire novel" (52).

With Sally's encouragement, John had returned to Sanford to see his friend Hambo and announce his revival; he is married to a propertied woman and has been appointed the new pastor of a church in Plant City. John's dalliance with Ora Patton who is described by Hambo as "fresh ez dishwater" (196), however, leaves him cold. The result is that he does not see the approaching train when he makes his way homeward: "He drove on but half-seeing the railroad from looking inward" (200).

The self-absorption that has characterized John repeatedly throughout the novel is evidenced here. He appears to be a man driven to self-destructiveness because he cannot learn from past behaviors and make a lifestyle adjustment. The pattern of deceit and contrition that was characteristic of John's relationship with Lucy is on the verge of being re-enacted in this third marriage as well: "Soon he would be in the shelter of Sally's presence. Faith and no questions asked. He had prayed for Lucy's return and God had answered with Sally" (200). Rita Terezinha Schmidt observes that John has some awareness at the end in his identification of himself as a "False pretender" (200), but argues, in a manner characteristic of his relationship with Lucy, his determination to manipulate Sally's good faith, in order to ensure the survival of the marriage: "The fact that he perceives Sally as a reincarnation of Lucy is one indication that the old pattern is about to be reenacted and that he is about to manipulate Sally's good faith. The text substantiates obliquely such a reading" (132-33).

The inability of some black men to alter their behavior to accommodate circumstances becomes, in part, the basis for their destruction. Such is the theme as well in Alice Walker's *The Third Life of Grange Copeland* and in Buchi Emecheta's novel *Second-Class Citizen.* The critic Klaus Ensslen in the article "History and Fiction in Alice Walker's *The Third Life of Grange Copeland* and Ernest Gaines' *The Autobiography of Miss Jane Pittman"* has described the character Brownfield in *The Third Life of Grange Copeland,* one of the works under review, in the following terms: "The semantic axis of Brownfield as a fictional character is defined as animal-like sensualism, incapacity or unwillingness for learning, envy towards any kind of education or constructive change" (156). The sacrifice of the women on the altar of gender oppression is likewise a constant theme in the literature under review.

WORKS CITED

Brakeley, Theresa C. "Drum." *Funk and Wagnalls Standard Dictionary of Folklore, Mythology and Legend.* New York: Funk and Wagnalls, 1972.

Brickell, Herschel. "A Woman Saved." Rev. of *Seraph on the Suwanee,* by Zora Neale Hurston. *Critical Essays on Zora Neale Hurston.* Ed. Gloria L. Cronin. New York: G.K. Hall, 1998. 195-96. Originally published in *Saturday Review of Literature,* 6 November 1948.

Brown, Alan. "'De Beast' Within: The Role of Nature in *Jonah's Gourd Vine.* " *Zora in Florida.* Eds. Steve Glassman and Kathryn Lee Seidel. Orlando: U of Central Florida P, 1991. 76-85.

Cronin, Gloria L. "Introduction: Going to the Far Horizon." *Critical Essays on Zora Neale Hurston.* Critical Essays on American Literature. Ed. James Nagel. New York: G.K. Hall, 1998. 1-29.

Dove, Rita. Foreword. *Jonah's Gourd Vine,* by Zora Neale Hurston. New York: Harper, 1990. vii-xv.

"Drum." *Larousse Dictionary of World Folklore.* Ed. Alison Jones. New York: Larousse, 1995.

Ensslen, Klaus. "History and Fiction in Alice Walker's *The Third Life of Grange Copeland* and Ernest Gaines' *The Autobiography of Miss Jane Pittman.* " *History and Tradition in Afro-American Culture.* Ed. Günter H. Lenz. Frankfurt: Campus Verlag, 1984.

Felton, Estelle. Review of *Jonah's Gourd Vine,* by Zora Neale Hurston. *The New Republic* 11 July 1934. Rpt. in Gates and Appiah, 4-5.

Gates, Henry Louis, Jr., and K.A. Appiah, ed. *Zora Neale Hurston: Critical Perspectives Past and Present.* New York: Amistad, 1993.

Gilroy, Beryl. *Frangipani House.* Oxford: Heinemann, 1989.

Glassman, Steve, and Kathryn Lee Seidel, eds. *Zora in Florida.* Orlando: U of Central Florida P, 1991.

Hemenway, Robert E. *Zora Neale Hurston: A Literary Biography.* With a Foreword by Alice Walker. Urbana: U of Illinois P, 1977.

Hurston, Zora Neale. *Dust Tracks on a Road: An Autobiography.* 1942. Reprint, edited and introduced by Robert E. Hemenway. 2nd ed. Urbana: U of Illinois P, 1984.

———. "High John De Conquer." *American Mercury* 57 (October-December 1931): 450-58.

———. "Hoodoo in America." *American Folklore* 44 (October-December 1931): 317-417.

———. *Jonah's Gourd Vine.* 1934. Reprint, with a foreword by Rita Dove. New York: HarperCollins, 1990.

———. "Mules and Men." 1935. Reprinted in *Zora Neale Hurston: Folklore, Memoirs, and Other Writings.* Comp. Cheryl A. Wall. New York: Library of America, 1995.

————. *Seraph on the Suwanee.* 1948. Reprint, with a foreword by Hazel V. Carby. New York: HarperCollins, 1991.

Jones, Kirland C. "Folk Humor and Comic Relief in Hurston's *Jonah's Gourd Vine.*" *The Zora Neale Hurston Forum* 1 (fall 1986): 26-31.

Litvinskii, B.A. "Mirrors." *The Encyclopedia of Religion* 9. Ed. Mircea Eliade. New York: Macmillan, 1987.

Mbiti, John S. *African Religions and Philosophy.* New York: Doubleday, 1970.

Meisenhelder, Susan Edwards. *Hitting a Straight Lick with a Crooked Stick: Race and Gender in the Work of Zora Neale Hurston.* Tuscaloosa and London: U of Alabama P, 1999.

"Mirrors." *A Dictionary of Superstitions.* Eds. Iona Opie and Moira Tatem. Oxford: Oxford UP, 1992.

Peters, Pearlie Mae Fisher. *The Assertive Woman in Zora Neale Hurston's Fiction, Folklore, and Drama.* Garland Series, ed. Graham Russell Hodges. New York: Garland, 1998.

Schmidt, Rita Terezinha. *"With My Sword in My Hand": The Politics of Race and Sex in the Fiction of Zora Neale Hurston.* Ph.D. diss., Univ. of Pittsburgh, 1983. Ann Arbor, MI: University Microfilms, 1988. 8411770

Schwarz-Bart, Simone. *The Bridge of Beyond.* Trans. Barbara Bray. Oxford: Heinemann, 1982.

Speisman, Barbara. "Voodoo as Symbol in *Jonah's Gourd Vine.*" Glassman and Seidel, 86-93.

Tate, Claudia. *Psychoanalysis and Black Novels: Desire and the Protocols of Race.* New York: Oxford UP, 1998.

Walker, Alice. "If the Present Looks Like the Past, What Does the Future Look Like?" *In Search of Our Mothers' Gardens: Womanist Prose.* New York: Harcourt, 1983. 290-312.

————. *The Temple of My Familiar.* New York: Pocket Books, 1989.

————. "Zora Neale Hurston: A Cautionary Tale and Partisan View." *In Search of Our Mothers' Gardens.* 83-92.

Wallace, Margaret. Rev. of *Jonah's Gourd Vine,* by Zora Neale Hurston. *The New York Times Book Review* 6 May 1934. Rpt. in Gates and Appiah, 8-9.

Chapter 4

ORPHANAGE IN BART'S *THE BRIDGE OF BEYOND* AND WALKER'S *THE THIRD LIFE OF GRANGE COPELAND*

Written in 1972 by Simone Schwarz-Bart, *The Bridge of Beyond* is a fictional autobiography that pays tribute to a remarkable woman, "Fannotte," of the author's native Guadeloupe (McKinney 58). The literal translation of the title from French, "Rain and Wind on Télumée Miracle" (Ormerod 108), encapsulates the theme of survival which is central to the novel. As Bridget Jones has remarked, "Just as Grandmother tells a folktale to reinforce the lesson: 'The horse mustn't ride you, you must ride it,' so Schwarz-Bart seems to adopt the same role, articulating her whole novel as the demonstration of a number of potent Creole sayings, especially those dealing with women and with resisting adversity" (xiii).

Télumée's fortitude links her to the other Lougandor women who "have always liked to fly high, grow wings, raise themselves up" (17). Her placement within a powerful matriarchy is contrasted with West Indian orphanage, a condition that functions in the novel as a motif for the dispossession of blacks. The result of their forced exile is an endless search to reclaim a lost motherland, a theme common to West Indian literature (Ormerod 1). Simone Schwarz-Bart's characters, however, do not undertake an odyssey to France, England, or Africa in order to recapture that which was lost. Instead, they seek to locate their country within themselves. These words of Télumée open the novel: "A man's country may be cramped or vast according to the size of his heart. I've never found my country too small, though that isn't to say my heart is great" (2).

Entwined with the sangfroid of the females is the theme of abandonment that afflicts five generations and that forces the women to
rely upon their inner reserve as well as on one another. Interest-
ingly enough, Télumée's great-grandmother Minerva settled in a
deserted hamlet that, because of its isolation, was given the name
L'Abandonnée (3). The name of the hamlet is significant since it
influences the relations of those inside its parameters. Minerva is
abandoned by the father of her child, "One Negro from Dominica
vanished as soon as he learned he had sired a child" (2-3), and it is
left to Xango to give Toussine, the daughter of Minerva, the affection that she deserves from a father.

This pattern of male behavior in *The Bridge of Beyond* is mirrored in Jeremiah, the husband of Télumée's grandmother, Toussine.
Although he is unlike the "Negro from Dominica" who deserted
Minerva, Toussine's mother, Jeremiah's death may be considered
abandonment of a different sort since the same set of circumstances
is created: a mother is left with the responsibility of fending for
herself and for her remaining daughter, Victory.

Télumée's mother, Victory, suffers a similar fate after Hubert
abandons her and her firstborn, Regina. His departure may be
viewed as a flight from responsibility, behavior which led to
Victory's dissipation, a progression slowed only by Angebert's show
of mercy toward her; however, the loss of Angebert, Télumée's
father, to murder, committed by the friend Germain, and the threat
of loss to Haut-Colbi of her daughter Télumée compelled Victory
to abandon the issue from her own womb; nonetheless, her abandonment of Télumée may be viewed as a safeguard against
Télumée's possible defilement, given Haut-Colbi's reputation as
"a great connoisseur of feminine flesh" (26). Significantly, Télumée
is not judgmental; rather, she shows great understanding of her
mother's resolve that is the consequence of an elusive happiness.

Not only do the females of five generations suffer abandonment on an individual plane, but on a spiritual plane as well. The
villagers consider themselves as having been abandoned by God,
who is identified as the white man incarnate. Ma Cia avers that
"For a long time now God has lived in the sky to set us free, and
lived in the white men's house at Belle-Feuille to flog us" (38).

The conception of a hostile, or godless, universe is decidedly
existentialist and adds another dimension to the theme of aban-

donment in the novel. In the work *Existentialism and Humanism,* Jean-Paul Sartre identified atheistic existentialism as founded on the premise of man's total subjectivism (28). Devoid of a creator who can bestow upon him an essence in the manner of an artisan who fashions a paper knife in accordance with his conception of its utility, man is obliged to invent himself. Subsequently, man's awareness of his utter aloneness in the world contributes to both his despair and anguish.

To illustrate man's state of abandonment, and the source of his anguish, Sartre related a personal anecdote of a pupil torn between remaining with his widowed mother or enlisting in the French army to avenge the death of his brother by German militia. Confronted with a choice between two courses of action, the pupil had sought Sartre's advice, but in coming to him, he had already committed himself, since his choice of counsel had been predicated on the advice he had deemed Sartre likely to give. Hence, the pupil's waiver of personal choice in itself constituted a choice. Sartre concludes that man's knowledge that he has no recourse other than to himself, since values or Christian doctrine is too abstract to be efficacious, contributes to his state of forlornness (35-39). Sartre goes on to label "cowards" those who forfeit their freedom by hiding behind deterministic excuses or adopting an attitude of fatalism.

In Simone Schwarz-Bart's novel, such an individual is represented in Letitia who is complicitous in her own and others' destruction, considering misery the common lot of the black woman. Hence, she has no qualms about pursuing Elie, Télumée's sawyer husband. Instead, she looks upon him as fair game, and when Elie's pride is at its lowest, she props him up with her attentions and simultaneously deals a death blow to Télumée by winning away from her the man whose identity has become inseparable from her own. As Abena P.B. Busia has noted in her article "This Gift of Metaphor: Symbolic Strategies and the Triumph of Survival in Simone Schwarz-Bart's *The Bridge of Beyond*":

> Télumée at the start of her life assumed that she would be
> bound to one man, the husband of her childhood choosing.
> She is deserted by him. When this happens, she incarcer-
> ates herself in their marital home in a desperate grief, a
> grief which is annihilating because in her love, she has seen

herself as mirrored in him. His rejection of her then becomes a fundamental self-negation. (297)

Beverley Ormerod in her work *An Introduction to the French Caribbean Novel* interprets Letitia's compulsion to sabotage Télumée's marriage to Elie as a symptom of the society's deracination which accepts misery as the black person's lot. Conditioned by history to consider themselves inadequate, black expectations become lowered, even non-existent: "In a society marked by grinding poverty and racial discrimination, the fatalistic acceptance of second-best becomes, in a twisted way, almost a source of pride" (117). Such is true of some of the characters in both *The Third Life of Grange Copeland* and *The Bridge of Beyond,* as Brownfield in *Grange* accepts with complete complacency his lowly status in life as a Southern sharecropper. As his wife Mem tells him (137): "The thing I done noticed about you a long time ago is that you acts like you is right where you belongs. *All* the time!" One could contend further that their "fatalistic acceptance of second-best" not only manifests itself in their dire predictions but lends itself to their willfully becoming the instruments of tragedy.

Such is true of Josie of *The Third Life of Grange Copeland.* Josie is comparable to Letitia of *The Bridge of Beyond* in that she likewise is an agent of destruction. Walker leads the reader to intimate that Josie's whoredom stems from the trauma caused by her rape when she was a teen (56). Her pain, however, has not made her more sensitive to the pain of others; instead, the obverse is true, as her pain has numbed her to the pain of others. The following is a case in point. When Brownfield becomes abusive of Mem, she has no place to turn, as Josie's plot of revenge against Grange has driven her to the brink of incest with Brownfield, the husband of her niece and the son of Grange.

Letitia's fatalistic attitude in *The Bridge of Beyond* is evidenced in her response to Télumée's question of whether it is Elie she seeks or Télumée's own ruination as demonstrated by her will to drive her ceremoniously from her marital home:

> 'Little coconut flower', she said woefully, 'where have the bells been ringing for you? Your house? What house is that? You're no more at home here than anywhere else.

Didn't you know the only place on earth that belongs to a
Negress is in the graveyard?' (113)

The tragedy of self-inflicted wounds that Schwarz-Bart laments in
The Bridge of Beyond finds an echo in Alice Walker's novel *The
Third Life of Grange Copeland.* In fact, the concern of both novelists is identical: the ability of subjugated peoples to survive whole.
Donna Haisty Winchell considers this theme—the survival of the
whole self—as central to Walker's oeuvre. In the Preface to her
work *Alice Walker,* she has written:

> The four novels, two collections of short stories, two col-
> lections of essays, and four collections of poems following
> those first poems represent her [Walker's] celebration of
> black women who have had the wherewithal to discover
> inside themselves from which to draw strength, and have
> thus survived whole, as Walker herself has done. (ix)

Comparable to Letitia of *The Bridge of Beyond* who is the nemesis of Télumée and Josie of *The Third Life of Grange Copeland*
who is the nemesis of Mem, Brownfield of *The Third Life of Grange
Copeland* sets himself up as the destroyer of his father Grange.
Embittered by his father's desertion of him and his mother which,
seemingly, made inevitable his economic slavery, or his future as a
Southern sharecropper, Brownfield becomes trapped in a vicious
circle. Inured by alcohol, back-breaking labor, chronic debt, and
habitual consignment of himself and his family to shacks that previously doubled as feed storehouses, Brownfield is progressively trans-
formed into a brute. He is described as having the table manners
of "a hog"; hands, of "gray leather on the outside, the inside scaly
and softly cracked, too deformed for any work except that done to
and for animals" (118); likewise, the catalogue of his brutish treatment of his wife Mem is evidentiary of his bestiality. He berates,
beats, and, finally, murders Mem after numerous pregnancies, deteriorating health, and exhaustion have robbed her of her emotional
defenses. His criminality he excuses, however, finding justification
for it in Mem's thinness, Grange's familial abandonment, and, concomitantly, his dehumanization by the Southern sharecropping system.

The inauguration of free labor in 1863 with the issuance of the Emancipation Proclamation introduced into the Southern economy the black laborer as sharecropper. The poor returns on crops in 1866 and 1867, caused by drought, boll worm and cotton caterpillar infestation (Jaynes 141-42), which made planters unable to pay either creditors or laborers, forced laborers to abandon farms and break contracts entered into with the expectation that profits from the previous year would sustain them until harvest time. Planters themselves defaulted on loans (Jaynes 144). Given the risk that the laborer entered into with a post-harvest payment, a share payment guaranteed by contract seemed preferable. Under the share payment, a share would be guaranteed the laborer; only its market value would fluctuate, depending upon crop return: "During poor seasons, the value of the laborer's fractional share might be low, but good seasons promised that this same fractional share would have a higher value. The *risky* money wage contract was an inferior asset relative to a share wage" (Jaynes 145).

For the planter as well, who obtained credit on the security of existing crops and who, because of failed crops, faced increasing difficulty in obtaining loans, the share system was a means of obtaining a secure, or stable, work force while, at the same time, dispensing with the wage obligation that many could ill afford to meet. Gerald David Jaynes enumerates in his work *Branches Without Roots: Genesis of the Black Working Class in the American South, 1862-1882* the advantages of the share system for both the planter and the laborer: "The share system 'in lieu of money wages' was 'an arrangement preferred by the laborers as more secure, and by the planter from his inability to pay until the crop was prepared for sale'" (155).

Notwithstanding the element of risk involved in both transactions to the sharecropper (neither could guard against foreclosure and seizure of property by creditors), Jaynes concludes that the share offered the laborer some measure of protection that the wage system did not; the responsibility for lawsuits over unpaid debts fell to the merchants who extended credit, not the laborer, whose share was, for the most part, guaranteed.

Given that the laborer was "liable for consumption debts" (Jaynes 157), the likelihood of fraud also increased the risk factor for the laborer. Alice Walker, in the novel *The Third Life of Grange*

Copeland, illuminates this pattern of fraud within the Southern sharecropping system during the 1940s.

The thirty-five-year-old Grange Copeland is unable to break even from sharecropping because he owes the planter Shipley $1200, and Shipley's design is to make certain that Grange and his son Brownfield never pay off the debt in order to create a condition of peonage. Grange, in hopelessness, abandons his wife Margaret, their son Brownfield, and Brownfield's half-brother, Star, who was born to Margaret out of wedlock. Three weeks later, Margaret, suffering from guilt and depression over Grange's desertion, takes her own life and that of the infant Star. On the day of the funeral, Shipley offers to build a new house for Brownfield if he will stay on; however, Brownfield, in a manner similar to his father, takes flight, reasoning that "The idea that he might continue to live in her [his mother's] house aroused nothing but revulsion. He knew too that the minute he accepted money from Shipley he was done for. If he borrowed from Shipley, Shipley would make sure he never finished paying it back" (31).

It is in Baker's County, Georgia, some years later that Brownfield's life is to become a re-enactment of his father's. Brownfield marries Mem, the niece of Josie whom "he thought of as of another mother" (66), enters into an agreement with a farmer to work "on shares for two years, or until Brownfield could make enough money to take his bride northward" (71), and, in so doing, similar to Grange, seals his own doom, as his indebtedness forges an iron-clad tie to the land that is destructive. Brownfield's constant moves from one sharecropper's cabin to another, in a desperate attempt to eke out a living, produces in turn depression, frustration, a profound self-hatred stemming from a life 'gone haywire' (85), aggression against others, namely Mem, whom he blames for his bad choices (80), and, finally, hopelessness:

> He no longer had, as his father had maintained, even the desire to run away from them. He had no faith that any other place would be better. He fitted himself to the slot in which he found himself; for fun he poured oil into streams to kill the fish and tickled his vanity by drowning cats. (85)

The author of *The Colonizer and the Colonized,* Albert Memmi, identifies himself as Tunisian, or North African. A Tunisian national, he deems himself categorized in his country as "a second-class citizen, deprived of political rights, refused admission to most civil service departments" (xiii). However, he relates that the portrait of the colonized extends beyond the borders of Africa to encompass vast multitudes everywhere—"Algerians, Moroccans, African Negroes, and American Negroes" (xi)—since, as he writes, the colonizer and the colonized have identifiable characteristics, namely, a mutual dependency, or reciprocity, that binds the colonizer and the colonized and that (1) creates for the colonizer privilege and for the colonized deprivation and that, (2) subsequently, molds character and dictates conduct:

> If his [the colonizer's] living standards are high, it is because those of the colonized are low; if he can benefit from plentiful and undemanding labor and servants, it is because the colonized can be exploited at will and are not protected by the laws of the colony; if he can easily obtain administrative positions, it is because they are reserved for him and the colonized are excluded from them; the more freely he breathes, the more the colonized are choked. (8)

The attempts by the colonizer, the usurper, to legitimize his privilege cause, in Memmi's estimation, the construction of the Nero complex (52). The colonizer falsifies history, re-writes laws and denigrates the usurped in order "to extol himself to the skies and to drive the usurped below the ground at the same time" (53). It is the momentum of these defense mechanisms, *i.e.,* the exaltation-resentment dialectics (65), that propels them by their own velocity. Thus, the colonizer finds it difficult, if not impossible, to escape the system of his own making:

> Having chosen to maintain the colonial system, he [the colonized] must contribute more vigor to its defense than would have been needed to dissolve it completely. Having become aware of the unjust relationship which ties him to the colonized, he must continually attempt to absolve himself. He never forgets to make a public show of his own virtues, and will argue with vehemence to appear heroic and great.

> At the same time his privileges arise just as much from his
> glory as from degrading the colonized. He will persist in
> degrading them, using the darkest colors to depict them. If
> need be, he will act to devalue them, annihilate them. But
> he can never escape from this circle. (54)

Just as the behavior of the colonizer imprisons him in his own
creation, so too does it entrap the colonized. Albert Memmi in his
work *The Colonizer and the Colonized* has argued that a consequence of colonization is the development in the colonized of a
"dependency complex" which manifests itself in the actualization
of cultural myths:

> The bond between colonizer and colonized is . . . destruc-
> tive and creative. It destroys and re-creates the two part-
> ners of colonization. . . . One is disfigured into an oppres-
> sor, a partial, unpatriotic and treacherous being, worrying
> only about his privileges and their defense; the other, into
> an oppressed creature, whose development is broken and
> who compromises by his defeat. (89)

In *The Third Life of Grange Copeland,* the defeatist attitude that
Memmi has identified as part of the transformation of the colonized is the consequence of mounting debt incurred by Brownfield
after five years of sharecropping. Inasmuch as his life as a sharecropper Brownfield considers as one that has not been chosen freely,
he absolves himself of responsibility and blames his failure on those
deemed to have control over his destiny (233-34).

Congruent with Schwarz-Bart's condemnation of the forfeiture
of personal freedom to cultural myths is the preponderance of nega-
tivist imagery surrounding the characters in *The Bridge of Beyond*
and in *The Third Life of Grange Copeland* who allow themselves
to be buffeted by either passion or the winds of fate; their behavior
is viewed as a form of madness. After Brownfield in *Grange* confesses to Josie, Grange's second wife and former mistress that the
death of his albino son from exposure had come from his own
hand because he tired of the strain of pretense, "of say[ing] he love
what he don't want" (314), Josie realizes that the horrific nature of
Brownfield has given way to insanity (313-14).

An example of madness in *The Bridge of Beyond* is contained in the tale of The Man Who Tried to Live on Air, as told to Télumée by her grandmother. Disillusioned by man's wickedness, a man called Wvabor Longlegs took comfort only in his mare and mounted her, never again being able to assert his will. When he wished to seize again the reins of life, after becoming enamored with a female image, he discovered that the control which he had relinquished to his mare could not be reclaimed. The moral of the fable, as told by Toussine, is to "keep good hold of the reins so that it's not the horse that rides you" (50-51).

Similarly, Elie's irrationality in *The Bridge of Beyond* is contained in the symbol of the horse, "the legendary example of human folly and disaster" (Ormerod 124). The reinvocation of the "bird of prey eyes" (99), representative of blind fate, also presages catastrophe as Elie, unemployed and despondent, begins to self-destruct: "I'd mounted a crazy horse, a man ill-grafted in his mother's womb, who was falling to pieces limb by limb" (106). Elie, a casualty of unemployment, soon makes Télumée the target of his aggression; he thrashes Télumée frequently and unmercifully and sadistically invites Letitia into their home in an effort to reduce Télumée to total abjection: "'And soon I'm going to teach you what the word woman means, and you'll roll on the ground and scream, as a woman does roll and scream when she's handled right'" (108).

Finally, the madness of Angel Medard, the male that Télumée had befriended following the death of Amboise, her second husband, is symbolized in *The Bridge of Beyond* by his "dancing brain" (161). Similar to Elie, Angel is orphaned, his brother having inflicted him with a head wound that has resulted in his dementia. Comparable to Elie, Angel misdirects his anger upon the one individual who is least deserving of it—Télumée. Angel, after ingratiating himself with Télumée and her adopted daughter, Sonore, effectively alienates Sonore's affection by deceiving her into believing that Télumée is "a charmer of children, [who] only wanted to make use of her in her innocence, delivered over body and soul, hair and sweat into [her] witch's hands" (163). Moreover, Angel's rage, like Elie's, seems to stem from Télumée's penchant for happiness. Frustrated by Télumée's outward show of adjustment to the loss of Sonore, Angel aims to destroy her, vowing to send her "hurtling down, me and my house and my bed, right down to the bottom of the hill, and forever" (164).

In contrast to individuals such as Letitia, Elie, and Angel Medard who renounce their free will in favor of social determinism is Télumée of *The Bridge of Beyond.* Distinct from individuals who allow themselves to be ruled either by passion, caprice, or circumstances, as connoted in the imagery that surrounds them, Télumée remains the arbiter of her destiny. Hence, in her refusal to allow herself to become manipulable by others, she becomes exemplary of a life lived in good faith. As Jean-Paul Sartre has written in *Existentialism and Humanism:* "The existentialist does not believe in the power of passion. He will never regard a grand passion as a destructive torrent upon which a man is swept into certain actions as by fate, and which, therefore, is an excuse for them. He thinks that man is responsible for his passion" (34).

Indicative of Télumée's personal freedom is the display of mercy toward her persecutors Elie and Angel. That is, after Angel's betrayal of their friendship by the attempted murder of Télumée, also Elie's abandonment of her, Télumée is without enmity toward them. Hence, she is aptly named "Télumée Miracle" by the villagers because of her serenity or her refusal to surrender her own subjectivity in the name of either passion or revenge.

Télumée's survival of Angel's murderous assault is expressive of her invincibility that emanates from her communal ties, as symbolized by the "web" that connects the village community of Fond-Zombi (Ormerod 117); Télumée's harmonious existence with the cosmos; and the nurturance of the grandmother, Toussine, whose love provided a safe harbor that is symbolized in her "great full skirt" (28).

Stanlie M. James in her article "Mothering: A Possible Black Feminist Link to Social Transformation?" defines as "Othermothers" those "who assist blood mothers in the responsibilities of child care for short- to long-term periods, in informal or formal arrangements. They can be, but are not confined to, such blood relatives as grandmothers, sisters, aunts, cousins or supportive fictive kin" (45).

The roots of othermothering, a practice unique to the African American community and throughout the Black Diaspora, James contends, may be found in the African world view that attaches great importance to mothering, conceiving of mothering as having not only a biological but a nurturing component as well, as illustrated by the following: cooperative child care in polygamous households and in foster care arrangements aimed toward the establishment within the child of a connectedness to the community (46).

Albeit these traditional family and communal patterns could not be replicated in the New World, which did not recognize legally the union between slaves, some traditions, such as othermothering, according to James, were adapted:

> If enslaved children were orphaned through the death or sale of their parents, other women within the quarters often assumed the additional responsibility for their care. Thus the African tradition of fostering was adapted to meet the needs of the enslaved community in the USA . . . and has since become known as othermothering. This practice of othermothering continues to this day to play a critical role in the African-American community. (47)

James concludes that inasmuch as othermothers personify Mamphela Ramphele's definition of power as "a range of interventions that achieve outcome" (51), they can be construed potentially as effective agencies for social transformation.

Othermothering is contained in Alice Walker's *The Third Life of Grange Copeland* and Simone Schwarz-Bart's *The Bridge of Beyond*. Toussine, of Simone Schwarz-Bart's *The Bridge of Beyond*, who has lost a twin daughter to an accidental fire and a husband Jeremiah to death, views the guardianship of her granddaughter Télumée as a godsend, as she is able to "put on [the] dress of life again" (106). Télumée's mother Victory had sent Télumée to live with the grandmother Toussine before running off with Haut-Colbi, a Carib who was passing through the hamlet, L'Abandonnée when he met Victory. It is precisely Victory's willingness to embrace life, despite prior disappointments, that mirrors Toussine's own faith and that causes Toussine to view her daughter's departure less harshly than do the other villagers of Fond-Zombi. In fact, her charge, as guardian to Télumée, has become to thwart the negativism of the villagers who wallow in self-pity, as can be seen in the following excerpt from the novel:

[A] lady by the name of Vitaline Brindosier, old, round, and fat, with snow-white hair and eyes full of innocence, had a special talent for upsetting people. When souls were heavy and everything proclaimed the futility of the black man's existence, Madame Brindosier would flap her arms triumphantly, like wings, and declare that life was a torn garment, an old rag beyond all mending. Then, beside herself with delight, laughing, waving her fine round arms, she would add in a bittersweet voice: 'Yes, we Negroes of Guadeloupe really are flat on our bellies!' (30)

Toussine, upon hearing these words, had whispered to Télumée (30), "Come away, Télumée, as fast as you can. They're only big whales left high and dry by the sea, and if the little fish listen to them, why, they'll lose their fins!"

Télumée, so orphaned by Victory, feels as though she had been "put on earth by mistake" (30, 39), while Toussine, widowed and alone, finds in Télumée a reason for living: "In fact, she was overjoyed at the mere idea of having my innocence cast a halo around her white hair, and when she came to fetch me she went away from L'Abandonnée blessing my mother" (27). In effect, the relationship between the two is symbiotic in nature, as their spirits are in perfect accord: "[Grandmother] looked at Elie through the same eyes as I did, heard him with my ears, loved him with my heart" (45-46). The 'doubling' that the two represent is also contained in the following passage descriptive of Télumée after her grandmother's death and her move to La Folie: "Ever since I'd come to La Folie I'd been supported by the presence of Queen Without a Name, who wielded half my hoe, held half my machete, and bore half my troubles, so that thanks to her I really was a Negress that was a drum with two hearts" (133).

Toussine envelops Télumée with a plentitude of love that armors her against life's vicissitudes; song, as conveyed to Télumée by one of her grandmother's tales, is also an antidote to tragedy. After Toussine had told to Télumée the story of a bird Zemba (158) that prevented its own destruction by its display of lyricism, Télumée is heartened: "I too set off dreaming, flew away, took myself for the bird that couldn't be hit by any bullet because it invoked life with its song" (47-48). Moreover, Elie's sadistic treatment of Télumée seems to stem from his resentment of her ebullient disposition, as the reference to flying would indicate (108): "'Where are your tears and cries now, spirit of the highways, flying Negress—where are they now?'"

Télumée's ebullience is reminiscent of that of her mother, Victory. Supporting herself and her two children as a laundress, she is remembered by Télumée as "singing like a happy magpie" (16) in order to disguise any pain that she might have felt rather than invite the pity of the villagers, which she considered a worst punishment. Télumée recalls Victory cajoling herself with the words (16): "Suffering brings scorn. Better to be envied than pitied. Sing, Victory, sing!"

The attraction of Ruth to her guardian and grandfather Grange of *The Third Life of Grange Copeland* stems in part from his love of life: "But Grange's crimes, she believed, were never aimed at anyone but himself, and his total triumph over his life's failures was the joy in him that drew her to him" (194). Evidentiary of his enjoyment of life are the Uncle Remus stories that he tells that have become for Ruth as cherished as his Christmas ambrosia and his love of dancing that he likewise shares with his granddaughter that, collectively, become for her a transmission of culture as well as history: "Grange taught her untaught history through his dance; she glimpsed a homeland she had never known and felt the pattering of the drums. Dancing was a warm electricity that stretched, connecting them with other dancers moving across the seas" (190).

On the other hand, imparted to Télumée in conversations with Ma Cia and her grandmother, Toussine, is also knowledge of the West Indian slave past interlaced with rules of conduct necessary to survive in a hostile, prejudicial world. Ma Cia commands Télumée to "Be a fine little Negress, a drum with two sides. Let life bang and thump, but keep the underside always intact" (*The Bridge of Beyond* 39). Later, as Télumée hires herself out to work for the Desaragnes, a white family, she and other members of her culture are denigrated as "savages" and "cannibals" incapable of self-improvement borne of their contact with European culture. Télumée, remembering Ma Cia's advice, disengages herself from her physical body, shielding herself from the dart thrusts of Madame Desaragne by withdrawing inward:

> I glided in and out between the words as if I were swimming
> in the clearest water, feeling the cooling breeze on my neck,
> my arms, the back of my legs. And, thankful to be a little
> Negress that was irreducible, a real drum with two sides, as
> Ma Cia put it, I left one side to her, the mistress, for her to
> amuse herself, for her to thump on, and I, underneath, I
> remained intact. (61-62)

Another potential threat to Télumée's serenity is Monsieur
Desaragne whose sexual advances toward the female workers were
common knowledge. Although Télumée seemed to have been
spared initially the advances of the males in the Desaragne household, she later becomes a target of assault. With a silk dress as his
calling card, Monsieur Desaragne reveals himself as operating under
two fundamental assumptions: one, the belief that sexual favors
can be bartered; and two, that Télumée will offer no resistance.
He is wrong on both counts as Télumée brandishes her nails and
threatens him with castration. Following this episode, Télumée's
success in preserving her purity is registered in allusions to the
drum: "There was a respite for the Negro, who became, I thought,
all the more ingenious through doing all these magic tricks, dancing
and drumming simultaneously, at once both wind and sail" (73).

The principle of inviolability is contained in the images of the
drum (39) and a cathedral (35), which become emblematic of freedom and resistance rather than restrictive enclosures. In Ormerod's
words, "The drum, symbol of African ancestry, slave resistance,
racial solidarity and rhythmic energy is here endowed with the sound
enduring quality of the tree and of the wooden boat that defies the
tempests" (120).

Another individual who possesses "an inner sovereignty, a core
of self" (*The Third Life of Grange Copeland* 314) is Grange
Copeland of the novel by Alice Walker that bears his name.
Brownfield, in his death-in-life existence, conveyed imagistically
through recurrent references to "silence" (9, 10, 14, 30, 33, 105,
153, etc.), is a replica of the young Grange, or Grange in his first
life; likewise, his complete irresponsibility links him to the young
Grange, an example of which is Brownfield's neglect to pay the
rent during Mem's convalescence from two failed pregnancies, thus
leading to their eviction from the house in the city that Mem had

struggled to obtain. However, Grange in his second life, which spans his years spent in the North, has learned well the price of hate, namely, that it is an anathema to personhood. Hence, the elder Grange, by virtue of his guardianship of his granddaughter Ruth, following the murder of Mem by Brownfield, becomes a man re-born. In a confrontation with his son who is intent on re-gaining custody of his sixteen-year-old daughter, Grange attempts to impart to Brownfield the wisdom acquired from his own life experiences—the danger of bartering one's soul in a quest for ven-geance. He beseeches Brownfield: *"You got to hold tight a place in you where they can't come.* You can't take this young girl here and make her wish she was dead just to git back at some white folks that you don't even *know"* (290-91). That refuge for Grange is the land that he has been able to acquire as a result of his mar-riage to Josie and the subsequent pooling of their assets that has secured for him independence from economic slavery: "For the time being, he would withdraw completely from them, find a sanc-tuary, make a life that need not acknowledge them, and be always prepared, with his life, to defend it, to protect it, to keep it . . . inviolate" (221).

Ruth is also an incarnation of the "core of self" (314) that should remain inviolate. She is associated in her grandfather's eyes with innocence (223): "[H]e could only teach hate by inspiring it. And how could he spoil her innocence, kill the freshness of her look, becloud the brightness of her too inquisitive eyes?" For his part, Brownfield is incensed that Ruth is forward-looking; consequently, his attempts are to induce in her the very feelings of nothingness with which he associates the world: "What did she see in the world that made her even wish to grow up? he wondered. He had to make her see that there was nothing, *nothing,* no matter what Grange promised her" (315). Grange murders Brownfield after his son has been awarded custody of Ruth rather than risk her defilement. Although the murder, according to Barbara Christian, re-enacts "the old pattern of kin-killing" (203), it nonetheless establishes a new pattern in that it affirms Grange's belief in Ruth's right to life. Grange's actions, which nestle in the paradox of destruction as essential to construction, therefore correlates with Albert Camus' concept of rebellion.

Resistance, according to Albert Camus, is inspired by the rebel's defense of non-negotiable rights. In *The Rebel,* Camus attempts to answer the question left pending at the end of *The Myth of Sisyphus,* namely, whether it is possible to move beyond nihilism and live without appeal. In *The Myth of Sisyphus,* Camus had rejected suicide because it destroyed one of the elements foundational to the absurd—man's desire for order and the indifference of the universe: "To say that life is absurd, the conscience must be alive" (*The Rebel* 6). In *The Rebel,* he repudiates wanton murder for the same reason that he repudiated suicide—a respect for life: "From the moment that life is recognized as good, it becomes good for all men. Murder cannot be made coherent when suicide is not considered coherent" (6).

Camus in *The Rebel* examines the revolutions of the last two centuries, the philosophies and literatures that have influenced them and concludes that ideologies have become degenerate and petrified into totalitarianism. A moralist, Camus advocates *la mesure,* or limits, derivative of the Mediterranean tradition deemed antithetical to the German ideology that deifies history and destroys nature:

> The profound conflict of this century is perhaps not so much between the German ideologies of history and Christian political concepts, which in a certain way are accomplices, as between German dreams and Mediterranean traditions, between the violence of eternal adolescence and virile strength, between nostalgia, rendered more acute by knowledge and by books and courage reinforced and enlightened by the experience of life—in other words, between history and nature. (299)

Essential to Camus' dialectic is the ideal of the rebel. In Part One of *The Rebel,* Camus speaks of the rebel slave who has taken orders unhesitatingly from his master until the moment of awareness, or his recognition of limits which cannot be transgressed. The slave's negation, therefore, affirms a respect for principle, without which "crime and disorder would reign throughout the world. An act of rebellion on his part seems like a demand for clarity and unity. The most elementary form of rebellion, paradoxically, expresses an aspiration to order" (23).

Grange Copeland of *The Third Life of Grange Copeland,* in his respect for limits, may be described as a rebel. Albert Camus defines a rebel in his philosophical work *The Rebel* as "a man who says no, but whose refusal does not imply a renunciation" (13). The rebel rejects an incursion that he considers intolerable, but, in so doing, affirms his respect for a borderline that should not be transgressed. For example, if the slave risks death as a consequence of his rebellion, he reveals by his actions that he attaches greater value to freedom than his own life: "If he prefers the risk of death to the negation of the rights that he defends, it is because he considers these rights more important than himself" (15-16). By the same token, Grange Copeland reveals himself as willing to die in order to keep inviolate that interior space that Alice Walker has referred to in the "Afterword" of *The Third Life of Grange Copeland* as "the soul": "I believe wholeheartedly in the necessity of keeping inviolate the interior space that is given to all. I believe in the soul" (345).

The heroism of "The Just Assassins" stems likewise from their respect for limits. In the "Author's Preface" to *Caligula and Three Other Plays,* Albert Camus specifies the nature of the heroism of "the just assassins":

> My admiration for my heroes, Kaliayev and Dora, is complete. I merely wanted to show that action itself had limits. There is no good and just action but what recognizes those limits and, if it must go beyond them, at least accepts death. (x)

Members of The Revolutionary Socialist Party, "the just assassins" are self-described terrorists who seek to put an end to tyranny by the assassination of the Grand Duke Serge. Ivan "Yanek" Kaliayev, the one designated by Boris Annenkov, the group's leader, to throw the bomb at the carriage of the Duke while en route from the palace to the theater, cannot bring himself to do so because he cannot reconcile the wanton murder of the Duke's niece and nephew who accompany the Duke with the goal of the revolution—justice. As Dora, one of Kaliayev's comrades, puts it:

> DORA: Yanek's ready to kill the Grand Duke because his death may help to bring nearer the time when Russian chil-

dren will no longer die of hunger. That in itself is none too easy for him. But the death of the Grand Duke's niece and nephew won't prevent any child from dying of hunger. Even in destruction there's a right way and a wrong way—and there are limits. (258; Act II)

Another Party principle, in addition to a respect for limits, is a belief in the solidarity of man founded on common suffering. In *The Rebel,* Camus identifies "the just assassins" as models of the rebel in their respect for human life and, in turn, their refusal to play god: "Kaliayev, and his brothers throughout the entire world, refuse, on the contrary, to be deified in that they refuse the unlimited power to inflict death. They choose, and give us as an example the only original rule of life today: to learn to live and to die, and, in order to be a man, to refuse to be a god" (305-6). Kaliayev carries out his terroristic mission two days later when the Duke, unaccompanied, makes his scheduled outing to the theater. The assassination of the Duke by Kaliayev makes his execution by hanging a surety; however, Kaliayev is steadfast in his willingness to offer his own life in exchange for the one taken. Hence, clemency, contingent upon his admission of guilt, as offered by the policeman Skuratov, is non-negotiable, as Kaliayev considers his death a matter of honor: "If I did not die—it's then I'd be a murderer" (288; Act IV). One of Kaliayev's comrades, Dora, upon learning the news of Kaliayev's hanging, philosophizes on the meaning of his execution to the Party:

DORA: There is no need for tears. Don't you realize this is the day of our justification? Something has come to pass which testifies for us; a sign for all the revolutionaries of the world. Yanek is a murderer no longer. (301: Act V)

Alice Walker has acknowledged in her collection of essays *In Search of Our Mothers' Gardens* her indebtedness to Albert Camus. She credits Helen Merrell Lynd, a professor at Sarah Lawrence College, for both having introduced her to Camus and for making philosophy understandable; its study, natural (38). In her own work, the influence of the philosopher Camus is evident both in Walker's embrace of the existential concept of *la mesure,* or limits, as in *The*

Third Life of Grange Copeland, wherein Grange acknowledges, reminiscent of the view expressed by Camus, his respect for life, "He never ceased to believe this, adding only to this belief in later years, that if one kills he must not shun death in his turn" (218), and in the choice of title for her second novel *Meridian.*

Set in the era of the 60s, the character for whom the novel is titled is dogged by the question of whether or not commitment to civil rights will lead to a justification of murder. The question is answered in the affirmative at the end of the novel. In April 1968, the civil rights activist Meridian had seen eulogized Rev. Dr. Martin Luther King, Jr., the victim of an assassin's bullet. It is later in the spring when she visits a Baptist church on the occasion of the congregation's memorial to a local fallen hero that she experiences her epiphany: wanton destruction is indefensible; however, violence in defense of life is justifiable; also, resistance that holds true to its origins or to a people's collective memory (200).

In the chapter entitled "Meridian," Camus contrasts rebellion and revolution. The rebel, in his quest for justice, does not betray the memory that has authenticated his insurrection. The revolutionary, on the other hand, sacrifices the individual toward the realization of a Utopian end, or an abstraction:

> When the end is absolute, historically speaking, and when it is believed certain of realization, it is possible to go so far as to sacrifice others. When it is not, only oneself can be sacrificed, in the hazards of a struggle for the common dignity of man. Does the end justify the means? That is possible. But what will justify the end? To that question, which historical thought leaves pending, rebellion replies: the means. (292)

Stepan Fedorov of "The Just Assassins" is emblematic of the revolutionary that Camus has represented as the antithesis of the rebel. In contrast to Kaliayev who avows himself to be a lover of life, Stepan identifies himself as a lover of justice. Whereas Kaliayev considers that the lives of the innocent should take precedence over Party principles, Stepan recognizes no limits and is willing to subordinate the lives of the innocent to the pursuit of justice. Hazel E.

Barnes in her work *Humanistic Existentialism: The Literature of Possibility* summarizes the polar differences between the two:

> Stepan insists that there can be no limits for those who believe in revolution, a doctrine which Camus constantly emphasizes. But Kaliayev will not give in. He has determined to give his life to overthrow despotism; but he sees in the words of Stepan the annunciation of another despotism which, if it is ever brought into being, would make of him an assassin by the same acts by which he sought to establish justice. (257)

Symbolic of the concept of limits is Nemesis, "the goddess of moderation and the implacable enemy of the immoderate" (296). In *Portrait of Camus: An Illustrated Biography,* Morvan Lebesque identifies as a symbol of moderation in Camus' works "the bow stretched to its farthest point and yet not launching the shaft" (162). Similarly, the meridian, which represents a balance between two extremes, divinity and humanity, symbolizes moderation. Camus writes in *The Rebel:*

> At this meridian of thought, the rebel thus rejects divinity in order to share in the struggles and destiny of all men. We shall choose Ithaca, the faithful land, frugal and audacious thought, lucid action, and the generosity of the man who understands. In the light, the earth remains our first and our last love. (306)

Hence, Alice Walker's novels *The Third Life of Grange Copeland* and *Meridian* and Simone Schwarz-Bart's novel *The Bridge of Beyond* are related in terms of their illumination of the valued existential concepts of personhood and authenticity to counteract metaphysical abandonment, the contingency of lives lived in bad faith, and nihilism. The metaphor relating Brownfield's ineffectuality to that of "a [pygmy] in a world of giants" (311), therefore, links him to the characters Letitia, Elie, and Angel Medard in *The Bridge of Beyond* who similarly are dwarfed by the choices made, namely, that of taking refuge behind fatalistic excuses in response to the challenge of forging their own personal identities and to the challenge of Nemesis.

WORKS CITED

Barnes, Hazel E. *Humanistic Existentialism: The Literature of Possibility.* Lincoln: U of Nebraska P, 1959.

Busia, Abena P.B. "This Gift of Metaphor: Symbolic Strategies and the Triumph of Survival in Simone Schwarz-Bart's *The Bridge of Beyond.*" *Out of the Kumbla: Caribbean Women and Literature.* Eds. Carole Boyce Davies and Elaine Savory Fido. Trenton: Africa World Press, 1990. 289-301.

Camus, Albert. "Author's Preface." *Caligula and Three Other Plays.* By Camus. Trans. Justin O'Brien. New York: Knopf, 1958. v-x.

———. "The Just Assassins." *Caligula and Three Other Plays.* Trans. Stuart Gilbert. New York: Knopf, 1958. 233-302.

———. *The Rebel: An Essay on Man in Revolt.* Trans. Anthony Bower. New York: Knopf, 1956. Originally published as *L'Homme Révolté* (Paris: Gallimard, 1951).

Christian, Barbara. *Black Women Novelists: The Development of a Tradition, 1892-1976.* Westport, CT: Greenwood, 1980.

James, Stanlie M. "Mothering: A Possible Black Feminist Transformation?" *Theorizing Black Feminisms: The Visionary Pragmatism of Black Women.* Eds. Stanlie M. James and Abena P. A. Busia. New York: Routledge, 1993. 44-53.

Jaynes, Gerald David. *Branches Without Roots: Genesis of the Black Working Class in the American South, 1862-1882.* New York: Oxford UP, 1986.

Jones, Bridget. Introduction. *The Bridge of Beyond.* By Simone Schwarz-Bart. Portsmouth, NH: Heinemann, 1982. iv-xviii.

Lebesque, Morvan. *Portrait of Camus: An Illustrated Biography.* Trans. T.C. Sharman. New York: Herder and Herder, 1971. Originally published in French as *Camus par lui-même* (Paris: Editions du Seuil, 1963).

McKinney, Kitzie. "Second Vision: Antillean Versions of the Quest in Two Novels by Simone Schwarz-Bart." *The French Review* 62 (1989): 650-60.

———. "Télumée's Miracle: The Language of the Other and the Composition of the Self in Simone Schwarz-Bart's *Pluie et vent sur Télumée Miracle.*" *Modern Language Studies* 19 (1989): 58-65.

Memmi, Albert. *The Colonizer and the Colonized.* New York: Orion Press, 1965.

Ormerod, Beverley. *An Introduction to the French Caribbean Novel.* Portsmouth, NH: Heinemann, 1985.

Sartre, Jean-Paul. *Existentialism and Humanism.* Translated and introduced by Philip Mairet. London: Methuen, 1948.

Schwarz-Bart, Simone. *The Bridge of Beyond.* Trans. Barbara Bray. Oxford: Heinemann, 1982. First published in French as *Pluie et vent sur Télumée Miracle, 1972.*

Walker, Alice. *In Search of Our Mothers' Gardens: Womanist Prose.* New York: Harcourt, 1983.

———. *The Third Life of Grange Copeland.* New York: Pocket Books, 1988.

Winchell, Donna Haisty. *Alice Walker.* New York: Twayne, 1992.

Chapter 5

THE POLYPHONIC TEXTURE OF THE TROPE 'JUNKHEAPED' IN TONI MORRISON'S *BELOVED*

Toni Morrison has articulated the importance of symbols in her novels. In a published interview with Jane Bakerman (1977), Morrison observed that the symbols in her novels "are often the route into a character or a scene": "I have to get a hook. . . . I need it, the phrase or the picture or the word or some gesture" (35). In another interview with Gail Caldwell (1987), Morrison has spoken of working from the ground up, of conceptualizing a novel in images before the architectural design of the novel has crystalized itself in her imagination (241). The richness of her novels stems, in Morrison's view, from the elastic quality of her imagery. In an interview with Marsha Darling (1988), she is quoted as saying: "What's rich, if there is any richness, is what the reader gets and brings him or herself. That's part of the way in which the tale is told. The folk tales are told in such a way that whoever is listening is in it and can shape and figure it out. . . . It's passed on and somebody else can alter it later" (253). In effect, readers are invited to bring their own experiences to bear on her novels in order to extrapolate meaning, as Morrison eschews didacticism in writing. To be sure, it is the "haunting," or incomplete quality of her fiction, as described by Nellie McKay in her interview with Morrison, that Morrison seeks in her prose: "I manipulate. When I'm good at it, it [the prose] is not heavy-handed. But I want a very strong visceral and emotional response as well as a very clear intellectual response, and the haunting that you describe is testimony to that" (147). The porous quality of her prose Morrison likens to the folk tale, as well as to jazz that simultaneously suggests and provokes. In an interview with Thomas Le Clair (1981), Morrison averred: "There is a level of appreciation that might be available only to people who understand the context of the language. The analogy that occurs to me is jazz: it is open on the one hand and both complicated and inaccessible on the other" (124).

To be sure, Morrison's words on her literature echo those of Jack Chambers on Miles Davis' experimentation with jazz fusion, a blend of jazz, rock, funk, soul, and blues, that the jazz artist recorded during the 1970s. While Davis' use of pop elements in his music provided the basis for mass appeal, its avant-garde nature made the music, according to Chambers, "probably the most forbidding and least accessible . . . that Davis ever made. [It] is self-contained but hard to grasp, compact but hard to comprehend. It includes more than its fair share of contradictions" (281).

One recurrent image in Morrison's novels is that of "detritus," the trope even finding its way into her interviews. On the detritus in *Sula,* Morrison has noted in the interview with Thomas Le Clair (1981): "The detritus of white people, the rejects from the respectable white world, which appears in *Sula* was in our neighborhood" (125). Morrison also identifies social pariahs, such as Sula and Shadrack of *Sula,* as well as black people who are marginalized and therefore transmogrified into social orphans, as common to her novels. In the interview with Claudia Tate (1983), Morrison commented on the various levels of meaning in her novels relative to the trope of the pariah:

> There are several levels of the pariah figure working in my writing. The black community is a pariah community. Black people are pariahs. The civilization of black people that lives apart from but in juxtaposition to other civilizations is a pariah relationship. In fact, the concept of the black in this country is almost always one of the pariah. (168)

In the novel *Beloved,* the concepts of "detritus" and "pariah" become conflated in the image "junkheaped" (174), a condition descriptive not only of Sethe's prison sentence for the infanticide of Beloved, social exclusion, and Paul D's desertion upon hearing from Stamp Paid "his graveyard information" (186), but, as well, of the psychological trauma caused by the Diaspora. In the view of Gail Caldwell, *"Beloved . . .* is as much about the mother-daughter relationship bond as it is the crimes of slavery" (241).

The description by Morrison of Sethe's possessing "irises the same color as her skin" (9) underscores the psychological diaspora caused by the dispersion. As well, the lacerations on Sethe's back, which Amy Denver identifies as a "chokecherry tree," are a signifier, in Carole Boyce Davies' view, of Sethe's captivity. Davies in her article "Mother Right/Write Revisited: *Beloved* and *Dessa Rose* and the Construction of Motherhood in Black Women's Fiction" identifies Sethe's body as the site of a series of markings dating from her pregnancy that are exhibitive of her bestialization:

> Sethe, then, is a marked woman, marked physically by
> abuse, pregnancy, motherhood, and other societal inscrip-
> tions (by the white female, by black male, and by the male
> white inflicter of the abuse which marks her initially). The
> marking which is re-identified as the branches of a tree . . .
> and thus as life, with myriad reference points, when looked
> at differently, becomes the signifier for captivity. (47)

Sethe's scarification, which mirrors the internal condition, literalizes the character's victimization. In the same manner, Sethe's mother's face is scarred, ruined by a permanently transfixed smile that has distorted her features: "She'd had the bit so many times she smiled. When she wasn't smiling she smiled, and I never saw her own smile" (203). Her disfigurement, like that of Sethe's, metaphorically illustrates the legacy of the past, or the effects of the past on present reality, and the need to reconcile oneself with the past in order to achieve wholeness. As Jacqueline de Weever has written in her work *Mythmaking and Metaphor in Black Women's Fiction:*

> For those Americans most intimately acquainted with the
> horrors of slavery and its aftereffects, the African-Ameri-
> cans, the path to wholeness lies in claiming the slave past
> through identification with it, living with it, and then leav-
> ing it consciously and decidedly for the sake of life itself.
> (160)

Jennifer Fitzgerald in her article "Selfhood and Community: Psychoanalysis and Discourse in *Beloved*" draws upon Melanie Klein's objects relations psychoanalysis, which identifies self-hood as a social construct bound to one's relations with others, to illuminate characterization. The infant projects emotions onto external "objects," namely, principal caregivers, namely, parents, and transforms these persons into "imagoes," or fantasy objects, which are then internalized into the infant's psyche. The process of socialization is complete only after the infant recognizes principal caregivers as autonomous beings. Fitzgerald contends that Beloved's obsessiveness with Sethe and, concomitantly, Sethe's own disrespect for boundaries, which stems from the traumatic separation from the mother, identify them both as pre-Oedipal. Fitzgerald writes in her article: "Slavery severed Sethe's bond with her mother before she had developed a separate identity; consequently, her sense of self and of the boundaries to that self is dangerously weak. Like a pre-Oedipal infant, she didn't know where the world stopped and she began" (677).

In a modification of Melanie Klein's objects relations theory, Jessica Benjamin in *Bonds of Love* maintains that the development of self occurs in relations with another subject rather than with another object. According to Benjamin, the self and the other are inter-related beings who mutually seek recognition from one another. Exhibitive of the balance sought between two woven but distinct entities is the concept of attunement, a "combination of resonance and difference" in which self and other are empathically in tune while maintaining their distinct boundaries and separateness (Benjamin 26). Benjamin compares the tension between self-assertion and mutual recognition to the optical illusion created by Escher's birds, which appear to fly in both directions: "What makes his drawings visually difficult is a parallel to what makes the idea of self-other reciprocity conceptually difficult: the drawing asks us to look two ways simultaneously, quite in opposition to our usual sequential orientation" (26). The failure to achieve what Benjamin terms "intersubjectivity" results, according to Schapiro, in a profound narcissistic wound that manifests itself in a terrifying greediness, what objects relations theorists call "love made hungry, . . . in which the baby fears it will devour and thus destroy mother and, conversely, that mother (due to projection) will devour and destroy the self" (Schapiro 197-98). According to Schapiro, this "terrifying greediness" accounts for the preponderance of oral imagery in the novel, such as the following: "Beloved ate up her [Sethe's] life, took it, swelled up with it, grew taller on it" (250).

The references to "milk for all" (100, 198) inscribe the pre-Oedipal nature of a number of the characters in *Beloved*. They attest to Sethe's successful defense of her right to motherhood and her potential to nurture not only her own offspring, but others, like Paul D, who are in need of nurturance. More to the point, they allude to a deprivation that plagues all of the characters; Baby Suggs' desire for color, Beloved's insatiable thirst and craven appetite for sweets, and Denver's need for companionship parallel Sethe's own desire for her mother's milk since her wet nurse "never had enough for all" (203). According to Barbara Schapiro, this emotional hunger is the legacy of slavery which makes impossible the self-affirmation that comes from the acknowledgement by the other of one's subjectivity:

> For Morrison's characters, African Americans in a racist, slave society, there is no reliable other to recognize and affirm their existence. The mother, the child's first vital other, is made unreliable or unavailable by a slave system which either separates her from her child or so enervates and depletes her that she has no self with which to confer recognition. The consequences on the inner life of the child—the emotional hunger, the obsessive and terrifying narcissistic fantasies—constitute the underlying psychological drama of the novel. (194)

Concomitant to the excessive need of the infant that stems from the failure of "intersubjectivity" is also hate. Jennifer Fitzgerald contends that the mother aboard the ship that Beloved describes in her narration fits the description, in psychological terms, of the "internal mother," who is a "double" of the external caregiver onto whom Beloved can alternately project idealized and demonized feelings of both love and hate:

> The double is psychologically created by the infant's ambivalent emotions—of both love (and dependence) and hate

(and fear of dependence)—for the person who looks after it. She is both idealized and demonized, both all loving and all abandoning. (673)

Beloved in her monologue relates her attachment to a woman with "the face that is mine" (211) and abandonment by the woman with whom she wishes "to join": "my own face has left me" (213). Expressive of Beloved's ambivalence of love and hate, according to Fitzgerald, are the attempts of mergence with the woman that are replicated later in Beloved's extreme dependency on Sethe, "Like a familiar, she [Beloved] hovered, never leaving the room Sethe was in unless required and told to" (57), and the accusations by Beloved of Sethe's desertion, "Beloved accused her [Sethe] of leaving her behind" (241). Fitzgerald contends that such split projections can result in anxiety, "in the feeling that the ego is in bits" (674), and can intensify in aggression, or an attack on the mother, such as the one described below.

The rage and ambivalence surrounding the love hunger is represented in the scene in the Clearing, where Sethe had gone with her daughters to seek solace upon receipt of the news from Paul D, a former slave at Sweet Home, of her husband's insanity. The solace had come in the form of a touch similar to the one belonging to Baby Suggs that had nursed Sethe back to health following her escape from Sweet Home. Gradually, however, the strokes had become bolder to the point where she was being strangled. The hands are associated in this instance with both Baby Suggs and Beloved, with mother and daughter. Afterwards, when Denver accuses Beloved of attempted strangulation, Beloved demurs, "I kissed her neck. I didn't choke it. The circle of iron choked it" (191). The scene clearly calls to mind Sethe's murder of Beloved with the hand saw, a remembrance that, despite Beloved's attachment to Sethe, triggers painful memories and subsequent aggression towards her.

The trope of splintered selves in *Beloved* is paradigmatic of the psychic death, or the denial of one's being as a subject. Sethe refers to herself as being "split in two" (202) and is described as having fly-away parts; Beloved, on the other hand, is in fear of either exploding into bits (133) or dissolving like Denver into nothingness (123). The cross-connections of the characters are clear.

Paul D's punishment—that of having to wear the bit in his mouth—parallels the lashings of Sethe that have produced the chokecherry tree on her back; too, the tobacco tin of Paul D emblematizes repressed memory that neither Paul D nor Sethe can countenance. Paul D's tobacco tin therefore serves the same function as the ghost: to dramatize the fissure created in the characters as a result of the psychic trauma that undermines their sense of self: "He would keep the rest where it belonged: in that tobacco tin buried in his chest where a red heart used to be. Its lid rusted shut. He would not pry it loose now. . ." (72-73). The denial of the two produces a blockage which hinders their psychological freedom. Sethe's psychological entrapment is figuratively represented in her person. Near the end of the novel, a complete role reversal has taken place; as Beloved has gotten bigger, so Sethe has become smaller. Morrison writes: "She [Sethe] sat in the chair licking her lips like a chastised child while Beloved ate up her life, took it, swelled up with it, grew tall on it" (250). The role of daughter and role of mother have become hopelessly entangled as Sethe attempts to compensate for her deprivation as a daughter by excessive indulgence toward Beloved. Resultant of the mother-daughter dyad is a narcissism that is destructive (Schapiro 204). In the words of Jennifer Fitzgerald: "Objects relations theory suggests that just as the infant refuses to see the mother as a separate individual, so the mother may be tempted to treat her child as a part of herself" (678).

Barbara Schapiro in her article "The Bonds of Love and the Boundaries of Self in Toni Morrison's *Beloved"* speaks of the destructive nature of Beloved's and Sethe's narcissism. That is, neither character respects the agency of the other; instead, each attempts to appropriate the other as part of her being:

> Both sides of the power dynamic, both surrender to and incorporation of the other, are apparent in the relationship between Sethe and Beloved. Toward the end of the novel, Sethe relinquishes herself completely to the will and desire of Beloved. She neglects to feed or care for herself and becomes physically drained and emotionally depleted. Sethe literally shrinks while Beloved literally expands and swells; both are caught up in a mutually destructive, frighteningly boundless narcissism. (203)

In addition to the psychological diaspora created by slavery that undermines self-hood, another legacy of slavery is wanderlust, a condition which prevents Paul D from staying in any one location for more than three months. Simone Schwarz-Bart in *The Bridge of Beyond* writes that the settlers of the village L'Abandonnée were comprised of runaway slaves, and the fear of their return to captivity kept a countless number of them on the move: "Some runaway slaves came there afterwards, and a village grew up. The wanderers seeking refuge were countless, and many would not settle anywhere permanently for fear the old days might return" (2). By the same token, Paul D's fear of re-incarceration has likewise been the impetus for his fugitive existence: "Slavery has birthed a fear of place that is quieted only when he is moving" (Furman 77). Subsequently, he is prone to "house fits" (115). When he arrives in Cincinnati eighteen years after he has been sold from Sweet Home by schoolteacher to a Southern trader, Paul D responds to the news by Sethe of the desertion of her sons Howard and Buglar from the vantage point of his own experiences: "Probably best, he thought. If a Negro got legs he ought to use them. Sit down too long, somebody will figure out a way to tie them up" (10). Philip Page in his work *Dangerous Freedom: Fusion and Fragmentation in Toni Morrison's Novels* considers that the flux of jazz, which Toni Morrison's works mimic, becomes likewise a metaphor for the African American experience:

> Just as jazz and the blues are open-ended forms, constantly under revision, always in question, denying fixity, so the historical places and roles of African Americans have been necessarily fluid. African American music is always shifting, always seeking the next variation, just as the African diaspora, the slave trade, the resale of slaves within the United States, the longed-for and sometimes achieved escape to the North, the myth of the return to Africa, and the northern migrations have kept African Americans literally on the move and metaphorically unfixed within the larger culture. (16)

Jennifer Fitzgerald has noted in the article "Selfhood and Community: Psychoanalysis and Discourse in *Beloved*" the grave reservations about psychoanalysis that some black and female theorists hold due to the following: Freud and his successors have posited a normative and universalized psychic model that isolates experiences from diversities such as class and gender thus "pathologiz[ing] non-normative families [and] privileging the healthy development of individual autonomy" (669). These reservations aside, Fitzgerald argues the manner in which the discourse of psychoanalysis and the discourse of slavery may be juxtaposed to reveal both significations and divisions. For example, in her view both the discourse of slavery and psychoanalysis "circulate the same meaning. . . . Pre-Oedipal dependence refuses to acknowledge the separate selfhood of the other; the brutal possessiveness of slavery . . . refuses to recognize [the slaves'] humanity" (684). Fitzgerald, however, notes that from the juxtaposition of the two discourses, the following division emerges. That is, in Fitzgerald's view, the novel *Beloved* extends a challenge to the classic psychoanalytic discourse that privileges separateness and autonomy. According to the revised version, "identity is constructed not within the narrow confines of the hegemonic nuclear family but in relation to the whole community" (683).

Stamp Paid, an example of "reciprocal self-love" (Fitzgerald 685), embodies the community spirit that is given life form by Morrison in Baby Suggs' "mission of love," or ministry (88), and in Ella and the thirty other women who effectively exorcised the ghost of Beloved from 124 (257). Considering the relinquishment of his wife to the slavemaster had satisfied any debt that he owed in the past and would owe in the future, he had renamed himself Stamp Paid and had committed his life to helping others satisfy any debts owed in misery. In return, Stamp Paid was welcomed at every door on which he had the occasion to knock and was granted any favor that he dared to request, as when he sought better sleeping arrangements for Paul D, since it was his actions, namely, showing Paul D the newspaper clipping of Sethe, that had driven him from 124. Ella, upon hearing Stamp Paid's confession, is more than willing to oblige her friend. The attitude of reciprocity apparent between the two reflects on a personal level the interdependence distinct to the community. In a manner of speaking, Stamp Paid, who is without a wife, husbands the entire community, as the following description intimates:

> Underneath his legal vegetables were the contraband hu-
> mans that he ferried across the river. Even the pigs he
> worked in the spring served his purposes. Whole families
> lived on the bones and guts he distributed to them. He
> wrote their letters and read to them the ones they received.
> He knew who had dropsy and who needed stovewood;
> which children had a gift and which needed correction. He
> knew the secrets of the Ohio River and its banks. (169-70)

The concept of communal mothering is encapsulated as well in the group of shackled prisoners, led by Hi Man in *Beloved*. Not only did the group of prisoners provide one another with anchorage, but by acting as one, they were able to circumvent their fate of certain death after mudslides produced by torrential rains flooded their underground prison, which consisted of wooden boxes measuring five feet deep, five feet wide for each of the forty-six prisoners (106-7).

Paul D also articulates an alternative version of the mother. He returns after the exorcism of the ghost from 124 to nurture Sethe back to health. Paul D's character as carpenter is in concert with the role of caregiver. Just as he had repaired the damage to 124 after driving away the ghost at the beginning of the novel, he returns at the end to repair the broken spirit of Sethe:

> Paul D washes her [Sethe] in sections, taking up where Baby
> Suggs left off. This functions as an alternative version of
> mothering, articulated in ways quite opposed to the dis-
> course of the good mother, dispensing with both the exclu-
> sivity of biology (only biological parents have responsibil-
> ity) and of gender (only women can be mothers). Paul D
> gives her back her self. (Fitzgerald 679)

Thus African Americans, denied the pre-Oedipal bonding with caregivers, develop the capacity to nurture themselves. Jennifer Fitgerald in her article "Selfhood and Community: Psychoanalysis and Discourse in *Beloved"* has identified the import of a psychological reading of the novel *Beloved:*

> [A] psychoanalytic reading of the novel allows us to ex-
> plore not only the psychic damage of slavery but its thera-

peutic alternative, the cooperative self-healing of a community of survivors, forging a "livable" (198) life for themselves. (685)

In Doreatha Mbalia's view, the theme of collectivism is reinforced
in the unmarked chapters of *Beloved*, which convey to the reader
the sense of a common struggle. Mbalia writes in *Toni Morrison's
Developing Class Consciousness:*

> Unmarked chapters reinforce the theme of Beloved by con-
> stantly reminding the reader that collective struggle then
> and now is the only practical way to alleviate the oppres-
> sion African people experience. Since the people are one,
> the history is the same, and the plight remains unchanged,
> clearly the solution is the same. (100)

The basis for *Beloved* was a newsclipping of a slavewoman who
had murdered her child rather than have her child experience the
life of a slave. The article "A Visit to the Slave Mother Who Killed
Her Child" was contained in *The Black Book,* a "compendium of
newsclippings and advertisements chronicling the life of African
people in the United States from slavery through the civil rights
movement" that Toni Morrison edited in 1974 (Mbalia 113; McKay
9). The article both inspired the book and the creation of characters. According to Nellie Y. McKay, "While she worked on The
Black Book Morrison came across an old newspaper report of a
runaway slave woman who tried to kill her children to save them
from recapture and re-enslavement. Almost a decade later the account would become the nucleus of her fifth and most celebrated
novel, *Beloved"* (9).

Noting Morrison's penchant for "borrowing kernels of ideas
from historical and literary works" (112), as reflected in the newspaper clipping, Doreatha Drummond Mbalia reasons that
Morrison's likely exposure, as editor at Random House, to
Chinweizu's work *The West and the Rest of Us,* which identifies
capitalism as the core of racism and black solidarity as a means to
combat it, invariably must have influenced Morrison's developing
socialist thought. Her work *Toni Morrison's Developing Class
Consciousness* is devoted to delineating that influence.

The eclectic, or jazz, quality of Morrison's work is also rendered in its affinity to female African and Caribbean authors. In an interview with Kay Bonetti, conducted in 1983, Morrison acknowledged that the "loose" structure of some African literature, derivative of the African oral tradition, was a model for her literature. Likewise, in "Rootedness: The Ancestor as Foundation," Morrison has spoken of her attempts to achieve orality in her fiction:

> There are things that I try to incorporate into my fiction that are directly and deliberately related to what I regard as the major characteristics of Black art. . . . One of which is the ability to be both print and oral literature. . . . To make the story appear oral, meandering, effortless, spoken—to have the reader *feel* the narrator without *identifying* that narrator, or hearing him or her knock about, and to have the reader work *with* the author in the construction of the book—is what's important. (341)

Albeit uncertain that the works of African author Buchi Emecheta are ones with which Morrison is familiar, the description of Beloved, in the words of Marcia Ann Gillespie, as "a succubus leeching Sethe's energy, resources, and spirit, using Sethe's mother love as a means of enslavement" (68) parallels the ironic effects of mother love, induced by the denial of selfhood to the black female, that both Emecheta has given treatment to in her novel *The Joys of Motherhood* and the Caribbean author Simone Schwarz-Bart has alluded to in *The Bridge of Beyond*. Karla F. C. Holloway in her work *Moorings & Metaphors: Figures of Culture and Gender in Black Women's Literature* contends that for women of the African Diaspora who often had to endure the "absent presence" of progeny from whom they were separated, motherhood was often construed as inimical to survival: "Black women's experience with motherhood has not encouraged a romantic 'life renewing itself' metaphor" (171). Expressive of the sentiment are the words of the character Elie of *The Bridge of Beyond* who makes to Télumée the following pronouncement: "Man has strength, woman has cunning, but however cunning she may be her womb is there to betray her. It is her ruin" (45).

The statement is expressive of the attitude of the male character Brownfield in Alice Walker's *The Third Life of Grange
Copeland;* he considers his wife's "big belly her own tomb" (210),
and it is there that he has planted his seeds of destruction. Similar
to the characters Elie and Letitia of Simone Schwarz-Bart's *The
Bridge of Beyond,* Brownfield has imbibed all the racist stereotypes of blacks; that is, he has accepted failure as his due. Hence,
he sets out to sabotage all Mem's attempts at self-improvement,
namely, her attempt to purchase a home. When earnings had been
put away toward the purchase, Brownfield had stolen, consecu-
tively, the money and had squandered it to buy a boar that he had
hoped to breed, only to have it later die, and to make a down payment on a car that later was repossessed: "She was furious, but
more than furious, unable to comprehend that all her moves up-
wards and toward something of their own would be checked by
him. In the end, as with the pig, his luck was bad and the finance
company took the car" (83).

After nine years, Mem had taken matters into her own hands
and had signed a lease on a home, deciding that the "decision to let
him [Brownfield] be man of the house for nine years had cost her
and him nine years of unrelenting misery" (122). What has goaded
Brownfield about the improvement in their standard of living is
that it has exposed his own lack of resourcefulness. Hence, he has
bided his time, plotting to give Mem her comeuppance by using
her body as a weapon against her:

> Her body would do to her what he could not, without the
> support of his former bravado. The swelling of the womb,
> again and again pushing the backbone inward, the belly
> outward. He surveyed with sly interest the bleaching out
> of every crease on her wrinkled stomach. Waiting. She
> could not hold out against him with nausea, aching feet and
> teeth, swollen legs, bursting veins and head; or the grim
> and dizzying reality of her trapped self and her children's
> despair. He could bring her back to lowness she had not
> even guessed at before. (143)

Hence, it is both Alice Walker's and Toni Morrison's disparate
views on motherhood, which "deny and affirm the popular percep-

tions of motherlove" (DeLancey 15), in addition to the central trope, or groundbeat, of orphanhood, descriptive of the fragmentation created—both social and psychological—by slavery, and, in general, the eclectic, improvisational, or jazz, quality of Morrison's fiction, a feature that Karla F.C. Holloway defines in her work *Moorings & Metaphors* as "plurisignance" (55), that would appear to warrant, respectively, the writers' correspondence both with female African and Caribbean authors.

WORKS CITED

Benjamin, Jessica. *The Bonds of Love: Psychoanalysis, Feminism, and the Problem of Domination.* New York: Random, 1988.

Chambers, Jack. *Milestones 2: The Music and Times of Miles Davis Since 1960.* 2 vols. New York: Morrow, 1985.

Davies, Carole Boyce. "Mother Right/Write Revisited: *Beloved* and *Dessa Rose* and the Construction of Motherhood in Black Women's Fiction." *Narrating Mothers: Theorizing Maternal Subjectivities.* Eds. Brenda O. Daly and Maureen T. Reddy. Knoxville: U of Tennessee P, 1991. 44-57.

Delancey, Dayle B. "Motherlove Is a Killer: *Sula, Beloved,* and the Deadly Trinity of Motherlove." *SAGE* 3, no. 2 (fall 1990): 15-18.

Fitzgerald, Jennifer. "Selfhood and Community: Psychoanalysis and Discourse in *Beloved.*" *Modern Fiction Studies* 39, nos., 3 & 4 (fall/ winter 1993): 669-687.

Furman, Jan. *Toni Morrison's Fiction.* Columbia: U of South Carolina P, 1996.

Gillespie, Marcia Ann. "Out of Slavery's Inferno." Rev. of *Beloved,* by Toni Morrison. *Ms.* 16 November 1987: 68.

Holloway, Karla F.C. *Moorings & Metaphors: Figures of Culture and Gender in Black Women's Literature.* New Brunswick, N.J.: Rutgers UP, 1992.

Mbalia, Doreatha Drummond. *Toni Morrison's Developing Class Consciousness.* Selinsgrove: Susquehanna UP, 1991.

McKay, Nellie Y. "Part One: Materials." *Approaches to Teaching the Novels of Toni Morrison.* Eds. Nellie Y. McKay and Kathryn Earle. New York: Modern Language Association, 1997. 3-18.

Morrison, Toni. *Beloved.* New York: New American Library, 1987. All subsequent references are to this edition.

———. Interview by Jane Bakerman. Taylor-Guthrie, 30-42.

—————. Interview by Kay Bonetti. Columbia, Mo.: American Audio Prose Library, 1983.

—————. Interview by Gail Caldwell. Taylor-Guthrie, 239-45.

—————. Interview by Marsha Darling. Taylor-Guthrie, 246-54.

—————. Interview by Thomas Le Clair. Taylor-Guthrie, 119-28.

—————. Interview by Amanda Smith. *Publishers Weekly* 21 Aug. 1987: 50-51.

—————. Interview by Claudia Tate. Taylor-Guthrie, 156-70.

—————. "Rootedness: The Ancestor as Foundation." *Black Women Writers, 1950-1980: A Critical Evaluation.* Ed. Mari Evans. New York: Doubleday, 1984. 339-45.

—————. *Sula.* New York: New American Library, 1973.

Page, Philip. *Dangerous Freedom: Fusion and Fragmentation in Toni Morrison's Novels.* Jackson: UP of Mississippi, 1995.

Schapiro, Barbara. "The Bonds of Love and the Boundaries of Self in Toni Morrison's *Beloved.*" *Contemporary Literature* 32.2 (summer 1991): 194-210.

Schwarz-Bart. *The Bridge of Beyond.* Trans. Barbara Bray. London: Heinemann, 1982.

Taylor-Guthrie, Danielle, ed. *Conversations with Toni Morrison.* Jackson: UP of Mississippi, 1994.

Walker, Alice. *The Third Life of Grange Copeland.* New York: Simon, 1970.

Weever, Jacqueline de. *Mythmaking and Metaphor in Black Women's Fiction.* New York: St. Martin's, 1991.

Chapter 6

THE SOCIOLOGICAL IMPLICATIONS OF FEMALE ABANDONMENT IN EMECHETA'S *SECOND-CLASS CITIZEN* AND *THE JOYS OF MOTHERHOOD*

Buchi Emecheta is one of the most prolific African writers. She has published twelve novels, four children's books, and three plays. Her novels include *In the Ditch* (1972), *Second-Class Citizen* (1974), *The Bride Price* (1976), *The Slave Girl* (1977), *The Joys of Motherhood* (1979), *Destination Biafra* (1982), *Double Yoke* (1982), *Naira Power* (1982), *The Rape of Shavi* (1983), *A Kind of Marriage* (1986), *Gwendolen* (1989), and *Kehinde* (1994). Her children's books include *Titch the Cat* (1979), *Nowhere to Play* (1979), *The Moonlight Bride* (1980), and *The Wrestling Match* (1980). Her three plays include *Juju Landlord* (1975), *A Kind of Marriage* (1975), and *Family Bargain* (1986).

She has received a number of prestigious awards, among them the 1978 Best Black Writer in Britain, the 1979 Jock Campbell, and the Daughter of Mark Twain, an American Literature Award. In 1992, she received an honorary Doctor of Literature degree from Farleigh Dickinson University, Madison, New Jersey, in recognition of her literary accomplishments. By all accounts, Buchi Emecheta has conquered the success phobia that the psychoanalysts Abram Kardiner and Lionel Ovesey have identified as symptomatic of displacement and that is mirrored in Emecheta's fictional surrogate Adah in her respective works *In the Ditch* and *Second-Class Citizen*.

The psychoanalysts Abram Kardiner and Lionel Ovesey undertook a study *The Mark of Oppression* conceived on the premise that group characteristics are adaptive rather than acquired. Hence, the book disputes the claim of inborn "Negro characteristics"; rather, it describes the Negro personality as defined by the cultural institutions that have produced it. The social scientists conclude: "Adaptive patterns are not inherited; each individual creates them anew according to need, within the framework of culturally determined possibilities" (xviii). The authors go on to observe that although their findings pertain to African Americans, they are "equally applicable to oppressed people anywhere, irrespective of color" (ix-x). Of particular concern to this writer in a survey of abandonment in the literature of selected female authors of the African diaspora is the psychodynamics of the group in relation to this phenomenon.

Of the twenty-five case studies, representing both the lower and the middle and upper classes, of particular interest was a twenty-seven-year-old male subject who was demonstrative of the "success phobia" that seems to have afflicted both Adah of *In the Ditch* and Francis of Buchi Emecheta's *Second-Class Citizen.*

Described by the psychoanalysts as a government clerk, the subject, referred to as W.S., had dropped out of high school in his junior year. The failure to graduate from high school, however, had not precluded his enlistment in the Army, where he was promoted to sergeant. Suffering a loss of rank because of insubordination, W.S. had declined the offer to attend Officers' Candidate School, rationalizing that "he wanted to stay with his buddies" (172). The psychotherapists opine the real reason is that "he feared advancement, though he was constantly striving for it" (172) and concludes that the struggle for status by blacks weakens the already fragile relationship among blacks in that it "creates more intra-Negro animosity than it alleviates" (214).

A case in point is Adah's Nigerian neighbors in *Second-Class Citizen.* Adah, Francis, and their children are evicted from their one-room apartment because the neighbors cannot abide Adah's success. Not only has Adah acquired "a white man's job" (69) at the North Finchley Library, but unlike most Nigerian immigrants who have been forced to foster out their children because of inadequate living accommodations (46), their two have remained with them. The childless landlord's jealousy of Adah's fertility, as Adah is, after only six months in London, expecting a third child, has been another factor that has led to their eviction. Consequently, Francis' attempts to ingratiate himself with his Nigerian neighbors have been futile, since Adah's successes have served as an unpleasant reminder of their own failures:

> [Francis] thought that by confiding in them and adapting to their standards they would accept him. But he was forgetting the Yoruba saying that goes, "a hungry dog does not play with one with a full stomach." Francis forgot that, to most of their neighbours, he had what they did not have. He was doing his studies full time, and did not have to worry about money because his wife was earning enough to keep them going. He could see his children every day and even had the audacity to give his wife another. (69-70)

The intra-racial rivalry in *Second-Class Citizen* stems in part from the adaptation by Adah of white prototypes, such as her decision to rear their children similar to the Britons rather than to have them fostered out, as ideals to be emulated. An example of the idealization of the European ideal in *The Mark of Oppression: Explorations in the Personality of the American Negro* is the preference by the male for the light-skinned female. As a result of this preference, group cohesion is hampered. To be sure, the animosity directed by the darker-skinned females against the lighter females due to their appeal to black males is compounded against those who pass, as passing is regarded as "a blow against other Negroes" (365). The response elicited by passing among blacks becomes then the barometer by which the psychotherapists Kardiner and Ovesey gauge attitudes among blacks toward other forms of success: "The same fear that is associated with passing attends any other kind of *success*. It is also regarded as a blow against other Negroes. This fear of success is a powerful deterrent in many cases of successful Negroes we have observed" (365).

The fear of success by Adah of *In the Ditch* and Francis of *Second-Class Citizen*, success being deemed a hostile act for which one is likely to suffer retaliation, accounts, in part, for their joblessness and creates for them an emotional cul de sac. Notwithstanding that Adah of *In the Ditch* is a Nigerian immigrant striving to accommodate herself to British society, her desire for acceptance is no less keen. Subsequently, when forced to choose between self-sufficiency and isolation or joblessness and acceptance, Adah chooses the latter and is baptised into the community of the Mansions:

> She couldn't claim to be working-class, because the working class had a code for daily living. She had none. Hers was then a complete problem family. Joblessness baptised her into the Mansions' society. Like most of the tenants there, she became a regular visitor at Carol's office. (31)

Kardiner and Ovesey theorize on the related causes for adaptational failure by the lower middle-class black: "All compensatory efforts fail and terminate in a reinforcement of the originally low self-esteem with which he started. . . . No course of compensation leads to any adequate outcome. All lead to blocked action or to aggression of which he himself ultimately becomes the victim" (178-79).

The decision to have numerous children as "a way of making the society that forced them into the ditch suffer" (54) is an example of the displaced aggression of the residents of the Mansions in *Ditch*. By the same token, Francis' displacement of aggression in *Second-Class Citizen* is similar to that of Brownfield in Alice Walker's *The Third Life of Grange Copeland* who similarly blames all his failures on his wife, Mem. Thus, one of Mem's ten-point resolutions governing Brownfield's move into her house is the following: "Eighth, you going to take the blame for every wrong thing you do and stop blaming it on me and Captain Davis and Daphne and Ornette and Ruth and everybody else for fifty miles around" (138). In *Second-Class Citizen,* notwithstanding that Francis has had to take each accounting examination approximately four times before passing (32), with each failure, he blames his wife. Notwithstanding, too, that Adah, when she sits for part of her library exam is able to "scrape through" (148), even as she works full-time as a library assistant and cares for their three children, Francis still considers his wife and children a hindrance to his studies. In his view, his failure to pass the exam is the result of her coming to England, producing so many children, and refusing to have them fostered out:

> Things got even worse for her when Francis failed his sum-
> mer examinations. He blamed it all on her. If she had not
> brought her children and saddled him with them, if she had
> allowed them to be fostered, if she had not become preg-
> nant so soon after her arrival, he would have passed. (50)

The upshot is that Francis's failure to attend lectures and his extra-
marital affairs get in the way of his academic pursuits. When the
son Vicky becomes ill with meningitis, Adah is loathe to contact
Francis because she is uncertain of his whereabouts.

Basic to the disorganization of the Black family, according to
Kardiner and Ovesey, is the lesser opportunity of the Negro male.
Because "the [black] female's chances for employment are better
and more constant than those of the [black] male" (54), the con-
ventional roles within the family are reversed. The result is resentment and enmity on the part of both partners that contribute to
familial disintegration: "Their roles are reversed. Since these values are just the opposite from what they are in white society, and
since the values of white society are inescapable, the male fears
and hates the female; the female mistrusts and has contempt for
the male because he cannot validate his nominal masculinity in
practice" (Kardiner and Ovesey 349).

The role reversal in the family in complete in *Second-Class
Citizen*. Francis accepts a one-time job as a postman, but quits
after two weeks, when Adah is on maternity leave following the
delivery of their third child. The measure of the couple's role reversal is Adah's guilt regarding her disability, so accustomed has
she become to being the family's breadwinner: "Francis went to
work for two weeks. Adah felt very guilty about this. She knew
her man ought to go out to work for their living, but in her own
particular family she had been doing all the work. It seemed to her
that she was failing, by staying at home and letting Francis go out
to work in that terrible winter" (127).

The inability of Francis to provide for his family leads him to
resort to hedonism; Grange Copeland of *The Third Life of Grange
Copeland,* to whoredom with his mistress Josie. As Kardiner and
Ovesey have noted, the discrepancy between the ideal and the real
self often leads the individual to fill alternately the gap by either
depression or abandon (271). For Brownfield Copeland of *The*

Third Life of Grange Copeland, both the former and the latter are the case, as Brownfield orbits between the two extremes that are inextricably linked one to the other. Kardiner and Ovesey observe the interconnectedness of the various adaptational processes, or constellations: "It would be very convenient if we could arrange these various factors into a simple causal sequence; but this is relatively impossible. They are a group of constantly interacting factors, which feed into each other" (364). Brownfield's indebtedness depresses him; he attempts to ameliorate the condition in the arms of his father's former mistress, Josie. For Francis of *Second-Class Citizen,* the latter is the case. Witness Adah's observations in *Second-Class Citizen* on the symptoms of their deteriorating marriage: ". . . the women in the house wrote Adah an open petition begging her to control her husband, because he was chasing them all. The letter was posted unsealed, and sent to the wrong branch of the library. So other library assistants could read it if they liked" (154).

Without question, Emecheta depicts Adah as victimized by displaced aggression similar to that displayed by the subject W.S. in the study by Kardiner and Ovesey who is described thusly: "He was passive in the major situations of life and permitted himself aggressions mainly with his equals or subordinates. These displaced aggressions upon his equals or inferiors had some expressive and tension-releasing function" (177). Emecheta is careful, however, to show the cyclic nature of oppression. She has stated of her works:

> [T]he main themes of my novel are African society and family: the historical, social and political life as seen by a woman through events. I always try to show that the African male is oppressed and he too oppresses the African woman. (qtd. in Mezu 67)

The men, however, do not bear sole responsibility for the plight of the women as second-class citizens. The females, too, seem to sanction the patriarchal values that denigrate women, namely, the belief that "a boy was like four children put together" (62), or as Adaku expresses it in *The Joys of Motherhood,* in reference to Nnu Ego's eldest son Oshia, "You are worth more than ten Dumbis"

(128). Adah of *Second-Class Citizen* likewise shares the mentality that, because of its identification with the revered male object (Ovesey 47), ends up enslaving women. When asked by a nurse if Vicky is the only child, Adah had responded that "there was another, but she was only a girl" (62). Such deprecating attitudes of women make them more susceptible to exploitation, inasmuch as they believe that they are deserving of it. Adah, for instance, begins to believe that it is because of her that Francis is a failure:

> Again it struck her that their plan had failed, and that it had all been her fault. She should not have agreed to work all the time. She should have encouraged Francis to work, just like this man's wife, whom she had not seen, had encouraged her husband to work. Francis would have met other men, like this one, and he would have copied them. (156-57)

Emecheta seems to imply in both *Second-Class Citizen* and *The Joys of Motherhood* that unless the attitudes toward females are altered, by males and females alike, society will remain "a man's world, which women will always help to build" (*The Joys of Motherhood* 187).

Adah's marriage to Francis is destined for disintegration not only because Adah is collusive in its destruction, but, as well, because the marriage has been one of expediency. Adah's father had died when she was approximately eight years old. Consequently, she was destined to live with her mother's elder brother as a servant (17); Adah's brother, Boy, with one of her father's cousins, while her mother was destined to be inherited by her father's brother. Thus it was for the sake of a home that Adah was to marry Francis Ofili, a student of accountancy. After obtaining a secondary school degree through sheer obstinacy, Adah was determined to continue her education. The rub, though, was that she was an orphan, and the continuation of her education, which was subject to social dictates due to her gender, required marriage:

> Well, there was one thing she had not bargained for. To read for a degree, to read for the entrance examination, or even for more "A" levels, one needed a home. Not just any home where there would be trouble today and fights to-

morrow, but a good, quiet atmosphere where she could study in peace.

Adah could not find a home like that. In Lagos, at that time, teenagers were not allowed to live by themselves, and if the teenager happened to be a girl as well, living alone would be asking for trouble. In short, Adah had to marry. (23)

Adah's disillusionment following the marriage is predictable (28). It coincides with that of A.T., a female participant in the Kardiner-Ovesey study, who likewise was reared in a foster home and succumbed to a marriage of expediency in order to escape a household of turbulence: "The foster father was an habitual drinker who liked to talk, and the more he drank, the more he talked. . . . At times he got very violent and struck the foster mother" (215). Accordingly, the marriage is described as doomed. Kardiner and Ovesey note, however, that "she cannot give up her husband for he serves her too well as a reliable whipping boy" (223).

Evidence of the adaptational pattern demonstrative of A.T. is also demonstrative of Adah in *Second-Class Citizen.* Adah is so completely cowed by Francis that her health remains secondary to Francis' welfare. For example, she continues to work while in her final month of pregnancy with her third child, and she decides upon a home delivery because she stands to earn six pounds with a home delivery. One day in December when she has been unable to go to work, she is convinced that the "go-slow" of the railwaymen is her fault (96); consequently, upon her return to their flat, she busies herself with explanations that Francis will accept. Francis, upon hearing from Adah the news of a railway strike, lectures her on diligence, albeit "at half past ten in the morning . . ., he was still in his pyjamas" (99). Adah remains silent during the lecture by Francis, but the revenge of Adah, the fictional surrogate of Emecheta, is the fictional demonization as "Lucifer" (106) of the husband who has abused her physically and psychologically. Emecheta drops completely the facade late in the novel, as she refers to her own titles, namely, *The Bride Price* (164); the writers who have influenced her, namely, Flora Nwapa, her interest in sociology (167), "What discipline teaches about people? Psychology? Sociology? Anthropology or history? She knew about the others, but what does a sociologist study?"; and the process by which she acquired her liberation, as well as that of her four children (174).

Abram Kardiner and Lionel Ovesey argue in their work the following import of the study of personality, or psychodynamics—a determination of the efficacy of institutional structures upon the individual has the potential to promote institutional changes: "Institutional changes proceed from dynamic sources within the personality. For this reason, a knowledge of the composition and structure of the personality in specific groups is a basic preliminary to social engineering" (10).

We have already seen the manner in which the family has influenced personality. The absence of parental care obliges individuals such as Adah of *Second-Class Citizen* and the subject A.T. to rely upon their own resources. On the other hand, according to Kardiner and Ovesey, "Excessive maternal care can . . . create a proclivity to passivity" (23). It is, in part, the latter that produces in Francis a proclivity toward passivity. Adah, for instance, silently curses her mother-in-law "for spoiling all her sons. There were so many girls in the family that the boys grew up thinking they were something special, superhuman creatures" (*Second-Class Citizen* 99). The condition can be seen in part in Francis' complacency, or his inability to take responsibility for the well-being of the family. Francis, however, finds justification for his complacency in religion. He becomes a Jehovah's Witness and rationalizes his sloth as piety. Because the Bible is often used to condone a multitude of vices and prejudices, Emecheta writes that it is "the greatest book on human psychology. . . . If you were lazy and did not wish to work, or if you had failed to make your way in society, you could always say, 'My kingdom is not of this world'" (100). Kardiner and Ovesey are in concurrence on the narcotic value of cults: "They offer 'escape' from hardships of life. . ." (353).

Education, as identified in Emecheta's autobiographical works, is one means for women to overcome the enslavement by traditional norms that "fiercely defy efforts at modernity." According to Rose U. Mezu,

> For Buchi Emecheta as for all the progressive feminist/
> womanist writers, education is the desideratum for an en-

lightened, independent, self-fulfilling life. The writer's personae in her autobiographical novels transcend near-impossible situations by virtue of knowledge and wisdom conferred by education. Education, therefore, becomes the panacea to combat all ills for it heightens self-awareness, sharpens perceptions and goals and forges a will of steel. (74)

Emecheta seems to advocate as well in *The Joys of Motherhood* and *Gwendolen* the formation of female alliances as one means of coping with abandonment. According to Nancy Topping Bazin in her article "Venturing into Feminist Consciousness," "Nnu Ego's experiences have made her realize that women must work together to 'change all this' (187). Nnu Ego has ventured into feminist consciousness, but it is not until after her death that she is free to take action by denying fertility to the young women. She knows that the continuous pressure to bear sons that drives them to her shrine will enslave them as it did her. Freedom for them must begin with rejecting the patriarchal glorification of motherhood" (50-51). At the very least, the group alliances would provide an emotional support system that would lessen the distress related to their abandonment by sons who have adopted Western lifestyles and values and by husbands who seek to distance themselves from failures toward whom they seem to feel little, if any, responsibility:

> Nnu Ego told herself that she would have been better off had she had time to cultivate those women who had offered her hands of friendship; but she had never had the time. What with worrying over this child, this pregnancy, and the lack of money, coupled with the fact that she never had adequate outfits to wear to visit her friends, she had shied away from friendship, telling herself she did not need any friends, she had enough in her family. (219)

In *Gwendolen*, Emecheta's latest novel, Emecheta delineates a sisterhood transcendent of cultural boundaries. When Sonia Brillianton returns to Jamaica after receiving a telegram apprising her of her mother's death, she discovers that she no longer has anything in common with her childhood friend, Roza. Instead, her kinship is with Mrs. Gladys Odowis, a Nigerian and fellow immigrant to Britain with whom she has shared common experiences. In a moment of epiphany, she realizes "that though Mrs. Odowis came from Africa, and she from Jamaica, they had more in common. She could no longer relate to Roza the way she used to before she left for London all those years ago" (140).

On the subject of sisterhood, Emecheta, in the 1988 interview with Susheila Nasta, averred that "It's about time women start cultivating each other rather than say, to survive, 'we must have children; we must have sons.' It does not necessarily follow. It's not that they [Nnu Ego's sons] hated her. They were so busy acquiring an education that they did not hear of her death."

Oladele Taiwo in his work *Female Novelists of Modern Africa* writes about Emecheta's craftsmanship, her attention to cause and effect in her novels as well as the central themes in her works. With respect to one of the novel's themes, the necessity for change, Taiwo writes regarding Francis's rigidity:

> The statement of the novel is clear. The social demands of London, representing the present for the Obis, are greater than those of their past in Lagos. Only strong-minded people, like Adah, can hope to survive in the new situation. Francis suffers mainly because he is unable to relate the past to the present. For, as Adah says, and she must know, 'Francis was not a bad man, just a man who could no longer cope with the over-demanding society he found himself in.' (106)

Just as Adah of *Second-Class Citizen* investigates the use of contraceptives and when she discovers that she is pregnant with her fourth child, takes the necessary precautions (160), her fiction reading also shows her ready adaptation of European culture. As a senior library assistant at the North Finchley Library (41), Adah was amazed at the patrons' love of fiction and began herself to emulate them, the result being that the works by contemporary novelists "helped her a great deal culturally" (44).

Adaku in *The Joys of Motherhood* also appears more adaptable and, therefore, able to thrive. She quits Nnaife's household rather than allow herself to be scandalized by conditions that she cannot change. She becomes self-supporting and recognizes the need to educate her daughters so that they too can become self-sufficient (170-71).

Contrarily, resistance to change is made analogous to death. Emecheta reports in her first work, *In the Ditch*, the sudden death of an elderly resident of the Mansions, the demise undoubtedly precipitated by the tenant's dread of re-settlement. The resident appeared to have been one of those "who had never had the courage to ask to be moved":

> In a little less than two months after the meeting at Haverstock Hill, the Mansions were almost empty. Most of the people had gone, leaving the dregs—those who owed enormous rent, or those who had never had the courage to ask to be moved. (115)

Simone de Beauvoir observes in *The Coming of Age* that although there are exceptions, imprisonment in the past is a characteristic of old age. The elderly person is, as Beauvoir describes him, "a dead man under suspended sentence. Blind to the rest of the world, to the end he stubbornly preserves the man he has been by means of his refusals and his memories" (385).

On the other hand, Francis of *Second-Class Citizen* was "an African through and through" (28) and was not inclined to alter any of his traditional beliefs, namely, that "a woman was a second-class human, to be slept with at any time, even during the day, and, if she refused, to have sense beaten into her until she gave in; to be ordered out of bed after he had done with her; to make sure she washed his clothes and got his meals ready at the right time. There was no need to have an intelligent conversation with his wife because, you see, she might start getting ideas" (164-65). The consequence of his stubbornness is his own emotional disintegration, as well as the disintegration of his family.

Francis's emotional disintegration is mirrored in the older Noble. Noble epitomizes the Nigerian male who, upon coming to England to educate himself for one of the "poshy jobs" (79) that were due to come in the wake of Nigeria's independence, had failed to get "a foothold" (80). To placate themselves for their failure, they had selected white wives who had little to recommend them other than their color. Calvin Hernton argues that marriage by a black man to a white woman represents more than a desire to achieve status; it represents a psychic need for "absolution":

> With black men who have to marry white women, much more than status or an attempt to escape a despised self is involved. There is something metaphysical about their need for white women. . . . In the disposition of the deformed, there is the organic craving to be loved by those who have crippled them, to be redeemed by those who have damned them. (83-84)

The extent of Mr. Noble's decline is reflected in his previous life in Nigeria. A chieftain's son, the husband of six wives, and the father of twenty children, he had abandoned all of them to study law in England (81). His inability to pass his law exams, his acceptance of low-level jobs to keep himself afloat, and his attempt to ameliorate his distress through a white wife are a projection of Francis's possible future.

Mr. Noble is also an example of the quiescent-aggressive tendencies constitutive of "the Negro personality," as Kardiner and Ovesey have described them:

> In the center of this adaptational scheme stand the low self-esteem (the self-referential part) and the aggression (the reactive part). The rest are maneuvers with these main constellations, to prevent their manifestation, to deny them and the sources from which they come, to make things look different from what they are, to replace aggressive activity which would be socially disastrous with more acceptable ingratiation and passivity. (303-4)

The aggression of Mr. Noble is directed toward the elderly female tenants in his building who, due to both their age and gender, would render them subordinates. Fittingly, Emecheta refers to them as "poor old things" (84). After receiving a disability pension from his job as a lift operator, Noble had invested his money in the purchase of an old, dilapidated, three-floor terrace house, occupied by two elderly English women, that he had hoped to renovate. Noble had assumed the quick departure of the two English women upon their discovery that their new landlord was black. He was proven wrong, as the tenants, who had been born in the house, refused to move. He miscalculated a second time when he raised their rent, and they refused to pay (83-84). Biding his time, Noble drowned his sorrows in drink. Soon he concocted another scheme: he would resort to witchcraft to drive them out of the property, but the elderly English women remained defiant. The brutal winter of 1962-63, however, produced the vacancy that Noble, in all his schemes, could not. The dilapidated building that provided little protection from the frigid elements precipitated their demise. The condition of the building, as well as Noble's reputation as a practitioner of witchcraft, however, effectively spoiled his chances for prosperity. Thus similar to W.S., whose half-hearted bids for status, such as leadership roles in social clubs, have failed, all avenues for Noble similarly appear blocked. Kardiner and Ovesey describe W.S. in terms suited as well for Noble: "He [W.S.] begins and ends with low self-esteem. All compensatory efforts fail and terminate in a reinforcement of the originally low self-esteem with which he started. . . . All lead to blocked action or to aggression of which he himself ultimately becomes the victim" (178-79).

The suppression of rage in order to avoid the socially disastrous consequences, can lead, according to Abram Kardiner and Lionel Ovesey, to other compensatory activities such as, among others, (a) disparaging the other fellow and (b) narcotizing the individual against traumatic impact in order "to help establish some semblance of internal harmony" (313). Evidence of the latter is seen in Noble of *Second-Class Citizen*, while evidence of disparagement, one of the above compensatory activities, is seen in Francis' belittlement of Adah's attempts at fiction-writing as "brainless" (170). On the other hand, evidence of both compensatory activities—disparagement of the Other and narcotization of self—is contained in Alice Walker's *The Third Life of Grange Copeland*.

Abram Kardiner and Lionel Ovesey observe in *The Mark of Oppression* that "Alcoholic psychoses in Negroes occur with twice the frequency that they do in whites" (313). In Walker's *The Third Life of Grange Copeland*, alcoholism is described as affecting at least two generations of Copelands. During Grange's first life, a drunken debauch had become a weekly ritual:

> Late Saturday night Grange would come home lurching
> drunk, threatening to kill his wife and Brownfield, stum-
> bling and shooting off his shotgun. He threatened Marga-
> ret and she ran and hid in the woods with Brownfield
> huddled at her feet. (15)

The scene is re-played at the end of the novel with serious consequences. It is Grange's son, Brownfield, who has returned home
"lurching drunk" and uttering terroristic threats. The daughters
Ornette and Ruth take cover in the chicken house (165), while the
oldest, Daphne, sets off to town to warn her mother of the possible
danger. As fate would have it, Mem is driven home from her job
as a domestic by her employer. The result is inevitable, as she is
gunned down by a crazed Brownfield. Her murder was to make
good on his threat that if Mem left him, as she had promised to do
after she had recovered her health and found a job, that he would
stop her forcibly with the barrel of a gun: "She had thought she
could best him. And he had warned her, if she tried, what he would
do. A man of his word, as he thought of himself, he had kept his
word. His word had even become his duty" (228-29).

That Brownfield is the replica of his father is clear. Not only
does their despair stem from the chronic debt of sharecropping,
but their displaced aggression against their wives leads, ultimately,
to their abandonment and, indirectly and directly, to their suicide
and murder. On the identical nature of Brownfield and Grange
Copeland, JoAnne Cornwell, in "Searching for Zora in Alice's
Garden," has established:

> Brownfield is in fact a body inhabited by the spirit of his
> absent father. As Grange Copeland's son, he is the con-
> tinuation of Grange's misery—he is Grange's first life, and
> it is through Brownfield that the contours of Grange's youth
> are revealed. . . . It comes as no surprise, then, that at the
> end of the novel, Grange must slay Brownfield, a vestige
> of his first life and a symbol of his second, for the sake of
> his third, which has been invested in Ruth. (104-5)

Brownfield's name had pre-figured his self-destructiveness. Named
for "the autumnal shades of Georgia cotton fields" (249),
Brownfield's name had been linked to the very source of his even-

tual despair: "Already she was giving him up to what stood ready to take his life. After only two years of marriage she knew that in her plantation world the mother was second in command, the father having no command at all" (249-50). Robert Butler lends the following interpretation to Brownfield's name:

> As [Brownfield's] name clearly suggests, his is a case of blighted growth; he is a person who has been physically and emotionally withered by the nearly pathological environment which surrounds him. By the end of the novel, he is portrayed as "a human being . . . completely destroyed" by the worst features of rural Southern life—ignorance, poverty, racism, and violence. (196)

In addition to displaced aggression, another correlation among the characters is their invisibility. Noble's name in *Second-Class Citizen* is not given. However, Noble's inculcation of the racist assumptions held about Africans compels him to accept readily the role of buffoon. It is because of his willingness to appease his white co-workers that he was nicknamed "Noble": "He was such a noble man that he would do anything for his mates, even taking his trousers off!" (82) Mr. Noble's deformity had resulted from his attempt to prove that Africans had superior strength by aiming to shoulder a lift. The disfigurement caused by the accident is symbolic of his profound self-hatred.

In the same vein, congruent with the exteriorization of the Copelands is their characterization in *The Third Life of Grange Copeland* as "workhorses." Their moves have been precipitated by transactions occurrent among members of the Davis family, for whom Brownfield is employed as dairyman. Brownfield had gone to work for Captain Davis after the death of the latter's sister-in-law. Mem, whose services were no longer needed, had been let go by Captain Davis' brother; in return, Captain Davis had allowed his brother the use of his tractor for a season: "The swap had been made exactly as if he and his family were a string of workhorses" (113). Captain Davis in Part V of the novel approaches Brownfield to negotiate yet another trade. Captain Davis' son J.L. is in need of a dairyman; hence, Brownfield's transfer is a fait accompli. It is precisely because of Mem's desire for security that she makes the decision to secure her own house: "I just done got sick and tired of being dragged around from dump to dump, traded off by white folks like I'm a piece of machinery" (122).

In the same way, Adah of *Second-Class Citizen* is defined by external aspects of her being: "To the other women in the ward, she was Caesar; to the strings of young doctors who kept trailing in the wake of the surgeon, she was 'Cord presentation,' whatever that meant. To the night nurses, she was the mother of Mohammed Ali, because her baby was loud-mouthed, troublesome and refused to be tamed" (113). A turning point comes at the end of the novel; her childhood friend calls her by her Igbo pet name "Nne nna" (174), hinting at the possibility of comradeship.

Readers are informed in *Head Above Water*, published in 1986, of the nature of Emecheta's friendship to Chidi, the childhood friend introduced at the conclusion of *Second-Class Citizen*. Following the disintegration of her marriage to Sylvester, the husband referred to in *Second-Class Citizen* as Francis, Chidi had become a confidant and advisor, introducing her to the Igbo community in Great Britain and later advising her to send her manuscript, variously called "Observersations," or "Social Realities" or "Life in London" (64), to the *New Statesman* where it was serialized before being published as the autobiography *In the Ditch*. Their friendship, as she writes about it in *Head Above Water*, has spanned twenty years (223), and although he had proposed marriage severally, she had rejected his proposals, neither wanting to risk the likelihood of trauma for her children nor additional children:

> I always remember my brother's running ears, due to slaps received at the hands of uncles and cousins, and his tattered khaki shirts. If our mother had stayed with us we would still have been very poor but our childhood would not have been so terrible. I did not want the kids I brought into the world to have a similar experience. And of course, with our people, marriage means more children. I did not want any more. (222)

Head Above Water often reads like a travelogue, *e.g.*, the chapter entitled "Job-Hunting." The autobiography is also poorly edited. Emecheta confesses that she rarely revises her work and loathes reading proofs sent to her by her publishers. On the advice of her agent that she revise *Second-Class Citizen*, Emecheta had refused, invoking creative license: "That was the way I wrote, pouring my heart out non-stop, and if I started to rewrite and correct my mistakes, it would be too artificial" (146). One wishes that Emecheta had seen the value of editing as, by her own admission in *In the Ditch*, "Her . . . words always betrayed the fact that she had learned her English via English for Foreign Students" (70).

Nonetheless, the relevance of *Head Above Water* is, to some extent, its insight into the creative process. Readers learn that *Joys of Motherhood* was inspired by her daughter's intractability. Chiedu had insisted on being transferred to a fee-paying private school, and when her mother had refused, she had gone to live with her father. Although she later returned after Emecheta's collapse from exhaustion, the incident had led the writer to contemplate the irony on which *The Joys of Motherhood* is based—that the mother who had sacrificed all would live to be mocked by her own children: "This was going to be my lot. I was going to give all I had to my children, only for them to spit on my face and tell me that I was a bad mother and then leave and run to a father who had never in all his life bought them a pair of pants" (224).

On the inspiration of *Second-Class Citizen*, Emecheta writes that she was responding to critics who had wondered how a mother who had described herself as educated could find herself "in the ditch" (104). The attitude of seriousness in the form of enslavement to custom, and/or "group think," and the prevalence of racism and sexism were the responses that Emecheta provided in *Second-Class Citizen.*

Finally, Alice Walker has described *Second-Class Citizen* as "one of the most informative books about contemporary African life that I have read" (70). The work speaks to her as a writer who is also a mother in that it discredits the long-standing belief that many have had about the means by which art is produced. Walker writes in *In Search of our Mothers' Gardens:*

> She integrates the profession of writer into the cultural concept of mother/worker that she retains from Ibo society. Just as the African mother has traditionally planted crops, pounded maize, and done her washing with her baby

strapped to her back, so Adah can write a novel with her children playing in the same room. (69)

In addition to re-defining our notions of how art is created, Emecheta, in *Second-Class Citizen* and *The Joys of Motherhood* writes of the dangers of imbibing racist and sexist stereotypes and the value of adapting oneself to changing circumstances without devaluing either one's gender or culture. Indeed, the sociological implications of Emecheta's works are clear. Trained as a social scientist, the focus in Emecheta's works is on "sociological issues—learning about male/female relationships; tradition versus modernity; what makes people do the things they do; why women are the way they are" (Mezu 79). Hence, *Second-Class Citizen, In the Ditch,* and *The Joys of Motherhood* are illuminative of the adaptational behavioral patterns of blacks, identified by Kardiner and Ovesey in *The Mark of Oppression* as derivative of their institutional and environmental conditions. So, too, is *Brown Girl, Brownstones,* by Afro-Caribbean author Paule Marshall, the focus of the succeeding chapter.

WORKS CITED

Bazin, Nancy Topping. "Venturing Into Feminine Consciousness: Bessie Head and Buchi Emecheta." In *The Tragic Life: Bessie Head and Literature in Southern Africa.* Ed. Cecil Abrahams. Trenton: Africa World Press, 1990. 45-58. Originally published in *SAGE: A Scholarly Journal on Black Women* 2, no. 1 (spring 1985): 32-36.

Beauvoir, Simone de. *The Coming of Age.* trans. Patrick O'Brian. New York: Norton, 1996. Originally published as *La Vieillesse* (Paris: Gallimard, 1970).

Butler, Robert James. "Alice Walker's Vision of the South in *The Third Life of Grange Copeland.*" *African American Review* 27 (summer 1993): 195-204.

Cornwell, JoAnne. "Searching for Zora in Alice's Garden: Rites of Passage in Hurston's *Their Eyes Were Watching God* and Walker's *The Third Life of Grange Copeland.*" *Alice Walker and Zora Neale Hurston: The Common Bond.* Ed. Lillie P. Howard. Contributions in Afro-American and African Studies 163. Westport: Greenwood, 1993.

Emecheta, Buchi. *The Family.* New York: George Braziller, 1990. Originally published as *Gwendolen.* Great Britain: Williams Collins Sons and Co., 1989.

———. *Head Above Water: An Autobiography.* London: Heinemann, 1986.

———. *In the Ditch.* London: Heinemann, 1972.

———. Interview with Susheila Nasta. *Guardian Conversations.* Videocassette. The Roland Collection of Films on Art, 1988.

———. *The Joys of Motherhood.* New York: George Braziller, Inc., 1979.

———. *Second-Class Citizen.* New York: George Braziller, Inc., 1975.

Hernton, Calvin C. *Sex and Racism in America.* New York: Anchor, 1965.

Kardiner, Abram, M.D., and Lionel Ovesey, M.D. *The Mark of Oppression: Explorations in the Personality of the American Negro.* Cleveland: World Publishing, 1951.

Mezu, Rose U. "Buchi Emecheta: The Enslaved African Woman and the Creative Process." *The Zora Neale Hurston Forum* 8 (fall 1993): 61-85.

Taiwo, Oladele. *Female Novelists of Modern Africa.* New York: St. Martin's, 1984.

Walker, Alice. *The Third Life of Grange Copeland.* New York: Simon, 1970.

———. "A Writer Because of, Not in Spite of, Her Children." *In Search of Our Mothers' Gardens: Womanist Prose.* New York: Harcourt, 1983.

Chapter 7

THE SUCCESS PHOBIA OF DEIGHTON
BOYCE IN PAULE MARSHALL'S
BROWN GIRL, BROWNSTONES

W.S., the subject alluded to in the previous chapter, is one of twenty-five subjects who participated in the study conducted by Abram Kardiner and Lionel Ovesey on "the Negro personality." A high school drop out, W.S.'s chances for social mobility are circumscribed. He has worked as a messenger and as an orderly, but his aspirations for bigger and better things are blocked by his fears of retaliation, as when he passes up the opportunity to attend Officers' Candidate School because "he wanted to stay with his buddies" (172). This quiescent-aggressive impulse produces blockage, or creates an impasse "which expresses itself in neurotic anxiety, so strong as to block off any action" (212).

W.S.'s quiescence, according to Kardiner and Ovesey, is reenforced by ethnicity. That is, W.S. has been conditioned to be compliant or to suffer the consequences of his non-compliance. His dreams are telling:

> His thoughts wandered on to a movie about Abraham Lincoln, who had a premonition of his own death in a dream. He, himself, had had a dream in which he saw himself dead and was mourned by many women. Lincoln struck out against injustice and was killed. The same may happen to him. (176)

Failure to act leads to a deflation of self-esteem, while aggressiveness runs the risk of incurring the hostility of those from whom he craves acceptance inasmuch as aggressiveness may produce status heretofore denied to the black population at large. Guilt related to his ambitions, in addition to the fear of retaliation, is another inhibitor of success, as seen in B.B., another middle and upper-class subject.

A twenty-six-year old and a college-trained technician, B.B. has a fixation with death that the psychotherapist relates to his desire to achieve more than accorded "the Negro" (205). The guilt which his aspirations inspire compels him toward masochism, as witnessed in the brother's exploitative behavior toward the subject, which resulted in the subject's flight from the South to New York, where he had sought therapy for his anxiety. In the North, the failure by the subject to extricate himself from a homosexual relationship in turn precipitated his flight South. The penchant of B.B. toward masochism and the anxiety centered around prestige and self-esteem on the part of the subjects W.S. and B.B. mirror the tendencies of Deighton Boyce in Paule Marshall's *Brown Girl, Brownstones* who likewise "feared advancement, though he was constantly striving for it" (Ovesey 172).

As noted in chapter two of this study, the body, according to Jean-Paul Sartre, makes one aware of one's existence in the world; so too does the Other who assigns a quality to one that is alien to one's being. Jean-Paul Sartre in *Being and Nothingness* speaks of the Look of the Other as possession, since the Other ascribes to one an identity that is elusive. An attempt by one to possess the freedom of the Other that fixes one's being is a singular response to one's being in the world. Sartre purports in *Being and Nothingness* that the ideal of love is to appropriate the freedom of the Other, to make it subject to one's own freedom and hence to become a supreme value. He observes, however, that to love is to demand to be loved, hence the inevitable conflict since "neither of the two can be held without contradiction. Better yet, each of them is in the other and endangers the death of the other. Thus we can never get outside the circle" (339). Sartre identifies the deceptive nature of love as part of its destructibility; another is the existence of a third party that nullifies the fiction of love as an absolute value.

Jean-Paul Sartre's drama *No Exit* is demonstrative of the destructibility of love caused by the appearance of the Other. Estelle Rigault, Joseph Garcin, and Inez Serrano are the occupants of Hell,

and each is destined to be the torturer of the Other: Inez, the torturer of Garcin, a pacifist and war deserter; and Estelle, a femme
fatale, the torturer of Inez, who is a lesbian. Inez aims to become
Estelle's mirror and, in so doing, transform Estelle into the ideal of
causa sui, or Self-cause; however, Estelle is only interested in the
attention of Garcin who is only interested in the self-redemption
that Inez can impart. Thus each attempt by Garcin to forge an
alliance with Estelle and, hence, have himself mirrored affirma-
tively in her eyes is thwarted by the presence of the Other, in the
form of Inez. Alfred Stern in his work *Sartre: His Philosophy
and Existential Psychoanalysis* summarizes the philosophical concepts contained in the play, namely, the destructibility of love occasioned by the appearance of the Other:

> In *No Exit,* the scene of which is hell, these attempts of
> Garcin and Estelle [to escape into bad faith and an unau-
> thentic existence] are frustrated by the permanent presence
> of a third person, Inez, representing other people. By her
> gaze both lovers are petrified into objects and compelled
> to be what they are in the eyes of other people, and, through
> them, in their own eyes. (155)

The failure of one to assimilate the Other and hence become the
foundation of one's being, or Self-Cause, could provoke despair or
a new attempt at the reabsorption of the Other in order to become,
conversely, the foundation for the Other. The latter attitude Sartre
in *Being and Nothingness* describes as masochism:

> It is my own subjectivity which above all must be denied
> by my own freedom. I attempt therefore to engage myself
> wholly in my being-as-object. I refuse to be anything more
> than an object. I rest upon the Other, and as I experience
> this being-as-object in shame, I will and I love my shame
> as the profound sign of my objectivity. (353-54)

Deighton Boyce of Paule Marshall's *Brown Girl, Brownstones* is
demonstrative of the masochistic impulse in his flirtation with failure. Sartre in *Being and Nothingness* considers guilt respecting
one's personal failure and the subsequent loss of esteem in the
Look of the Other as integral to sadism and masochism: "Masoch-

ism, like sadism, is the assumption of guilt. I am guilty due to the very fact that I am an object, I am guilty toward myself since I consent to my absolute alienation. I am guilty toward the Other, for I furnish him with the occasion of being guilty—that is, of radically missing my freedom as such" (354).

The guilt of Deighton in *Brown Girl, Brownstones* stems in part from the premature death of the second-born who suffered from a congenital heart defect. Some twenty years following his death, Silla, incensed by Deighton's latest preoccupation, his involvement with the Divine movement, charges that it has been Deighton's neglect of his familial responsibility that has contributed to the premature demise of their son: "Then years back, it was the car. The piece of old car you had to have even though it was depression, just to make like a big sports in front the boy. That piece of old junk that made his heart worse and killed him before his time" (175-76). Deighton's response to Silla's accusation is one of gratitude, as her rage is expressive of his own self-condemnation:

> For she had unwittingly probed deep into that shadowy turn of his mind and found the doubt hidden there. She was the one who had driven it out, unmasked it and shaped it into words. Now there would be no need to question that uneasy guilt. He could embrace it. (176)

In a manner similar to Deighton, Clive Springer embraces the guilt associated with the Other's distress, namely, his mother's, and that is a sign of his objectivity. Silla, upon her discovery of Selina's surreptitious affair with Clive, catalogues Clive's unrealized potential:

> "Every morning Clytie carried that boy for somebody to keep so she could do day's work. Clytie wore one coat for years so the Great Master Clive could take piano lesson . . . . And what she get for it? I know every hair 'pon she head is white-white and she does walk the streets talking to sheself, swearing somebody begrudge she the houses and work obeah on the boy." (259)

Importantly, both Clive and Deighton are cast by Marshall as iconoclasts. Both live apart from their family, Deighton at the Peace restaurant that he manages and Clive at a rooming house that his family owns; both are dreamers and would-be artists whose plans never materialize. Deighton hopes to return to Barbados, and the twenty-nine-year-old Clive to become economically and psychologically independent of his family. However, their restive nature reveals their designs as vacuous. Clive, for instance, is described thusly: "[Clive's] lax form was strewn amid the cushions as if carelessly thrown there . . ." (242).

As the novel opens, Deighton is in a state of repose in the sun parlor of the brownstone studying a correspondence course in accounting that he has just begun (8). Other correspondence courses and lessons have included those on car and radio repair and trumpet playing, but none of the ventures have panned out (32). He has learned recently that he has inherited almost two acres of land from his deceased schoolteacher sister; his dream is to return to Barbados and build (12) "a house to end all house!"

The discrepancy between desire and actuality, however, is made clear by Marshall as she goes on in a subsequent chapter to describe Deighton's fetish for silken undershirts that parallels the tenant Suggie Skeete's fetish for perfumes, as described also in chapter two. Both are collectors of sorts, Deighton of shoes and Suggie, "the summer woman" (52), of perfumes that she sniffs, but never uses. Spendthrifts they are not, as evidenced when Silla inquires of Deighton whether he has put aside money for a down payment on the brownstone that they currently lease and receives the following negative response (24): "Not penny one!"

Given Deighton's languor, readers could erroneously assume that Deighton is unemployed; he is not. He works alongside Percy Challenor at the mattress factory. The difference, though, is that he holds a single job while Percy Challenor, "a workhorse" (54), holds two in order to meet two mortgages. The upshot is that "The Challenors had started buying the house two years ago" (54). By the Bajan standard that measures success in terms of home ownership, Deighton is "a disgrace" (55). Percy Challenor, for instance, cannot brook idleness of any sort, as can be inferred from his questioning of Selina regarding Deighton's land ownership (55): "He done anything about it? . . . . Sell it? . . . . He ain renting it either?"

His subsequent dismissal of Deighton as "a spree boy" who "don know a thing 'bout handling money and property and thing so" (55) is indicative of his disdain of Deighton's inertia.

Sartre in *Existentialism and Humanism* defines the existentialist as a man of action; that is, his being is inseparable from his actions. Sartre identifies as a misconception the view that a temperament predisposes one toward a particular behavior and argues instead that actions alone constitute one's being: "There are nervous temperaments; there is what is called impoverished blood, and there are also rich temperaments. But the man whose blood is poor is not a coward for all that, for what produces cowardice is the act of giving up or giving way; and a temperament is not an action" (43). Hence, the quietism that both Deighton and Clive personify is antithetical to the doctrine of self-commitment. In effect, their lassitude, similar to that displayed by some of the characters who have preceded them in this study—Letitia and Elie of Simone Schwarz-Bart's *The Bridge of Beyond*, Brownfield of Alice Walker's *The Third Life of Grange Copeland*, and the Breedloves of Toni Morrison's *The Bluest Eye*, who collectively take perverse pleasure in their doom and consider that it has been preordained—in its escapist nature, represents unauthenticity, or a form of bad faith. Alfred Stern summarizes the concept in his work *Sartre: His Philosophy and Existential Psychoanalysis:*

> The great majority of people . . . deny their freedom, hiding it from themselves with all kinds of deterministic excuses. They exist "unauthentically." They are "cowards" or, as far as they try to prove the necessity of their existence, they are "stinkers." By denying their freedom, they try to flee from anxiety by grasping themselves from outside, as things. (77)

Sartre in *Existential Psychoanalysis* had given properties to the modalities of being. He had identified water as a symbol of the for-itself; the viscous, as a symbol of the "in betweenity" of the for-itself and the in-itself. Another property of "in betweenity" is that of softness, which characterizes Clive and Deighton, respectively, in their inability to commit themselves to any course of action: "The slimy is *docile*. Only at the very moment when I believe that I possess it, behold by a curious reversal, *it* possesses me. . . . Its softness is leech-like" (136-37).

The languor of Deighton makes him the antithesis of his wife Silla whose materialistic values in turn make her an example of the attitude of seriousness. The attitude of seriousness "involves starting from the world and attributing more reality to the world than to oneself; at the very least the serious man confers reality on himself to the degree to which he belongs to the world" (*EP* 71). In other words, the individual afflicted with a spirit of seriousness looks to convention or societal norms, rather than himself, to govern his choices (Stern 78). Sartre notes in *Existential Psychoanalysis* that it is not by chance that "materialism is serious" inasmuch as materialists come to define themselves in terms of the world, or by their possessions (71-72). Thus, they assume the concreteness of the in-itself, or the rock.

When Silla secures a job at the defense factory making ammunition (78), she is one of a number of Barbadian women who are "working morning, noon, and night" (74) who often resort to unethical schemes to become owners of brownstones. Correspondingly, Silla is characterized as an automaton, possessed with a "hard center" (246), and at one with the machine mass of the defense factory. As she inveighs to her daughter Selina on the high costs of getting ahead, or making it: "[I]n this Christ world you got to be hard and sometimes misuse others, even your own" (224).

In contrast to Silla's hardness, Deighton is characterized by a slackness that is symptomatic of his despair. Silla, addressing her female friends, speaks of the hopelessness that she associates with Barbados:

> "It's a terrible thing to know that you gon be poor all yuh life, no matter how hard you work. You does stop trying after a time. People does see you so and call you lazy. But it ain laziness. It just that you does give up. You does kind of die inside. . . ." (70)

Ironically, it is Deighton's inertia that has been his undoing. Deighton, who has been warned by the daughter Selina that Silla had threatened fraudulent disposal of the land, for a year does nothing to counteract Silla's threat. After the correspondence course in accounting had failed to earn him a respectable job, he had turned his attention to another "get rich quick scheme," namely, becoming a musician or a trumpet player. His inertia on this score costs him dearly, as Silla not only disposes of the land which nets $900 through fraudulent means, but uses his own apathy as a weapon against him:

> "I say to myself that you don write to the sister so I gon write for you. I sat at this kitchen table late 'pon a night practicing to write your name till I had it down pat. Then I write the first letter. . . . I take it to a place near my job that does type out letters for people and pay to have it type and then all I had to do was sign yuh name. Yuh even tell she in the first letter that you was taking up typewriting. Ah yes, I figure for you good." (113)

The war between Deighton and Silla, paradigmatic of the circularity of relations with the Other, is one that neither can hope to win, as it is Silla, "the young woman with the soft smile" (103), the side that she suppresses, that surrenders to Deighton's sophistry. Arguing expediency, Deighton goes alone to a New York bank to claim the money draft. He returns hours later having splurged the $900 to buy gifts for "lady-folks," among them a ruffled pink evening gown for Ina to wear to Gatha Steed's daughter's wedding, a $100 book certificate for Selina, and a bold red coat for Silla (130). For himself, he has purchased a trumpet with ivory keys. His spending spree has left him spent, both literally and figuratively, as he questions Silla mockingly: "You satisfy? Good! 'cause I's well satisfy" (130). Silla, angered by her own susceptibility to Deighton's charm, becomes even more resolute in her purpose, vowing to (131) "steel my heart and bide my time and see you dead-dead at my feet!"

Importantly, either the literal or figurative negation of the masochist, according to Lynn S. Chancer, is a means to halt the sadomasochistic dynamic indicative of Silla and Deighton in *Brown Girl, Brownstones*:

> But once the masochist has been negated, the dynamic comes to an abrupt halt. This can happen either literally

through death, at the extreme end of the sado-masochistic continuum . . ., or figuratively by the sadist having exerted so much control that the masochist retains no independent powers of resistance. (54)

Guilt, according to Sartre, is essential to the sadomasochistic dynamic; another, in the view of Lynn Chancer, is dependency: "[A]n excessive attachment exists for both parties, extreme in that neither feels as though the other can be done without; dependence is of a symbiotic character in that both sadist and masochist feel a compulsive need for physical, but most critically for psychic, connection to the other" (3). Barbara Christian in her work *Black Women Novelists: The Development of a Tradition, 1892-1976* has commented on the symbiotic relationship existent between Silla and Deighton Boyce in *Brown Girl, Brownstones:*

> Both have tormented each other. Neither can understand the causes that have brought them to the turning when their essential natures were betrayed by each other. Both are intertwined in their defeat of each other. (97)

Yet another manifestation of the dynamic is, according to Chancer, the ritualistic behavior of the parties involved: "[I]nteraction has a repetitive and ritualistic character in that the sadist is consistently drawn toward a position of control while the masochist is just as constantly in the persona of the more controlled" (3). In Deighton and Silla Boyce, the ritualistic behavior assumes the demeanor of oneupmanship: Silla works doubly hard in order to earn money for a down payment on a brownstone, and Deighton works equally hard to squander his earnings and, hence, to thwart Silla's materialistic design. In Deighton's expenditure of his earnings on "flash," he is reminiscent of the subject G.R. in *The Mark of Oppression.*

In *The Mark of Oppression,* the subject G.R. is described as "a fashion plate" (98), albeit at the time of the interviews he is employed as a porter. Orphaned at the age of three, a school drop out at the age of ten, G.R. at the age of twelve struck out on his own, after receiving a blow from his caregiver uncle that left him "swolled up for weeks" (100). His series of menial, low-paying jobs—attendant in a shoe-shine parlor and men's room of a railroad station—have produced chronic debt. The authors summarize G.R.'s emotional outlook:

> There is a hopelessness and a futility about G.R. as he describes the repetitive frustration of his ambitions. No matter what he does, nothing works out the way he wants it, nothing seems to go right. Everything ends in failure. People are always taking advantage of him. They cheat him, make a fool of him, reject him, and derogate him. All of these attitudes are reflected in his dreams. (108)

To compensate for his lack of self-esteem, G.R. uses both clothing and women for "flash." Separated from his first wife, with whom he had fathered two children, G.R. had "taken up" with another and had fathered two additional children. At the time of the interviews, he is separated from his second "wife" and has no plans to settle down a third time. His relationships with women are, therefore, casual by design, as he explains his choices to the interviewer:

> "I figure what's the use of playing with fire when you know you'll be burnt. You mostly use them as flash. You know what I mean as a flash? You're out cabareting and you want somebody with you that don't look beat-up . . . someone who ain't going to make you ashamed." (109)

In *Brown Girl, Brownstones,* on the evening of carnage, symbolized by the red coat that Deighton has purchased for Silla, Silla acknowledges that she has been placed in checkmate by Deighton who, similar to the subject G.R., is associated with "flash": "You think I wasn't gon buy them dresses for the wedding? But he always got to be the big sport. . . . Always a lot of flash with nothing a-tall, a-tall behind it . . ." (133).

Similar to the experiences of the subjects in the study by Ovesey and Kardiner, Deighton's deflated self-esteem becomes an inhibitor that contributes to Deighton's downward spiral. After Deighton's accident at the factory led to lameness in one of his arms, Deighton had become a follower of the Father Peace, or Divine, movement. The accident had left him a broken man, a ghost of his former self. In the hospital, he had forbidden his daughters to see him since, in the words of Silla who had to break the tragic news to her daughters, "the last thing he would want would be for wunna to see him when he ain dress back and making like a big sports" (157). After Deighton's release from the hospital, the embrace of failure is registered in the relief that the disability affords him to no longer hope: "His good hand groped out to the limp arm and it stoked it almost fondly, as if instead of defeat this was a strange kind of fulfillment—the one thing he had been truly seeking even as he sought the job in accounting and the return home" (159). Silla's reminder of his failures, "You don belong here" (174), which had re-opened old wounds was thus the pretext that he needed in order to make finally the break from his family and become a true follower of the Divine sect that preached celibacy: "The word *mother* is a filthy word" (168). Deighton's spiritual death is apparent as he speaks of himself at the end of Book One in the past tense. When asked by the deportation authorities to identify himself, he responds, "Yes, officer, they did call me Deighton Boyce" (182).

Daryl Dance has noted that the inability of the black man "to bring home some bread and cut the ice" (307) leaves him psychologically emasculated. Such is illuminated by Marshall in *Brown Girl, Brownstones* who describes Deighton, a Peace follower, from the perspective of Selina, as a "shadow" whose "substance was irretrievably lost" (170).

The psychoanalysts Ovesey and Kardiner have noted in their work *The Mark of Oppression* that "the father deserts because his masculine prerogatives are undermined by the inability to find consistent and gainful employment" (39). The rationale would apply likewise to Deighton Boyce of *Brown Girl, Brownstones,* as he relinquishes to Father Peace the control of his destiny in order to belong. In the words of Clive Springer who is a fictive embodiment of Deighton: "Most people want to be with the lowing herd, to be told, to be led. They gladly hand over themselves to something" (264).

The fictional Father Peace is predicated on Father Divine, as the reference by Deighton to Father Peace's jail sentence and Deighton's imitative speech, "Peace! It is truly wonderful!," a phrase made famous by Father Divine (Weisbrot 87), would indicate.

The jail sentence in question is a one-year term, along with a $500 fine, meted out to Father Divine for being "a menace to society." Charges had been brought by the residents in Sayville in May, 1932 (51) for disturbing the peace. Father Divine had purchased an eight-room house in the formerly all-white community from a townsman who, according to Weisbrot, wanted "to spite a disagreeable neighbor by selling his home to a Negro buyer" (27). The influx of visitors to Sayville, many of whom were attracted by the Father Divine banquets that "built a reputation" (29), became the trigger to dormant racial sentiment as residents expressed fears of a black invasion. An attempt to discredit Father Divine was soon underway. An undercover investigation into Father Divine's finances, however, had uncovered no wrongdoing. The failure to find evidence of wrongdoing, nonetheless, was not, in Weisbrot's opinion, sufficient to shield Father Divine from 'justice' (47).

Police were summoned upon complaints by neighbors on November 1931 that Father Divine was disturbing the peace. A disruption of the gathering by authorities had led to the arrest of Father Divine, along with some eighty of his followers (47). Although a majority—fifty-five—paid the assessed fine of $5 each, some contested, including Father Divine, and were subsequently hauled before Judge Lewis S. Smith, "a Presbyterian of puritanical bent whose notion of religion was a world apart from the rollicking prayer sessions and cult-like worship of Divine's following," who, according to Weisbrot, "took an instant dislike to Father Divine" and who objected to the Divine message of "interracial harmony" (55). He therefore was intent on using the bench to send a message, despite the recommendations by the jury for leniency. He handed down the maximum sentence of one year in jail and a $500 fine. The stress, however, of the trial proved fatal, as "three days after sentencing Divine, he suddenly keeled over, dead" (53). For Divine and his followers, however, the death of the judge was merely evidence of Divine's providential powers:

> Father Divine himself revealed an exceedingly elastic sense of opportunity when informed of Smith's sudden demise. Previously, despite his impeccable demeanor and assurances of his willingness to stay in jail, Divine had seemed to visitors somewhat subdued and apprehensive. Now, however,

he was again in full command. Controlling whatever emotion he may have experienced on hearing of Smith's death, Divine paused a moment and then said sadly, "I hated to do it." (53)

Marshall's account is identical to the one related by Weisbrot. Deighton had reprimanded Selina after she had destroyed the frame that held Divine's photograph:

"You see? You see? Father struck you down! You interfere with him and he struck you down! Thank you, Father. Go ahead. Go ahead, keep interfering and he gon strike you down each time. Just like he does all them who interfere with him and refuse to believe he's God. Take that big-shot Judge Jones. He put Father in jail. And Father prophesy that he was gon die the next day. And he die!" (162)

The autobiographical nature of *Brown Girl, Brownstones* is apparent from an interview with Joyce Pettis. In response to a question by Pettis on the model for her character Beryl, Marshall had responded that she was a composite of a number of friends growing up who represented the typical Afro-West Indian family, quite in contrast to her own family who

never succeeded in purchasing the Brownstone house, you see. We were never an entire family. My father, after I was about age thirteen, became so involved with Father Divine that he was no longer part of our household. In a sense he had sort of abdicated his responsibilities as father. So the set pattern for families that was so true for most of the West Indians that I knew in Brooklyn was disrupted for me. Beryl represents the child of those families who went the so-called established route. (121)

Paule Marshall's novel *Daughters,* published in 1991 and dedicated to her father, is, according to Marshall, a means of coming to terms with her feelings of abandonment over her father's desertion of the family to become a follower of the Father Divine movement and of overcoming the fear of failure that she felt her father, "a natural-born poet," had courted. The PM, as he is affectionately called in *Daughters,* a barrister in the fictional Triunion, maintains such a psychological hold on his girl-child Ursa Bea that her relationships with other men, such as Lowell Carruthers, are threatened. Only after she had sabotaged his re-election in his Morlands district by revealing to his opponent the PM's plan to convert government lands into "a playground for the Fortune 500 and friends" (357) had she purged herself of her dependency and made possible, by the election of the young teacher Justin Beaufils, the PM's opponent who is running as an Independent, the restoration of PM's original mission of change and unity for the island that represented Dutch, Spanish, and English interests. Marshall has noted that *Daughters,* because it examines the ghosts that she herself has had to exorcise, is in fact, one of her most personal works:

> This father whom I adored became a devotee of someone who decreed there were no more mothers and fathers, parents and children, rather that *he,* Father Divine, was father and mother to *all.* So that Samuel Burke, my father, one day forbade my sister and myself to call him Daddy. Finally, he disappeared out of our lives altogether to go and live in Father Divine's "kingdom" in Harlem, abandoning us to a cycle of poverty and my mother's rapid decline into bitterness, cancer, and an early death. . . . It's taken me a long time and much interior work to get over my anger at him. And also to overcome the fear that I had been *contaminated* with what I sensed and saw as his failure. Failure it seemed he almost actively sought out. . . . [T]hat outrage and sense of inevitable rejection were, I think, to undermine the important relationships with men later on in my life. I've had to *really* struggle to undo that damaging pattern. (Dance 8)

In the work *Father Divine and the Struggle for Racial Equality,* Robert Weisbrot notes that the Peace Mission "represented every social background, economic level, and racial group in the nation" (59), one of which was West Indian immigrants who flocked to the Peace Mission seeking an antidote for their disenfranchisement:

Trapped in the ghettos by racism and isolated even within ghetto society, many West Indians were susceptible to appeals by cults that provided full acceptance and emotional release through religion. Father Divine extended a special welcome to foreigners as part of his crusade for universal brotherhood, thus making his Peace Mission a particularly inviting haven for those otherwise alienated people. (61)

In addition to seeking belongingness, Deighton's reasons for joining the Peace movement may be considered escapist, and hence demonstrative of Sartrean bad faith. The organization was largely egalitarian; that is, no distinction was made amongst "the angels." Given the obsessive struggle for home ownership, the classnessness of the Peace Mission must have been seen as a haven "from a society they found deeply troubling" (Weisbrot 192-93). On the appeal of the movement to blacks, Kardiner and Ovesey have written:

Since class distinctions are wiped out, the struggle for status is nominally non-existent. At least it is not played out on the standard of living stage, which is set by the organization. There is no special climbing on the status level and no struggle for existence on the subsistence level. The feeling tone of mutual dependence must be enhanced and the feeling of mutual hatred diminished. (356)

In the article "The Property of Being in Paule Marshall's *Brown Girl, Brownstones,*" Vannessa D. Dickerson argues the manner in which the brownstones both shape and reflect the communalism of the Divine movement. On the brownstone that has been converted by the Divine followers into a Kingdom Hall, she observes that its "wall-less . . . roomless" nature "bespeaks no individuality but a mindless reduction of humanity into mass . . ." (7).

On the other hand, Silla of *Brown Girl, Brownstones* considers Deighton's cult involvement as so much "foolishness," given its focus on an afterlife rather than on the struggle in the here and now (172). Such a sentiment was echoed by many who branded Divine's disciples as dwelling "on the fringes of life, hanging between sanity and insanity" (Weisbrot 176). Within the Sartrean ontology, Deighton's Divine discipleship may be construed as an example of bad faith, since by his discipleship, Deighton wants "to escape the responsibility of being-for-itself and still remain superior to being-in-itself. He wants to be an in-itself-for-itself. According to Sartre, man cherishes this wish whether he actually maintains a belief in an individualized God or not" (Barnes 106). These views of Divine's ministry and followers notwithstanding, Weisbrot in his work *Father Divine and the Struggle for Racial Equality* conceives of Divine's ministry as inseparable from the quest for social justice. In fact, Weisbrot identifies Divine's social activism in the 1930s and 40s as a precursor to the Civil Rights movement of the 1950s and 60s.

Robert Weisbrot in the Preface to his work has noted that he had begun his study on Father Divine "to explore why urban blacks would join an 'escapist' religious cult, as Divine's popular Peace Mission movement was widely portrayed during the 1930s." He discovered instead that "Divine stood for a socially progressive religion tied to a cooperative ethic and to demands for racial equality." His work is therefore his attempt to set the record straight on Father Divine's legacy.

One of the qualities that Father Divine attempted to inculcate in his followers was, according to Weisbrot, economic independence. Toward that end, welfare benefits related to unemployment were eschewed. Weisbrot notes that "one municipal official estimated in 1939 that Divine's forbearance had saved New York City alone over $2 million in welfare funds during the Depression" (92). It was felt by Divine that a dependency on welfare benefits undermined both the work ethic and the self-respect of those dependent upon them: "There is more respect for a person who can respect himself independently than that person who is dependent on charity" (qtd. in Weisbrot 91).

Father Divine himself became the model of the movement's entrepreneurial ethic. It is noted by Weisbrot that by the mid-1930s, the Peace Mission had become "the largest realty holder in Harlem, with three apartment houses, nine private houses, fifteen to twenty flats, and several meeting halls with dormitories on the upper floors. In addition, followers in Harlem operated some twenty-five restaurants, six groceries, ten barber shops, ten cleaning stores, two dozen huckster wagons with clams and oysters or fresh vegetables, and a coal business with three trucks ranging from Harlem to the mines in Pennsylvania" (122-23). In addition to the value of economic independence, Divine sought to instill ambition and hard work in his disciples in the hope that "they would rise from the slums and, through their example as model citizens, help defuse the racism simmering in the country" (91). With respect to the effects of racial uplift on social reform, Robert Weisbrot notes: "Father Divine's efforts to fashion independent, self-respecting people helped many in the ghettos to reach undreamed levels of achievement. . . . Men and women who had never held steady employment or learned to read discovered that they could do these things, and much more: their potential had just been awakened" (103). Personal reform was inseparable from social reform, as individuals who had begun to value themselves would be less inclined to tolerate their disvaluation by others.

In an interview with Daryl Cumber Dance, Paule Marshall, in response to a question related to the historical figures, namely, Cudjoe, who people her recent work *Daughters,* acknowledged that in all of her fiction there is a preoccupation with history in order to counter the negative stereotypes that too often have come to define Africa, African American and Caribbean culture: "History was an Africa without civilization and art, was West Indians as monkey chasers and African-Americans as mammies and Amos and Andies, black people denigrated at every turn. And so part of my preoccupation with history in the work is my need to set the record straight, if only for myself" (5).

In light of Marshall's articulated concern for verisimilitude, she would appreciate indeed the efforts by Weisbrot and Jill Watts whose works, respectively, attempt to "set the record straight" on Divine's legacy. For example, Jill Watts, in her Preface to *God, Harlem, U.S.A.: The Father Divine Story,* argues that the cult status of the Peace Mission movement marginalizes its import; hence, her research on Divine has been an attempt to garner for him his proper place in history (x).

The movement, which the religious and political paper *The Spoken Word* identified as constituting at least 30,000 followers (Watts 142), attracted members across racial, gender and cultural boundaries. Indicative of its cross-cultural appeal is the membership of Deighton Boyce, a West Indian immigrant, who manages a Peace restaurant on Fulton Street, where he also lives (178). Watts has noted also in her work that large numbers of females were attracted by the communal lifestyle that the movement offered because the communalism essentially liberated them from their restrictive roles: "Worshiping and living together as a collective unit challenged gender roles and freed women from their responsibilities as wives and mothers" (35). Common to all the followers, however, was the void in their own lives. Robert Weisbrot notes in his work *Father Divine and the Struggle for Racial Equality:* "Yet amid this diversity of circumstance and temperament, followers shared the powerful unifying belief that only Father Divine could fill some vital lack in each of their lives" (59). Deighton Boyce of Paule Marshall's *Brown Girl, Brownstones* becomes then the mirror by which the lives of the disinherited, namely, the West Indian immigrants, are refracted. Deighton remarks, for example, his tenuous legal status which has rendered him non-existent: "As far as the record goes I ain even in this country since I did enter illegally. Y'know that's a funny thing when you think of it. I don even exist as far as these people here go" (66).

In the same manner that Deighton is representative of the disinherited group of West Indian immigrants, Silla is representative as well of the disaffected group of domestic workers. For example, Silla is rendered faceless by the group to which she belongs—domestic workers. During the Depression, there was no ready market for their services, and as Robert Weisbrot notes in his book, these workers often had to subsist on day-to-day employment that earned them from $.35 to $.50 daily:

> The "Bronx Slave Market" was the most notorious example of the widespread mistreatment of domestic workers. Always a low-paid group, these workers suffered intensely from the Depression, where many former employers now regarded their services as dispensable. The result was to create a huge surplus of domestic laborers who lined up early each morning in front of homes that once regularly employed them. There these women would compete for the attention of housewives, often accepting work for 50 cents or even 35 cents a day. (141)

Silla of Paule Marshall's *Brown Girl, Brownstones* is representative of this disaffected group. Selina observes that "she could never think of the mother alone. It was always the mother and the others

. . . [who] took the train to Flatbrush and Sheepshead Bay to scrub floors. The lucky ones had their steady madams while the others wandered those neat blocks or waited on corners . . . until someone offered her a day's work" (10-11).

Another link between Deighton and Silla is their self-entrapment that is made symbolic in Miss Mary's self-immolation (204). Deighton had prophesied, "These old houses is more trouble than profit" (21). Silla's ownership of a brownstone, predictably, is tinged with regret, given the price that has been exacted: "Houses! When you does have to do some of everything short of murder to get them sometimes. I tell you, I tired enough hearing about them . . ." (142-43). So, too, is Florrie Trotman's home ownership tinged with regret; Trotman realizes that wealth she has, but not the youth to enjoy it: "I sorry for all the long years I din have nothing and my children din have and now I got little something I too fat and old to enjoy it and my only son dead in these people bloody war and he can't enjoy it. That's what I sorry for!" (224).

The tragedy of the novel relates to the elusiveness of the American dream, which is made synonymous with home ownership. One sees at the end of the novel the destruction caused by the obsession with materialism. Jean-Paul Sartre in *Existential Psychoanalysis* equates materialism to the attitude of seriousness precisely because the materialist externalizes himself into his objects of possession: "Marx proposed the original dogma of the serious when he asserted the priority of object over subject. Man is serious when he takes himself for an object" (72). As Selina walks through Fulton Park near the end of the novel, she observes that the brownstones, symbolic of the Bajan community, have been ravaged by time and are in the process of being destroyed to make way for a city project. Too, the face of the neighborhood has changed, as "the staccato beat of Spanish voices, the frenzied sensuous music joined the warm canorous Negro sounds to glut the air" (309). The rubble from the brownstones foretells the deteriorating value of the property, even as the Bajan community seeks to acquire more. The houses for the Bajan community have become their crucifix, or Sisyphean rock. As Paule Marshall has commented on Silla in her interview with Kay Bonetti: "She [Silla] gains, but she loses."

Not only has Deighton been lost at sea during his deportation—he either jumped overboard or was drowned—thus holding true to pattern of sadomasochism in that the destruction of the masochist leads likewise to that of the sadist (Chancer 54), but the daughters have been alienated. Ina has announced her plans to marry, and Selina, at the end of the novel, is on the verge of returning to Barbados, a journey that Marshall seems to suggest is essential to her "completion of self." Considering that Selina had never been to Barbados, the journey is crucial for better understanding the forces that have shaped her father and, in turn, herself. Symbolically, too, in journeying to Barbados, she will complete the odyssey begun by her father, which will represent the fulfillment of his dream. Hence, Selina emerges at the end of the novel as both a dreamer, in deciding to journey to Barbados as her father had wanted to do, and as a pioneer, in deciding to defy her mother as Silla herself had once done.

In conclusion, then, it is Selina's pioneering spirit, softened by Deighton's romanticism, that makes the novel resonate with hope. It may be noted as well that from Marshall's cast of characters, Selina comes closest to the existentialist ethic. She rejects the quietism of Deighton and the materialism of Silla and instead charts her own course. As Sartre has summarized in *Existentialism and Humanism:* "[Existentialism] cannot be regarded as a philosophy of quietism since it defines man [woman] by his [her] action; nor as a pessimistic description of man [woman], for no doctrine is more optimistic, the destiny of man [woman] is placed within himself [herself]" (44).

WORKS CITED

Barnes, Hazel. Humanistic Existentialism: The Literature of Possibility. Lincoln: U of Nebraska P, 1959.

Chancer, Lynn S. *Sadomasochism in Everyday Life: The Dynamics of Power and Powerlessness*. New Brunswick: Rutgers UP, 1992.

Christian, Barbara. *Black Women Novelists: The Development of a Tradition, 1892-1976*. Westport, CT: Greenwood, 1980.

Dance, Daryl C. "Daddy May Bring Home Some Bread, But He Don't Cut No Ice: The Economic Plight of the Father Figure in Black American Literature." *Journal of Afro-American Issues* 3 (summer/fall 1975): 297-308.

Dickerson, Vannessa D. "The Property of Being in Paule Marshall's *Brown Girl, Brownstones." Obsidian II: Black Literature in Review* 6 (winter 1991): 1-13.

Kapai, Leela. "Dominant Themes and Technique in Paule Marshall's Fiction." *College Language Association Journal* 16 (1972): 49-59.

Kardiner, Abram, M.D. and Lionel Ovesey, M.D. *The Mark of Oppression: Explorations in the Personality of the American Negro.* Cleveland: World Publishing, 1962.

Marshall, Paule. *Brown Girl, Brownstones.* New York: Feminist Press, 1981.

————. *Daughters.* New York: Plume, 1992.

————. An Interview by Kay Bonetti. Columbia, Mo.: Audio Prose Library, 1984.

————. An Interview by Daryl Cumber Dance. *The Southern Review* 28 (winter 1992): 1-20.

————. An Interview by Joyce Pettis. *MELUS* 17 (1991): 117-29.

Sartre, Jean-Paul. *Being and Nothingness: An Essay in Phenomenological Ontology.* Trans. Hazel E. Barnes. Secaucus: Philosophical Library, 1956.

————. *Existentialism and Humanism.* Trans. Philip Mairet. London: Methuen, 1948.

————. *Existential Psychoanalysis.* Trans. Hazel E. Barnes. New York: Philosophical Library, 1953.

————. *No Exit. No Exit and Three Other Plays.* Trans. Stuart Gilbert. New York: Knopf, 1948. 3-47. Originally published as *Huis Clos* (Paris: Gallimard, 1945).

Stern, Alfred. *Sartre: His Philosophy and Existential Psychoanalysis.* 2nd rev. ed. New York: Delacorte, 1967.

Watts, Jill. *God, Harlem, U.S.A.: The Father Divine Story.* Berkeley: U of California P, 1992.

Weisbrot, Robert. *Father Divine and the Struggle for Racial Equality.* Urbana: U of Illinois P, 1983.

Chapter 8

MADNESS AS A RESPONSE TO THE FEMALE SITUATION OF DISINHERITANCE IN MARIAMA BÂ'S *SO LONG A LETTER* AND *SCARLET SONG*

As Buchi Emecheta has shown in *Second-Class Citizen,* the threat of polygamy, even among non-Muslims, is an all too real one. When Adah is hospitalized with her third child, she meets other women who set in sharp relief her plight as an African female, one of whom is an English woman who has waited seventeen years to have a child and who "never stopped showing this child around, even when she was not strong enough to walk properly" (111). Although Adah takes comfort and pride in being able to claim two successful pregnancies, one of which has yielded a boy, Vicky, she is aware of the precariousness of the existence of the African woman who is unendowed with children. Imagining the woman's condition to have been her own, Adah concluded that "she would have either died of psychological pressures or another wife would have been bought for Francis. He would have declared himself a Moslem, for he was once a Moslem when he was younger" (112).

Adah's postulation takes the form of reality in Mariama Bâ's *So Long a Letter.* Ramatoulaye, after twenty-five years of marriage to Modou Fall and twelve children (39), is stunned with the news by the emissaries Tamsir, Modou's oldest brother, Mawdo Bâ, and the local Imam that Modou has taken a second wife, Binetou, "a child the same age of [her] daughter Daba" (39). The male privilege in traditional African society, which makes possible the conjugal betrayal, the greed of mothers-in-law which sanctions male dominance, and the struggle of the abandoned females to re-claim their dignity and self-hood after desertion by their husbands are the subject matter of Mariama Bâ's award-winning novel.

The prevalence of female abandonment in Senegalese society is demonstrated in Jacqueline, the Ivorian, and Aïssatou, Ramatoulaye's childhood friend. Jacqueline, despite the protests of her Protestant parents, had married Samba Diack, a Muslim. Compounding the differences in religious faith was also the prejudice of some Africans against those in the hinterlands, a bias that the husband himself came to share, given the infidelities with Senegalese women that he took no pains in concealing.

Jacqueline's public humiliation manifested itself in signs of physical illness that the medical doctors, after prescribing a battery of tests—from an electrocardiogram to blood tests—could not find a diagnosis for. Only after a month of negative results did the Head of the Neurology Department declare her as suffering from depression over her circumstances and exhaustion related to her recent pregnancies. Assured that her cure resided in her own hands, Jacqueline then became determined to ward off the death that she had previously invited (45): "Re-animated, she related the discussion to us and confided that she had left the interview already half-cured. She knew the heart of her illness and would fight against it. She was morally uplifted. She had come a long way, had Jacqueline!" Her surprising recovery anticipates that of Rama who has been similarly discarded by her husband of twenty-five years.

Insanity is identified in Mariama Bâ's two novels, *So Long a Letter* and *Scarlet Song* as a response to abandonment; both dramatize the psychic damage caused by social oppression or, more specifically, the institution of polygamy. Barbara Hill Rigney in her work *Madness and Sexual Politics in the Feminist Novel: Studies in Brontë, Woolf, Lessing, and Atwood* argues that insanity is a political response to the "collusive madness" (7) of society in the form of sexual oppression that threatens feminine survival. The psychosis of women is viewed hence as a defense mechanism that enables the self to achieve a measure of ontological security: "If the world is in truth inhospitable, unhomelike, then perhaps withdrawal from that world is a sane and reasonable method of self preservation" (47). On the prevalence of the madwoman in literature, Sandra M. Gilbert and Susan Gubar in their work *The Madwoman in the Attic* posit that the creation is a projection of the authors' own anxiety and rage onto a fictional double who embodies their own vacillation between conformity and rebellion: "Indeed, much of the poetry and fiction written by women conjures up this mad creature so that female authors can come to terms with their own uniquely female feelings of fragmentation, their own keen sense of the discrepancies between what they are and what they are supposed to be" (78).

Mireille's insanity in *Scarlet Song* seems precipitated by profound loneliness, a condition that Ousmane has exploited to his own end. Since the marriage to Ousmane has required Mireille to disavow her parents, homeland, and cultural ties, the acceptance of her by the parents-in-law has been essential to her ability to adapt to her new homeland. From the beginning, however, the breach caused by race, caste, and nationality seems irreparable. The mother-in-law's resentment over what she considers a forfeiture of her traditional rights as a mother-in-law creates antagonism and later a determination to usurp the wife's authority and to restore an erstwhile lost equilibrium. Hence, when Ouleymatou, the sister of Ousseynou, Ousmane's former hut brother, sets out to ensnare Ousmane, Yaye Khady, Ousmane's mother, becomes an ally. Ouleymatou, to ingratiate herself with Yaye Khady, relieves her of some of the domestic chores that are considered the duties of a daughter-in-law. In so doing, she not only wins over Yaye Khady as an ally and ensnares Ousmane, but sets in motion a series of events that lead to Mireille's emotional breakdown. Bâ narrates the principal cause for her complete vulnerability: "Ousmane had built his double life on Mireille's isolation. He had told Boly, 'Mireille will never be any the wiser. The world she lives in is impervious to tittle-tattle. . .'" (154).

The victimization of women which could lead to their despair and untimely death was a theme contained in Zora Neale Hurston's novel *Jonah's Gourd Vine*. Lucy's illness is not defined, but the suggestion is that the mistress of John, Hattie Tyson, seeing Lucy as an obstacle to be removed, had had her hoodooed. Hattie Tyson's visit to the conjurer, which is described in the chapter prior to Lucy's physical decline, suggests the correlation between the two. In addition, Hurston's description elsewhere, namely, in *Mules and Men,* of "a killing ceremony" (213) would corroborate the conclusion that Lucy's death is the result of voodoo. Rita Terezinha Schmidt, however, dismisses that interpretation in favor of another—Lucy's despair occasioned by her husband's infidelity that had robbed her of the will to live:

> The movement of the narrative warrants the fact that the deterioration of Lucy's health is the consequence of a life of toil, abuse and disappointments. In these terms, Hurston does not intend to portray Lucy as a super woman, with a limitless capacity for endurance, but to convey essentially, her humanness. There are limits beyond which a woman cannot stand being ignored as a person and relegated to the status of an object. (127-28)

The betrayal of trust that is prominent in the fiction of female African-American and African authors is illustrated as well in Aïssatou, Rama's confidante and fictional double in *So Long a Letter* whose abandonment just three years prior (13) had prefigured her own and whose independence she both emulates and espouses as the antidote to male oppression in Senegalese society.

Contrary to Modou whose seduction of Binetou was related to his vanishing youth, Mawdo, Aïssatou's estranged husband, had been subject to the manipulation of his mother who had resented her son's marriage to a blacksmith's daughter. She had thus bided her time and plotted her revenge by making his marriage to her namesake Nabou a certainty. On the pretext of loneliness, she had visited her brother, Farba Diouf, "a customary chief in Diakhao" (26), with the request that one of his daughters be placed in her charge, but as Rama writes in her letter to Aïssatou, "She was thinking of you, working out her vengeance, but was very careful not to speak of you, of her hatred for you" (29). Through the financing of the niece's primary and secondary school education, Nabou had produced an obligation that could be compensated only through the marriage of the young Nabou to her only son, Mawdo. Mawdo's entrapment was a surety; however, in Mawdo's offer of little, if any resistance, to "antiquated laws" (30), Bâ indicts him for succumbing to the male desire for "variety":

> It was 'so as not to see his mother die of shame and cha-grin' that Mawdo agreed to go to the rendez-vous of the

wedding night. Faced with this rigid mother moulded by the old morality, burning with the fierce ardour of antiquated laws, what could Mawdo Bâ do? He was getting on in years, worn out by his arduous work. And then, did he really want to fight, to make a gesture of resistance? Young Nabou was so tempting. . . . (30)

Aïssatou, when faced with Mawdo's betrayal, acted decisively. She left Mawdo, taking her four sons with her. Unlike Rama, she rejected the arguments that immobilize women by making their well-being secondary to those of the men, for instance, their concern for the children (31). Aïssatou's independence has brought success; she has educated herself and has landed a job as an interpreter for the Senegalese embassy in the United States. Emblematic of her success is her gift of a car to Rama that provides her with greater mobility and independence (53).

Rama and Aïssatou share a deep bond of friendship not only because they are childhood friends, but because they have experienced the same abandonment: "There was your own case, Aïssatou, the cases of many other women, despised, relegated or exchanged, who were abandoned like a worn-out or out-dated *boubou*"(41). Rama, however, had responded differently to her betrayal. She had chosen to remain with Modou, despite the protests of her children, and to share her husband in accordance with the Islamic precepts of polygamic life. The irony is that her loyalty had gone unacknowledged by Modou, who, when faced with a jealous wife in Binetou, had twice abandoned Rama (52).

J.O.J. Nwachukwu-Agbada in the article "'One Wife Be For One Man': Mariama Bâ's Doctrine for Matrimony" calls attention to the rather superficial portrayal of the male characters in *So Long a Letter*. In the words of Nwachukwu-Agbada: "[A]ll the men are made to be guilty of this [adultery]: Modou Fall, Mawdo Bâ, Daouda Dieng, and Tamsir. There seem to be sexual itches in each of them that can only be taken care of by polygyny" (567). The critic finds it curious that for their second wives Modou and Mawdo would choose women whose lack of sophistication, seemingly, would put them at a disadvantage and voices dissatisfaction with the ratiocination proffered by Bâ:

What makes a man prefer the "simpler" wife to the perfume-wearing, richly clad, gold-bangled, and enlightened woman? Mariama Bâ never worried her male characters long enough to elicit an appropriate response to the question. Certainly, being a woman, the author could not put herself in an empathic position to establish men's inner motivations and the permanency of such embedded psychological urges. Rather than be concerned with a thrust in that direction, Bâ seems to have been content to leave the answer at the level of the lechery and sexual insatiation of men and their constant desire for "variety." (568)

The social justification for polygamy is, according to John Cairncross, largely economic. In the work *After Polygamy Was Made a Sin: The Social History of Christian Polygamy,* he writes: "Polygamy is a means of indicating and obtaining social prestige, of securing a good labour force in an area where women usually till the fields, and, probably most important of all, a sexual necessity since intercourse during pregnancy and lactation is frequently forbidden" (213).

Eugene Hillman in his work *Polygamy Reconsidered* affirms the view that polygamy subsists on economic grounds. He asserts that "male lust does not figure at all among the factors that make this a preferential form of marriage." Instead, he cites as factors, among others, the sex ratio among the mainland population of 95.1 males per 100 females (89), notions of prestige, "Some women even regard it as a disgrace to be the only wife of a man" (120), and the desire for a large family for economic subsistence as supportive of the custom of African polygamy:

A large number of offspring is regarded as a matter of socioeconomic urgency in an area where subsistence food production depends on the labor force that each family provides for itself, where the average rate of child mortality is very high, where the continuation of the family through male heirs is a grave responsibility, where each marriage contract multiplies the number of mutually helpful relatives, where leadership qualities are developed only through the good management of large families, where personal relationships are always regarded as more valuable than the possession of things, and where a large number of well-

> brought-up children is looked upon as the greatest of hu-
> man achievements. Where the desire for as many children
> as possible is paramount . . . , the practice of polygamy may
> be seen as an efficient means of realizing socially approved
> goals and social ideals. (114-15)

Although the aim of Hillman's work is to warn its target audience, namely, missionaries, of the dangers of ethnocentrism, of attempting to prescribe social customs for another culture that are antithetical to their way of life, the author occasionally falls victim to the same superciliousness that he criticizes, as when he makes claims such as the following: "It is not the members of polygamous families, but outside observers, who see polygamy as something undignified or even debasing for women" (126).

The publication of Bâ's two novels, which treat polygamy as a product of a male-centered culture, gives the lie to Hillman's assertions. Given the parallel content of both *So Long a Letter* and *Scarlet Song,* it is quite apparent that Bâ looks disdainfully upon polygamy as sanctioned by the Islamic faith. Although it is decreed that a practicing Muslim may take four wives (*Scarlet Song* 127), Bâ's sympathies are clearly with those such as Ousmane's father, Djebriel Gueye, whose decision to take a single wife has been governed by affordability and common sense. He therefore compares favorably with his neighbor Pathé Ngom whose multiple wives caused no cessation of domestic strife:

> Ousmane had witnessed scenes in Pathé Ngom's compound,
> caused by the rivalry among his wives. Children sided with
> their mothers and were dragged into their quarrels, sharing
> their deep-seated resentment. In these confrontations ev-
> erything to hand was used as a weapon: the basin full of
> dirty water, the brazier full of burning coals, the saucepan
> of boiling water, ladle, pestle, broken bottles. (7-8)

Ousmane recalls the performance of a *ndeup,* the exorcism dance, subsequent to a physical match between Ma Fatim, Pathé Ngom's first wife, and Maïmouna, a co-wife, which had produced paralysis in the former, a condition that was excused by her sister Pikine as caused by neglect of the *rab* (142). That Ousmane, cognizant of the domestic discord of the neighbor, would take a second wife, rejecting his father's own noble example, is indicative of the self-indulgence that Bâ is critical of in both novels. For example, it cannot be argued that a desire for additional progeny is the basis for the second marriage of Modou Fall in *Letter,* since Rama had already borne him twelve children (12); neither can it be argued that the basis for the second marriage was material necessity, since Modou Fall, a government minister, is, by any standard, one of the Senegalese elite. Charles Ponnuthurai Sarvan has observed that

> The wealth and social position of the family becomes clear at the funeral of Modou Fall with which the novel commences. The procession consists of official and private cars, buses, and lorries, and most of those who come to condole are dressed in expensive clothes. It is the duty of the dead man's sisters to buy the widows' mourning clothes, and the sum raised, in this instance, is 200,000 francs (7). In 1980, around the time in which the novel is set, the average lowest income of someone in public employment was 29,587 francs per month whereas the highest was 231,288. (457)

Given that the reasons for taking a second wife have neither to do with progeny nor financial security, one can concur with Nwachukwu Agbada that the men are depicted as "appropriat[ing] what is 'good' in Western culture and turn[ing] to their hitherto rejected culture to seek legitimacy for their palpably animal passion for more marital partners" (562).

Lynn S. Chancer has shed additional light on this sadomasochistic type of interaction in her work *Sadomasochism in Everyday Life: The Dynamics of Power and Powerlessness.* In her view, patriarchal, or male-dominated, societies produce features akin to those of the sadomasochistic dynamic: the devaluation of the subordinate party or parties and a suppression of neediness so that both males and females seek to live vicariously through the Other:

> Each gender comes to feel an extreme need for the other, for seizing back aspects of oneself that have been forcibly displaced onto the other. This is because patriarchy is organized to prevent the realization that both sides—the de-

sire to depend on someone else as well as the desire to preserve a sense of independence from them—exist within oneself. (138)

The failure of the dynamic is in its design. The subordination of women forecloses the possibility that either the masochist or the sadist will be able to acknowledge the free agency of the Other. Hence, the sadist may search over and over for the acknowledgement unattainable within the parameters that have been established and that he perpetuates. This perpetual search for "recognition" characterizes the "itches" of the men that Nwachukwu-Agbada has referred to euphemistically in his article "'One Wife Be For One Man': Mariama Bâ's Doctrine for Matrimony."

Readers opine from the details that are offered in *Letter* that, in addition to the thrill of conquest (39), Modou aims, from his marriage to Binetou, to re-capture a vanishing youth, while in the second novel *Scarlet Song,* Ousmane feels the need to assert his négritude by taking an African wife. The argument, however, is a rationalization, since as his friend Ali bluntly tells him, he is seeking "cultural justifications for what is simply a physical infatuation" (139). On the other hand, readers make the inference that Ousmane is captivated by the pursuit itself, as has been the case with Mireille.

Ousmane seemed to have been attracted to Mireille because of her Europeanness. That is, she represented the ultimate conquest; however, after winning the object of his desire, the appeal had waned: "One dreams of something. One fights to obtain it. One sacrifices everything for it, and once you possess it, it is no longer enough" (127). For Senegalese men, marriage to a white woman was viewed as a means of social mobility. In a climate of cultural enlightenment, though, such unions were deemed imprudent. Ironically, it is some of Ousmane's friends, who themselves have chosen white partners, who condemn his choice (122): "We chose this way during the colonial period, out of self-interest, laziness, weakness or opportunism. But you! With the rebirth of our country and the evolution of the black woman! You were the black woman's hope!" By Ousmane's own admission, marriage to Mireille constituted proof, or validation, of his manhood: "What about Mireille? What was I trying to prove? My ability to attract someone so far above me? I was excited by the difficulty of the enterprise" (136). Mbye B. Cham in his article "Contemporary Society and the Female Imagination: A Study of the Novels of Mariama Bâ" has echoed that expressed sentiment by Ousmane. Cham writes: "Rejected by Ouleymatou, he [Ousmane] turns to Mireille for personal validation; challenged by Mireille to be responsible, he seeks escape in Oulaymatou who panders to his vanity and who now represents Africa and African culture in his eyes" (99).

Common to both Binetou and Ouleymatou, however, is their objectness, a trait that explains the choices of the men who seek supremacy rather than equality in marriage. Daba, the eldest daughter of Rama, eschews politics because in her view it is the province of men who lust after power:

> "When I look at the fruitless wranglings even within the ranks of the same party, when I see men's greed for power, I prefer not to participate. No, I am not afraid of ideological struggle, but in a political party it is rare for a woman to make an easy break-through." (74)

Related to this point, the bid for power, Glenn W. Fetzer has identified in his article "Women's Search for Voice and the Problem of Knowing in the Novels of Mariama Bâ" Binetou's manipulable nature. Discussing Bâ's characters in accordance with the five perspectives outlined in *Women's Ways of Knowing: The Development of Self, Voice and Mind*, namely, silence, received knowledge, subjective knowledge, procedural knowledge, and constructed knowledge, Fetzer asserts that contrary to Aïssatou and Rama who integrate well the subjective and the objective realms of experience and seek to foster self-hood in others, in other words, they are constructors of knowledge, Binetou, due to her impressionability, never becomes her own person:

> The one who most nearly reflects this perspective [received knower] is Binetou, the young bride of Modou Fall's old age and the co-wife of Ramatoulaye in *Une Si Longue lettre*. As a received knower, Binetou demonstrates a concept of self derived from her environment. Having listened too

much to the voice of her mother intent on self-aggrandizement and to the voices of her materialistic friends, Binetou adapts their view of reality to herself. Although initially manipulative of Modou—a way of behaving learned from her mother, Binetou soon finds herself locked into an unfulfilling marriage, without the resourcefulness to create for herself an identity. (35)

Likewise, Ouleymatou's conception of herself as an object, an *en-soi*, validates the values of society at large which deem the female as a means of male transcendence. Simone de Beauvoir has written in *The Second Sex:*

The Other can be incarnated in the sea, the mountain, as perfectly as in woman; they oppose to man the same passive and unforeseen resistance that enables him to fulfill himself; they are an unwillingness to overcome, a prey to take possession of. If segra and mountain are women, then woman is also sea and mountain. . . . (146)

Ouleymatou's petrification of herself into an object of allure, or the Other, through which she brings herself into being (*SS* 507), is typified in the following: "She groomed it [her body], she polished it, she perfumed it. She took every care of it, for it was her weapon of seduction" (115).

The vanity of the male which leads him to seek transcendence in a younger female and, it might be added, an *en soi* is criticized by Bâ in her novels; she also indicts the females, such as Binetou's mother in *Letter* and Yaye Khady in *Scarlet Song* who sacrifice, respectively, their young daughter and daughter-in-law "on the altar of affluence" (*So Long a Letter* 39). Hence, central to the novel is not only the victimization of females by males, but the victimization of females by other females. In the behavior of Rama, Bâ seems to advocate, similar to Emecheta, the solidarity of females and economic independence as means of counteracting their sexual oppression. For example, when Rama is approached by Daouda Dieng, her former suitor, after the sudden death of Modou, to become his second wife, she rejects his offer of marriage, not willing to make her happiness the root of another's sorrow: "Abandoned yesterday because of a woman, I cannot lightly bring myself between you and your family" (68).

Ramatoulaye had already rejected the proposal of Modou's elder brother, Tamsir, on her fortieth day of mourning, that she become his fourth wife, a proposal that violated the Islamic decree that the younger brother inherit the older brother's wife. Rama writes that after "thirty years of silence, thirty years of harassment" (57-58), she could no longer will herself to passivity and had burst forth contemptuously, accusing Tamsir of greed, insensitivity, and irresponsibility to his three wives:

> "What of your wives, Tamsir? Your income can meet neither their needs nor those of your numerous children. To help you out with your financial obligations, one of your wives dyes, another sells fruit, the third untiringly turns the handle of her sewing machine. You, the revered lord, you take it easy, obeyed at the crook of a finger. I shall never be the one to complete your collection. My house shall never be for you the coveted oasis: no extra burden; my 'turn' every day; cleanliness and luxury, abundance and calm!" (58)

Given Lady Mother-in-Law's own experiences of neglect as a senior wife, it would appear that she would be less willing to compromise her own daughter; nonetheless, her behavior affirms the truth of Chancer's assertion that gender relations are likewise stratified into layers of power and powerlessness, as the discomfiture of Lady Mother-in-Law over her own powerlessness is "displaced into the satisfaction found in possessing some degree of greater power relative to others" (Chancer 38). In the words of Rama in *Letter:* "A victim, she wanted to be the oppressor. Exiled in the world of adults, which was not her own, she wanted her prison gilded" (48).

The denial of the female as a free entity results in her complacency; that is to say, she is the first, according to Simone de Beauvoir, to rush to the defense of the old gods (566); to throw herself at the feet of the conqueror (566); to acquiesce to defeat; and to venerate the old ways. Her "character" is deemed therefore the effect of her situation:

It is evident that woman's "character"—her convictions, her values, her wisdom, her morality, her tastes, her behavior—are to be explained by her situation. The fact that transcendence is denied her keeps her as a rule from attaining the loftiest human attitudes: heroism, revolt, disinterestedness, imagination, creation. (588)

One solution, in de Beauvoir's view, to female resignation is engagement: "Let the future be opened to her and she will no longer cling desperately to the past. When women are called upon for concrete action, when they recognize their interest in the designated goals, they are as bold and courageous as men" (*The Second Sex* 567-68).

In an interview, Bâ has acknowledged that hope for the future resides in part in parenting techniques that may serve to erode the assumptions of a patriarchal society that produces this push-pull dialectic: "So now we mothers, we mothers who have had the privilege to understand a little and to play a part in the creations of our sons, we have tried to raise them so that they do not grow up thinking of themselves as 'kings of the family.' This is the hope for the future" (qtd. in Rueschmann 15). Inasmuch as social psychology is enmeshed with our everyday lives, Chancer in her work makes a similar call for a transformation that is both internal and external:

> At the same time, one would hope to do both, to effect changes both within and without: to try to affect our own self-awareness at the same time one tries to influence the course of social ideologies and institutions. One would hope to "fight the power," in the words of the rap group Public Enemy, while still trying to maintain one's humanity, minimizing the reproduction of sadistic dynamics this power tends to arouse—somehow keeping all of this in mind. (184)

The account of female solidarity ameliorates somewhat the tragic ending of Mariama Bâ's second novel, *Scarlet Song,* and provides it with its message of hope. Soukeyna, sister to Ousmane, sides with Mireille against her mother: "I am completely opposed to my brother's second marriage and consider that nothing can justify it except your self-interest. I'll have nothing to do with this second home" (152). Nonetheless, the effect on Mireille of Ousmane's betrayal has been catastrophic. She goes berserk. She murders their son Gorgui by giving him an overdose of sleeping pills and assaults Ousmane with a carving knife after his pre-dawn return from his second home. Miraculously, his wounds are not fatal, the flow of blood merely symbolic of dashed hopes: "Ousmane Gueye lay on the floor. Mireille did not seem to see him as she continued walking aimlessly to and fro. A scarlet song welled up from Ousmane's wounds, the scarlet song of lost hopes" (166). Seen from a psychological angle, Mireille's insanity could presage the figurative death of Ousmane, given the symbiotic nature of the sadomasochistic dynamic. Chancer has proffered in her work:

> Should the masochist become worn down, should she or he die either figuratively or literally, the sadist would be destroyed as well. (In this sense, when the sadist punishes the other, he or she is at the same time punishing himself or herself, engaging in an irrational pursuit.) Allegedly, the sadist takes pleasure in controlling the masochist and must continually innovate in order to keep the process moving and to perpetuate a sense of sadistic identity. But once the masochist has been negated, the dynamic comes to an abrupt halt. This can happen either literally through death, at the extreme end of the sadomasochistic continuum, or figuratively by the sadist having exerted so much control that the masochist retains no independent powers of resistance, *e.g.,* a nervous breakdown. (54-55)

Chancer's view is echoed by Jessica Benjamin in her work *The Bonds of Love: Psychoanalysis, Feminism, and the Problem of Domination,* wherein Benjamin remarks that the failure of the individual to recognize the Other results in literal and figurative death inasmuch as a denial of the agency of the Other is tantamount to a denial of self:

> The paradox of recognition, the need for acknowledgment that turns us back to dependence on the other, brings about a struggle for control. This struggle can result in the realization that if we fully negate the other, that is, if we assume

complete control over him and destroy his identity and will,
then we have negated ourselves as well. For then there is
no one there to recognize us, no one there for us to desire.
(39)

Mireille's insanity in *Scarlet Song* parallels that of Elizabeth in Bessie
Head's *A Question of Power* that is caused, in part, by
homelessness. Mireille's marriage to Ousmane had precipitated
the severance of ties to her French homeland, while, on the other
hand, Elizabeth's membership in a banned political party had rendered her "a stateless person in Botswana" (18). Her classification as Coloured compounds her dilemma, as it makes impossible
her assimilation into Motabeng, "a village of relatives who married
relatives, and nearly everyone had about six hundred relatives" (20).
To be sure, as Eleni Coundouriotis writes in her article "Authority
and Invention in the Fiction of Bessie Head," it is precisely Elizabeth's
dispossession that makes her vulnerable to "sexual molestation" at
the hands of several "large, looming soul personalities" and that
culminates in Elizabeth's schizophrenia:

> Sello and Medusa make clear in the first part of the novel
> that Elizabeth is viewed as an appropriate object of sexual
> assault because she is not sufficiently African. . . . Sexual-
> ity and belonging to a land thus are explicitly linked by the
> logic of their sequential presentation in Medusa's argument.
> Sex, the manifestation of the extensive mental and psycho-
> logical invasion of an entire society against Elizabeth, is a
> social, not a private act. (22)

Furthermore, Elizabeth's persecution—both real and imagined—
exemplifies the "permanent nervous tension" created by South
African apartheid. Head writes of Elizabeth's psychological state
in *A Question of Power:*

> In spite of her inability to like or to understand political
> ideologies, she had also lived the back-breaking life of all
> black people in South Africa. It was like living with *per-*
> *manent nervous tension* [my emphasis], because you did
> not know why white people there had to go out of their way
> to hate you or loathe you. (19)

It has been noted earlier, with regard to *Madness and Sexual Politics in the Feminist Novel: Studies in Brontë, Woolf, Lessing, and Atwood,* by Barbara Hill Rigney, that schizophrenia "is a special strategy that a person invents in order to live in an unlivable situation . . . a kind of temporary answer to social and political oppression" (8). One might add, in concurrence with Jean-Paul Sartre, that insanity is also a defense against racial oppression. Jean-Paul Sartre, in the Preface to *The Wretched of the Earth,* argued that neuroses is a weapon adopted by the oppressed against their dehumanization:

> The colonized people protect themselves against colonial estrangement by going one better in religious estrangement, with the unique result that finally they add the two estrangements together and each reinforces the other. Thus in certain psychoses the hallucinated person, tired of always being insulted by his demon, one fine day starts hearing the voice of an angel who pays him compliments; but the jeers don't stop for all that; only from then on, they alternate with congratulations. This is a defense, but it is also the end of the story; the self is disassociated, and the patient heads for madness. (19)

Sartre concludes that the status of the indigenous population is "a nervous condition introduced and maintained by the settler among colonized people *with their consent"* (20).

Nervous Conditions, a novel by Tsitsi Dangarembga, that takes its title from Jean-Paul Sartre's Preface to *The Wretched of the Earth,* dramatizes that neurosis. The collusive nature of the Africans is apparent in the realm of education, as the British or French education that makes possible their upward mobility inspires an allegiance to the colonial system responsible for their prosperity. Such allegiance is apparent in Babamukuru whose Bachelor's Degree in South Africa and Master's Degree in England, both funded by government scholarships, have produced "not a replica of Europe, but its caricature."

The reductio ad absurdum of Babamukuru's transformation is the arrangement of a Christian wedding for his brother Jeremiah and Mainini, after their union of nineteen years, as a safeguard against bigamy. Jeremiah is not opposed to marriage to Lucia, reasoning, in the view of the narrator, that "my mother and Lucia, being sisters, would get on comfortably together and reminded Babamukuru that as Lucia was a good worker, it would be useful to have her permanently about the home" (127). Takesure, a distant cousin of Babamukuru's who has come down at Babamukuru's behest to help work the land in order to relieve his indebtedness, is rumored to be the father of Lucia's unborn child; however, Takesure already has two wives and the accompanying debt of their brideprice. Given his obligations, readers are told, Jeremiah, rather than Takesure, is viewed by Lucia as a better prospect for marriage:

> [Takesure] did not like being a husband and Lucia knew that he neither wanted, nor could afford, nor was able to be one three times over. . . . Lucia, who had grown shrewd in her years of dealing with men, denied that the foetus was Takesure's. She accredited it instead to my father, although this could not have been true. (126)

A family *dare,* which constituted the patriarchy and "womb-sister" of Jeremiah, who accordingly had been given patriarchal status, was summoned to discuss the matter between Lucia and Takesure, one that Jeremiah had argued was one of a series of misfortunes that had originated with the mysterious death of his twelve-year-old son Nhamo while at the mission school near Umtali where Babamukuru was headmaster. To counteract this series of misfortunes, Jeremiah had proposed a cleansing ceremony, a measure to which Babamukuru was staunchly opposed since the ceremonies represented African unenlightenment. He had offered instead a counter-proposal—a Christian wedding to purge the household of sin:

> 'Yes, Jeremiah, even now, so many years after our mother passed away, you are still living in sin. You have not been married in church before God. This is a serious matter, so I have been saving a little, a very little bit of money, for a wedding for you and Mainini.' (147)

The outrageousness of the proposition, "a wedding that made a mockery of the people I belonged to and placed doubt on my legitimate existence in this world" (163), is not lost on the fourteen-year-old narrator Tambu who is a product of the union of nineteen years. A beneficiary of Babamukuru's magnanimity in that he has taken her into his home and has made himself responsible for her school fees following the death of the elder son Nhamo who had been expected to elevate the family branch by obtaining a university degree (44), neither Tambu nor her mother Mainini can object to Babamukuru's plan. The reasons for their silence have both to do with appearances; they wish neither to give the appearance of ingratitude nor the appearance of violating cultural norms. Tambu has noted at the outset of the novel: "The needs and sensibilities of the women in my family were not considered a priority, or even legitimate" (12).

That reality is adumbrated in the silent rage of Mainini who, along with her daughters, is expected to tend the crops and other household chores that are considered the domain of women, "My mother, lips pressed tight, would hitch little Rambanai more securely on her back and continue silently at her labours. The ferocious swings of her arms as she grabbed and stripped a maize stalk restrained Netsai and me from making the slightest murmur of rebellion" (7); also, in the repressed rage of Maiguru, the wife of Babamukuru who works to make possible his support of members of his extended family but is excluded from decisions affecting them:

> 'I am tired of being nothing in a home I am working myself sick to support. And now even that Lucia can walk in here and tell me that the things she discusses with you, here in my home, are none of my business. . . . And when I keep quiet you think I am enjoying it. So today I am telling you I am not happy.' (172)

Given the cultural silencing of females, Tambu can only rebel covertly against what she considers "a comic show" (163), and this she does by inducing paralysis that is the result of her internal struggle:

> The . . . morning of the wedding, I found I could not get out of bed. I tried several times but my muscles simply refused

to obey the half-hearted commands I was issuing to them.
Nyasha was worried. She thought I was ill, but I knew
better. I knew I could not get out of bed because I did not
want to. (166)

Tambu's rebellion is mirrored in Nyasha, Babamukuru's daughter,
who, along with her brother Chido, had journeyed to England and
had returned five years later Anglicized in dress, speech, and in
habits. Nyasha, for instance, surreptitiously smokes cigarettes (85),
wears mini skirts (37), reads novels, such as D.H. Lawrence's *Lady
Chatterley's Lover* (75), that are deemed by her parents to be "no
good for you," and subverts her father's dominance by becoming
anorexic. In the words of Janice E. Hill:

When Babamukuru connects obedience to the eating of
food, the effect on Nyasha is loss of appetite, an emotional
strategy that will become increasingly effective for her and
develop systematically into anorexia and bulimia. By saying "I'm full," Nyasha shifts the site of battle from the din-
ing table controlled by Babamukuru to the territory of her
own body, which she controls. Her refusal to eat food becomes a weapon of power in an otherwise powerless situation. (screen 4)

Hill views the women in the Sigauke family as symbolic of "the
discontent that Africans expressed with colonial power structures
during the 1960s and 1970s—structures that accorded them an inferior status and did not allow a legally acceptable means of expression" (screen 9).

A cultural hybrid, Nyasha is also a symbol of the assimilado; as
a result of her five-year sojourn in England, she can no longer
speak the native tongue Shona (42). She is hence reminiscent of
the French-educated Rama in Mariama Bâ's *So Long a Letter* who
likewise has been shaped by cross-cultural influences:

The assimilationist dream of the colonist drew into its cru-
cible our mode of thought and way of life. The sun helmet
worn over the natural protection of our kinky hair, smoke-
filled pipe in the mouth, white shorts just above the calves,
very short dresses displaying shapely legs: a whole gen-

eration suddenly become aware of the ridiculous situation festering in our midst. (*So Long a Letter* 24)

The divided self of Rama in *So Long a Letter*, the writer would contend, accounts for the mixed messages that the novel contains and that have been criticized by reviewers. That is, it has been contended by Femi Ojo-Ade that Rama, although she exculpates the Mother-in-Law for her sacrifice of Binetou on "the altar of materialism," Ramatoulaye and Aïssatou are worshippers before that very altar:

> [Ramatoulaye] establishes a hierarchy even among the female species. Aïssatou is superior to little Nabou; Nabou is superior to Binetou; Ramatoulaye, naturally, is superior to all. The yardstick for comparison is the level of civilization. Civilization, as in western culture. Civilization, as in acculturation. Civilization, as in capitalism. For the reader must be clear about one fact: Ramatoulaye's middle-class origins are to her a source of pride and her commitment as a pioneer is, first and foremost, to that class. (83)

Although it can be argued that Femi Ojo-Ade comes perilously close to the straw man argument, of attacking a prejudice similar to—classism—but different from, the one illuminated by Bâ, namely, sexism, and thus clouding the issue, similar reservations have been articulated by Yakini Kemp.

Yakini Kemp has noted that although the "tough individualism" of the women—Rama in Mariama Bâ's *So Long a Letter*, Akunna in Buchi Emecheta's *Bride Price*, and Margaret Cadmore in Bessie Head's *Maru*—makes them "iconoclasts" (12), the romantic themes and feminist elements in the works form a "tenuous partnership," with the romantic vision of the works ultimately restricting their feminist elements. Yakini Kemp concludes:

> Whereas each writer achieves a degree of success in utilizing her fiction as creative art and as social criticism, the idealism found in their romantic vision leads them away from criticizing fundamental social structures that help perpetuate the social ills they cite. Thus, Bessie Head wanted to see the Masarwa freed while leaving intact the elitist and

patriarchal social relations that continue to suppress her Masarwa protagonist. And Bâ wished dissolution of polygamous marriage while ignoring class privilege as equally exploitive of women. Even Emecheta, labelled by one critic, "a firebrand upholding the feminist faith". . . posits no need for such changes. (14)

Finally, Irène Assiba d'Almeida asserts that Rama is torn between modernity and tradition, and that the conflict results in ambivalence on women's issues. This conflict, according to d'Almeida, stems from Rama's plight of wanting to preserve tradition yet reject those social elements that bind women: "Ramatoulaye describes the plight of working women who have a double yoke to bear and she also demands recognition for the interminable work done by women who stay at home. Yet, on the other hand, she has internalized a number of stereotypes about women and women's behavior" (167).

The displeasure of the critics stems from the contradictory positions that *So Long a Letter* attempts to hold. First, it inscribes class ambivalence by appealing to the solidarity of women with the example of bourgeois and aristocratic leadership; second, the novel attempts to promulgate blackness while also venerating European culture and ideologies; and, third, the novel purports to venerate black womanhood while it expresses favor for the male gender ("I envy you [Aïssatou] for having had only boys!"). In this context, the stylistic features of the novel ultimately become inhospitable to the novel's propagandistic content. Charles Ponnuthurai Sarvan has summarized the "tug-of-war" existent in Mariama Bâ's fiction: "Mariama Bâ does not write from a clear and categorical standpoint; her novels are questioning and explorative rather than radical and imperative" (464). This concern aside—the authorial ambivalence in the novel that is a by product of the author's colonialist background—the strength of the fiction of both Mariama Bâ and Bessie Head lies in their courageousness in tackling social, cultural and religious norms that oppress women. By their disclosure of the psychic damage caused by these centuries-old practices, they join other feminine voices of African literature, such as the Zimbabwean author Tsitsi Dangarembga, who affirm the females' right to dignity by giving voice to their silence, a silence that Carol Margaret Davison construes as another form of disinheritance: "[I]n giving voice to her silenced sister, the woman writer underlines her own tragic legacy of voicelessness—an inheritance better described as a disinheritance" (19).

WORKS CITED

Abrahams, Cecil, ed. *The Tragic Life: Bessie Head and Literature in Southern Africa.* Trenton: Africa World Press, 1990.

Aegerter, Lindsay Pentolfe. "A Dialectic of Autonomy and Community: Tsitsi Dangarembga's Nervous Conditions." *Tulsa Studies in Women's Literature* 15 (1996): 231-40.

Bâ, Mariama. *So Long a Letter.* Trans. Modupé Bodé-Thomas. London: Heinemann, 1981.

———. *Scarlet Song.* Trans. Dorothy S. Blair. Essex, England: Longman, 1986.

Beauvoir, Simone de. *The Second Sex.* Trans. and edited by H.M. Parshley. New York: Knopf, 1952. Originally published in French as *Le Deuxième Sexe* (Paris: Gallimard, 1949).

Benjamin, Jessica. *The Bonds of Love: Psychoanalysis, Feminism, and the Problem of Domination.* New York: Random, 1988.

Berger, Roger A. "The Politics of Madness in Bessie Head's *A Question of Power.*" Abrahams, 31-43.

Cairncross, John. *After Polygamy Was Made a Sin: The Social History of Christian Polygamy.* London: Routledge and Kegan Paul, 1974.

Cham, Mbye B. "Contemporary Society and the Female Imagination: A Study of the Novels of Mariama Bâ." *Women in African Literature* 15 (1987): 89-101.

Chancer, Lynn S. *Sadomasochism in Everyday Life: The Dynamics of Power and Powerlessness.* New Brunswick, N.J.: Rutgers UP, 1992.

Coundouriotis, Eleni. "Authority and Invention in the Fiction of Bessie Head." *Research in African Literatures* 27 (1996): 17-32.

d'Almeida, Irène Assiba. "The Concept of Choice in Mariama Bâ's Fiction." *Ngambika: Studies of Women in African Literature.* Eds. Carole Boyce Davies, and Anne Adams Graves. Trenton: Africa World Press, 1986.

Dangarembga, Tsitsi. *Nervous Conditions.* Seattle: Seal Press, 1988.

Davison, Carol Margaret. "A Method in the Madness: Bessie Head's *A Question of Power.*" Abrahams, 19-29.

Emecheta, Buchi. *Second-Class Citizen.* New York: George Braziller, 1975.

Fanon, Frantz. *The Wretched of the Earth.* Trans. Constance Farrington.

New York: Grove, 1968.

Fetzer, Glenn W. "Women's Search for Voice and the Problem of Knowing in the Novels of Mariama Bâ." *College Language Association Journal* 35 (September 1991): 31-41.

Gilbert, Sandra M. and Susan Gubar. *The Madwoman in the Attic: The Woman Writer and the Nineteenth-Century Literary Imagination.* New Haven: Yale UP, 1979.

Gover, Daniel. "The Fairy Tale and the Nightmare." Abrahams, 113-21.

Head, Bessie. *Maru*. London: Heinemann, 1971.

———. *A Question of Power.* London: Heinemann, 1974.

Hill, Janice E. "Purging a Plate Full of Colonial History: The 'Nervous Conditions' of Silent Girls." *College Literature* 22 (1995): 78-91.

Hillman, Eugene. *Polygamy Reconsidered: African Plural Marriage and the Christian Churches.* Mary Knoll, NY: Orbis, 1975.

Hurston, Zora Neale. "Mules and Men." 1935. Reprinted in *Zora Neale Hurston: Folklore, Memoirs, and Other Writings.* Comp. Cheryl A. Wall. New York: Library of America, 1995.

Jackson, Kathy Dunn. "The Epistolary Text: A Voice of Affirmation and Liberation in *So Long a Letter* and *The Color Purple.*" *The Griot* 12, no. 2 (fall 1993): 13-20.

Kemp, Yakini. "Romantic Love and the Individual in Novels by Mariama Bâ, Buchi Emecheta and Bessie Head." *Obsidian II: Black Literature in Review* 3 (winter 1988): 1-16.

Nair, Supriya. "Melancholic Women: The Intellectual Hysteric(s) in *Nervous Conditions.*" *Research in African Literatures* 26 (1995): 130-39.

Nwachukwu-Agbada, J.O.J. "'One Wife Be For One Man': Mariama Bâ's Doctrine for Matrimony." *Modern Fiction Studies* 37 (autumn 1991): 561-73.

Ogundele, Olapido Joseph. "A Conversation with Dr. Buchi Emecheta." *Emerging Perspectives on Buchi Emecheta.* Ed. Marie Umeh. Trenton: Africa World Press, 1996. 445-56.

Ojo-Ade, Femi. "Still a Victim? Mariama Bâ's *Une si Longue Lettre.*" *African Literature Today* 12 (1982): 71-87.

Olagun, Modupe O. "Irony and Schizophrenia in Bessie Head's *Maru.*" *Research in African Literatures* 25 (1994): 69-87.

Phillips, Maggi. "Engaging Dreams: Alternative Perspectives on Flora Nwapa, Buchi Emecheta, Ama Ata Aidoo, Bessie Head, and Tsitsi Dangarembga's Writing." *Research in African Literatures* 25, no. 4 (1994): 89-103.

Rigney, Barbara Hill. *Madness and Sexual Politics in the Feminist Novel:*

Studies in Brontë, Woolf, Lessing, and Atwood. Madison: U of Wisconsin P, 1978.

Rose, Jacqueline. "On the 'Universality' of Madness: Bessie Head's *A Question of Power.*" *Critical Inquiry* 20 (1994): 401-18.

Rueschmann, Eva. "Female Self-Definition and the African Community in Mariama Bâ's Epistolary Novel *So Long a Letter.*" *International Women's Writing: New Landscapes of Identity.* Contributions in Women's Studies 147. Eds. Anne E. Brown and Marjanne E. Goozé. Westport: Greenwood, 1995.

Sartre, Jean-Paul. "Preface." *The Wretched of the Earth.* Trans. Constance Farrington. New York: Grove, 1968.

Sarvan, Charles Ponnuthurai. "Feminism and African Fiction: The Novels of Mariama Bâ." *Modern Fiction Studies* 34 (autumn 1988): 453-64.

Schmidt, Rita Terezinha. *"With My Sword in My Hand": The Politics of Race and Sex in the Fiction of Zora Neale Hurston.* Ph.D. diss., Univ. of Pittsburgh, 1983. Ann Arbor, MI: University Microfilms, 1988. 8411770

Uwakweh, Pauline Ada. "Debunking Patriarchy: The Liberational Quality of Voicing in Tsitsi Dangarembga's *Nervous Conditions.*" *Research in African Literatures* 26 (1995): 75-84.

Chapter 9

THE EXILE OF THE ELDERLY IN GILROY'S *FRANGIPANI HOUSE* AND *BOY-SANDWICH*

In Simone Schwarz-Bart's *The Bridge of Beyond* and Toni Morrison's *Beloved,* abandonment becomes a metaphor for the physical and psychological dispossession of blacks who were severed from their African homeland; in Buchi Emecheta's *Second-Class Citizen, The Joys of Motherhood* and in Mariama Bâ's *So Long a Letter* and *Scarlet Song,* abandonment becomes synonymous with female oppression whose culprit is male privilege, as it is practiced through the Islamic custom of polygamy. In Beryl Gilroy's two novels *Frangipani House* and *Boy-Sandwich,* however, abandonment characterizes the condition of the elderly whose basic rights are often undermined. Lucy Wilson in her article "Aging and Ageism in Paule Marshall's *Praisesong for the Widow* and Beryl Gilroy's *Frangipani House*" has written on the abandonment, or exile, of the elderly in *Frangipani House:*

> Typically, we think of exile as a fundamental dislocation brought about by distance from one's home and roots, intensified by race, religion, ethnic origins, class, as well as gender. Another kind of exile, however, is the separation and alienation that results from the inevitable and inexorable process of aging. It is exemplified by a character like Beryl Gilroy's Mama King, who has lived her entire life in one place. (189)

The setting in Frangipani House is Guyana, while the dominant setting in *Boy-Sandwich,* a sequel to *Frangipani House,* is London, England. The sixty-nine-year-old Mama King, who is widowed and suffers from a series of ailments, malaria, quinsey, and pleurisy, has been placed by her two daughters Token and Cyclette, who have immigrated to America, in Frangipani House, a rest home exclusively for black female inmates. In *Boy-Sandwich,* the couple Simon and Clara Grainger have been evicted from their home in London as many of the residential homes have been scheduled for demolition in order to make room for a new development. The solution for Robby, the only son of the Graingers, is to have them admitted to a nursing home, the Birches, that, after their admission, will boast an integration of three: Belladora, a woman of mixed race, and the Graingers who are of West Indian descent. Despite the changes wrought by time, *i.e.,* a dual-gender facility (the Birches in *Boy-Sandwich)* as opposed to the same-gender facility (Frangipani House), unchanged has been the victimization of the elderly that Simone de Beauvoir has written of in *The Coming of Age* and that Gilroy chronicles in both works. According to Beauvoir,

> Nowadays the adults take quite another kind of interest in the aged: they have become objects of exploitation. In the United States more than anywhere else, but also in France, there are greatly increasing numbers of nursing-homes, rest-homes, residences, villages and even towns where elderly people who have the means are made to pay as much as possible for an often inadequate comfort and care. (*The Coming of Age* 219-20)

The exploitation of the elderly is paramount in *Frangipani House.* The inmates are not only targets of theft, as many of their possessions are pilfered and sold for profit (*Frangipani House* 8, 91; *Boy-Sandwich* 14, 63), but, as evidenced in *Boy-Sandwich,* they are also forced to pay for services that are theirs by right of admission.

Grandpa Grainger requests of his grandson Tyrone that he give five pounds to the caretaker Juney rather than suffer negligence. He cannot afford the amount, since his pension funds have been confiscated. The bribe, he hopes, will lead to improved care for him and his wife:

'Give Juney a five pound,' he says. 'If I have my pension I
would pay. What happen to my pension book? I never
have money. Clara leave in de bath too long. She cold. I
try to take her out but I couldn't and Belladora went out so
no one give me a hand. You must give Juney five pound to
help us. Everybody payin' Juney. If you don't pay you get
by-pass.' (17)

The impression given is not only one of exploitation and inadequate care, but of unprofessionalism as well, as many of the
caregivers perform their duties while under the influence. Tyrone
barges into a secluded staff room and discovers the caregivers sit-
ting around a table sharing drinks (17). In *Frangipani House*, Olga
Trask, the proprietess of the nursing home, drowns her sorrows in
a bottle of rum after the escape of Mama King from the home and
her realization of the likely repercussions from the resident's disappearance:

She fumbled in her drawer and pulled out a flattie of rum
and took a long sip and soon the silence in the room was
broken by the rum gurgling its way to comfort her. . . .
More and more, drink had begun to take her into another
world. (74)

The victimization and neglect of the elderly by those assigned their
care are conveyed through the imagery. In *Frangipani House*, Olga
Trask is described as "a comely, honey-brown predator of a woman"
(2).

In *Frangipani House*, the abusive care stems from the exploitation of difference. As punishment for her delusional behavior, an
injection is given to Mama King to calm her, and she is forced, as
punishment, to eat without her dentures two big sausages (35).
Contrarily, in *Boy-Sandwich*, the abusiveness stems from the
caregivers' refusal to acknowledge difference, as the diet of the
elderly is no different from that of those not suffering from the
infirmities of age: "The old people sit at tables and are served
salad which many cannot eat because their false teeth can cope
with neither the coarsely chopped raw vegetables nor the leathery
baked potatoes" (24).

Simone de Beauvoir in *The Coming of Age* avers that the mental condition often reflects the physical and relates that, statistically, out of a hundred thousand subjects, the number of the mentally sick among the same age group is "2.3 under fifteen years of age, 76.3 between twenty-five and thirty-four, 93 between thirty-five and fifty-four, and 236.1 among the aged" (35). She characterizes neurosis among the aged as a defense against the threat of a possible loss of their identity:

> A person becomes neurotic when 'in the identification of his own character he is unable to find good relationships with others and a satisfactory internal equilibrium.' When this is the case, he presents a cluster of symptoms that are in fact so many defences against an intolerable situation. (493)

She also identifies melancholy as a widespread psychosis that is often triggered at the time of some emotional crisis, such as "bereavement, separation or transplantation" (496).

Mama King's emotional crisis in *Frangipani House* has been precipitated by her institutionalization. Symptomatic of her emotional crisis is her delusional behavior. According to de Beauvoir, "violent melancholia . . . is often accompanied by illusions, hallucinations and oneiric delirium" (497). Thus, Mama King conjures up her late husband Danny and carries on conversations with him in an effort to compensate for her loss of fellowship in the real world. For instance, when Mama King is being served her meal by the nurse, she demands an extra portion for her late husband:

> 'You want food Mama? Eat something! I have a nice sausage here for you.'
> 'I want two. One for me and one for Danny.'
> 'Which Danny? This is a woman only place. No Danny allowed!'
> Mama King began to cry. 'I want two! I want one for Danny!' (35)

Because "living conditions have great influence upon the appearance and evolution of the disease [melancholy]" (*The Coming of Age* 500), the turning point for Mama King in *Frangipani House* comes with her escape from the Eventide Home and her acceptance into a band of beggars, led by Pandit. What has been recaptured is a raison d'être that has been lost with the immigration of her daughters to the states and later the grandchildren that she had so lovingly nurtured: "Mama King was never more moved to contentment and happiness. One of the little girls approached her and curled up in her lap. And then drop by drop her mothering feeling returned to her. She slept well that night" (60).

Work has been also a means by which Mama King has defined her being. Confinement to a nursing home, hence, has effectively robbed her of her essence. When her grandson Markey visits her, he is amazed by her physical decline: "The sight of her overwhelmed him. He remembered her dark-haired and strong, able to get the stopper from a bottle with her teeth. She was purposeful and positive. Now here she was, a haunted ghost with a haunting past" (46).

Simone de Beauvoir in *The Coming of Age* has likened retirement to death:

> Hemingway said that the worst death for anyone was the loss of what formed the centre of his life and made him what he really was. Retirement was the most loathsome word in the language. Whether we chose it or whether we were compelled by fate, retiring, giving up one's calling— the calling that made us what we were—was the same as going down to the grave. (262)

Mama King in *Frangipani House* credits the beggars for having restored to her life. She tells one of her daughters Cyclette, who, along with Token and her grandchildren, has returned to Guyana upon the news of Mama King's disappearance:

> 'Cyclette, the only real kindness I ever get was from beggars. They was kind. They was good—sharing, protecting—giving me respect and friendship. They have little but they give a lot. They give me back my senses because they treat me like I was somebody.' (94)

On the other hand, the turning point in *Boy-Sandwich* is the admission of the ninety-year-old George into the Birches who brings with him the gift of song: "Voices, some cracked, some surprisingly melodious, are singing in accompaniment to several well-known old music hall tunes. At the piano sits a man I have never seen before. He is obviously a new admission" (52-53).

The therapeutic value that Gilroy accords music is reminiscent of the view of Paule Marshall, as expressed in *Praisesong for the Widow*. Avey Johnson, on a Caribbean cruise with two female companions, is haunted by memories of her early life with her late husband Jay (Jerome) Johnson. Characterized by poverty, Avey Johnson nonetheless associates with her past a passion for life that had been compromised by the couple's move to North White Plains (132) and, concomitantly, their acceptance of white middle-class values. She recalls, for instance, the role of music in their lives and its restorative impact:

> The Jay who emerged from the music of an evening, the self that would never be seen down at the store, was open, witty, playful, even outrageous at times: he might suddenly stage an impromptu dance just for the two of them in the living room, declaring it to be Rockland Palace or the Renny. (95)

Subsequent to George's admission, the narrator Tyrone remarks a similar change in the Graingers; that is, they have become more lucid: "My grandparents are becoming more coherent with the passing of each day. They have stopped deteriorating. I can hardly believe the evidence of my eyes. Grandma has moved from spasms to spans of clarity. She is becoming a part of things. . . . It is an almost miraculous change and I feel grateful for it" (57).

The conclusion of *Boy-Sandwich* also marks a new beginning. The sale of an original painting by the Spanish artist Jose Gutierrez Solana (1886-1945) to a private collector makes possible the return of the Graingers to the West Indies. Tyrone had discovered the painting while searching a trunk belonging to his grandmother for the rare coins, doubloons (11, 88). Officials at the British Museum, where Tyrone had taken it for appraisal, had apprised him of its worth and had instructed that "[he] should have it cleaned and insured" (89). The homecoming of the elderly couple, accompanied by their son, Robby, and his family, which has been funded by the sale of the painting, has provided the Graingers with a new lease on life, as they have become participants in life rather than spectators of life. The grandson, at a soiree planned by the grandparents for their Guyanian friends, describes their transfiguration, which is evident in the grandmother's storytelling, the participation in which acquires for her cathartic value: "I wish that the Matron could hear them now especially when Grandma tells them the humorous story of Buru Ananse—the spider man evicted from his hole. She acts it, dances, dips and turns and so gets the hidden fear out of her system" (105).

Simone de Beauvoir considers in *The Coming of Age* the symbiotic relationship of the elderly with their communities; that is, the esteem accorded by the community to the elderly determines the vitality of both the elderly and the traditions of their community:

> Where the authority of the old is still strong, the reason is that the community as a whole wishes to maintain its traditions by means of them. It is the community, according to its potentialities and its interests, that determines the fate of the old: and the old are subject to this determination even when they think themselves the strongest. (86)

The value accorded the elderly is evident in Beryl Gilroy's *Boy-Sandwich*. Gilroy writes of the regard for the elderly in the West Indies: "The people about her accept old age and its handicaps. They measure persons against life rather than against youth. In Britain the young alone matter and elderly people are regarded as used-up and intractable simply because they are old" (104). Cindy's husband Chuck in *Frangipani House* also reflects on the ancestral worship by African tribes that he had witnessed during his twelve-month sojourn in Africa: "Ancestors ever present stalked friend or foe in the African bush. Some were even buried in the family compound, worshipped, deified" (100).

The happy ending that characterizes *Boy-Sandwich* is also a feature of *Frangipani House*. Mama King, along with a mid-wife, presides over her granddaughter Cindy's delivery of twin sons, two symbols of hope (108). One twin is named for Mama King's brother Abel, whose legacy has been one of generosity. The late brother

of Mama King not only has purchased a home for her in Guyana
(109), but has financed the medical degree of his nephew Solo
(94).

Similar to the appellation of the twin Abel in *Frangipani House*,
which signifies continuity with the past, Grandpa Grainger's photo
album in *Boy-Sandwich* is used by Gilroy as a structural device,
suggesting life's continuum. The photo album allows Grandpa
Grainger, a raconteur, to recount to his grandson his personal history, as well as that of his family. The photo album therefore forms
a pictorial history of the Graingers' West Indian roots:

> All through my youth and in the early days of his retire-
> ment, he [Grandpa] had talked to me about times long since
> gone and had pointed out friends and family in the album
> to prove the most important points of argument and reason.
> It is the most treasured of his possessions—this album of
> pages overburdened with photographs. . . . In a voice
> marked with the twang of his Island he would often talk of
> those yesterdays when he kept his many assignations with
> destiny, across seas and oceans and in the countries be-
> yond. (5)

Simone de Beauvoir in *The Coming of Age* sees the fixation of the
elderly on the past less positively, as they are not simply a means
of preserving a cultural history, but of clinging to a lost youth by
the complete alliance with their former selves:

> [The elderly] refuse time because they do not wish to de-
> cline; they define their former I as that which they still are—
> they assert their solidarity with their youth. Even if they
> have overcome the identification-crises and have accepted
> a new image of themselves—each in his heart preserves
> the conviction of having remained unalterable: when they
> summon their memories they justify this assertion. They
> set up a fixed, unchanging essence against the deteriora-
> tions of age, and tirelessly they tell stories of this being that
> they were, this being that lives on inside them. . . . All their
> life, whether they are thirty or whether they are fifty, they
> have still continued to be that child though at the same time
> they were that child no more. (362)

The habits that the elderly acquire also represent a form of on-tological security in that they solidify their being by ensuring them that the past, present, and future will remain fixed: "Because of habit he [the old person] knows who he is. It protects him from his generalized anxieties by assuring him that tomorrow will be a rep-etition of today" (469). Commitment to habit Beauvoir describes as an aggressive act, since it is one means by which the powerless, the elderly, can impose their will on others by obliging others to respect that will (*The Coming of Age* 467). Hence, Simon Grainger, despite his list of complaints against the Birches initially balks at plans to return to the Caribbean, citing comfort in the familiar: "It ent de best but I get use to it" (*Boy-Sandwich* 97). However, ulti-mately Simon's desire to please both Clara and his grandson, whose devotion to his grandparents has compelled him to postpone for one year his undergraduate education (59), leads him to abide by the family's joint decision to return to the Caribbean.

Simone de Beauvoir in *The Coming of Age* also notes that the special tie between the grandchildren and the grandparents stems from their liminality, or their peripheral roles in society:

> In status the granddaughter and grandfather are both on the fringe of society. For the Greek tragedians a child and an aged man were alike because both were powerless: among many . . . peoples the connexion is carried much further—a single age-class includes both the child, who has scarcely emerged from the other world, and the ancient, who will soon return to it. Both are in a state of transition that frees them from certain taboos. (206-7)

As has been seen in Alice Walker's *The Third Life of Grange Copeland,* the bond between Grange and Ruth is reflective like-wise of the duality of self, the body and soul, or spirit, the latter which Grange is intent on preserving, even if the preservation car-ries as its price the destruction of his son Brownfield, "a beast Grange himself has created" (291). The symbolism of Ruth is seen in her description as "something of a miracle, something of immense value to him, to his pride, to his will to live, to his soul" (236). In this sense, the sacrificial nature of Grange's love for his granddaughter Ruth is similar to that of Sethe in Toni Morrison's *Beloved* for her daughter Beloved.

The title of Beryl Gilroy's novel *Boy-Sandwich* affirms the "betweenity" of the two generations. Tyrone recalls that "Walking between my parents or between my grandparents I felt sandwiched-in and safe. I thought of myself as a boy-sandwich. I was the filling and they the slices of bread" (36).

In *Boy-Sandwich,* Gilroy reveals that she is not only concerned with preserving the dignity of the elderly, which confinement in nursing homes effectively robs them of, but as well with dramatizing the conflicting loyalties of West Indian immigrants. Tyrone, for instance, experiences problems of adjustment following his return to the West Indies, in part due to the denial by the community of the individuation he has come to value:

> In Picktown I am trapped—in my family identity, the identity of my community and the identity of my opportunity. In London I had lived another life, grown other feelings, got to know myself as 'Tyrone.' I know how and where I am vulnerable. (110)

In light of the concerns in *Boy-Sandwich,* the novel may be considered a West Indian contribution to the been-to literature that African authors such as Chinua Achebe and Ayi Kwei Armah helped to usher in with the publication, respectively, of *No Longer at Ease* and *Fragments.*

Gilroy's preoccupation, too, with the absurd reality of death, revelatory of life's utter contingency, links the author to the existentialists Jean-Paul Sartre and Albert Camus. Death in *Frangipani House* is a constant reality. The inmate Miss Mason expires on her ninetieth birthday (40), and Mama King's childhood friend Miss Ginchi dies from breast cancer while Mama King lies recuperating in the hospital following a 'choke-and-rob' attack by thieves. In *Frangipani House,* upon the news brought by Carleton, the grandson of Miss Ginchi, of her death, Mama King muses on life's frailty:

> Mama saw Death and Life, both children of the same father, both legitimate. Death, dominant and conclusive. Life

uncertain and accidental, friable as dry earth, malleable as clay, and finally fragile as gossamer in the hands of Death. (78)

In *The Coming of Age,* Beauvoir argues that the despair suffered by the elderly over the constant loss of contemporaries is comparable to death itself, since with the loss of their peers, the elderly also lose an image of themselves that is irrevocable:

> There are people in their sixties who suffer, when they lose friends or relatives of their own generation, from the loss of a certain image of themselves that the dead possessed: with him there vanishes a part of youth or childhood that he alone remembered. . . . They have carried it away with them into the grave; and my memory can recover only a frigid imitation of it. In the 'monuments of the dead' that stud my history, it is I who am buried. (366-67)

Albeit *Boy-Sandwich* reflects a wider range of themes than its predecessor, *Frangipani House,* the novel lacks "rhetorical intensity" (Wilson 197), as when Gilroy writes of the adversarial persona of the Matron, who is actively involved in union politics and wishes to restrict Tyrone's visits to his grandparents. Tyrone had launched the following fusillade:

> There are no set visiting hours and, as long as I do not get in the way of the domestic staff, I feel free to come and go. Sometimes I visit between twelve and one, at other times between three and four-thirty. What harm is there in that? I remind her that this is a 'democratic country' in which I am allowed to make a 'democratic decision' to visit my elderly relatives whom I fear are in danger of being intimidated. All this sounds like a union minute and as a consequence they stop trying to *lid me in.* (my emphasis) (26-27)

Later in the novel, the contents of Grandma Grainger's handbag, which Grandma Grainger had placed in Tyrone's custody, are described as "sick-making" (88). Notwithstanding the "English in Translation" timbre of the language in *Boy-Sandwich,* Gilroy should be praised for giving voice in both novels to the plight of elderly nursing home inmates whose despair stems from feelings of social and psychological abandonment. According to Lucy Wilson in her article "Aging and Ageism in Paule Marshall's *Praisesong for the Widow* and Beryl Gilroy's *Frangipani House,*" the strength of the novel *Frangipani House* lies in Gilroy's use of the exile of the elderly as a metaphor for the human condition: "Mama King rise[s] Phoenix-like from the ashes of [her] past [life] to face new challenges in [her] remaining years. [She] achieves a renewed sense of self-worth after a shattering encounter with her own mortality. . . . In a sense, [she has] turned the exile of old age into a metaphor for the human condition, since ultimately we must all relinquish our hold on the familiar and embrace non-being" (197).

WORKS CITED

Beauvoir de, Simone. *The Coming of Age.* Trans. Patrick O'Brian. New York: Norton, 1996. Originally published as *La Vieillesse* (Paris: Gallimard, 1970).

Gilroy, Beryl. *Boy-Sandwich.* Oxford: Heinemann, 1989.

———. *Frangipani House.* Oxford: Heinemann, 1986.

Walker, Alice. *The Third Life of Grange Copeland.* New York: Simon & Schuster, 1970.

Wilson, Lucy. "Aging and Ageism in Paule Marshall's *Praisesong for the Widow* and Beryl Gilroy's *Frangipani House.*" *The Journal of Caribbean Studies* 7 (1989-90): 189-99.

Chapter 10

CONCLUSION:
ABANDONMENT AS A TROPE
FOR THE HUMAN CONDITION

On the threshold of a decision whether or not to travel abroad to attend a psychoanalytical congress in New York (185), the thirty-nine-year-old Anne Dubreuilh realizes that she has accommodated herself to circumstances, namely, age, rather than assume the burdensome task of altering them. Her dispassionate attitude toward life has prompted her teen-age daughter Nadine to describe her as wearing "Immaculate kid gloves" (72). In an act of defiance, Anne has a romantic fling with Scriassine; ironically, though, the failure of the affair confirms only what she suspected all along; that she has lost the ardor of her youth:

> "I might have dressed more elegantly, gone out more often,
> known the little pleasures of vanity or the burning fevers of
> the senses. But it was too late. And then all at once I
> understood why my past sometimes seemed to me to be
> someone else's. Because now I am someone else, a woman
> of thirty-nine, a woman who's aware of her age!" (86)

In that Anne's response to life is a denial of her free subjectivity, her being as a for-itself, which is associated with mutability, and her acceptance of her self-for-others, *i.e.*, her identity as a psychoanalyst, the character is demonstrative of bad faith. Hazel Barnes describes in *Humanistic Existentialism* the manner in which sincerity, an allegiance to the past, or a state of being, can lead to bad faith *(mauvaise foi):*

> With regard to the past, sincerity is possible and neces-
> sary; if a person is to be in good faith, then he must admit
> that he has been what he was, he must acknowledge his
> own acts. With regard to the present, I should go further
> than Sartre; it seems to me that sincerity is in good faith in
> so far as one describes his projects as they actually seem to
> him to be rather than as he merely desires another to see
> them. But if a person makes of himself the project of *being*
> what he is, this is not sincerity but bad faith. For the indi-
> vidual does not have a fixed nature; to assume that he must
> continue to be what he is becomes the equivalent of saying
> that some gift of heredity or previous experience is deter-
> mining his being, is cutting off his future. (54)

To illustrate the individual's potential for change, Barnes compares
the human life to a blank canvas with the individual free to concep-
tualize his own future: "[I]f one confronts a blank canvas, there
are other alternatives beside committing suicide or throwing mud at
it. One can set about scraping the surface and hope to find a
painting underneath. Or one can set about painting a picture which
will be personally gratifying" (175). The creative potential of individuals Simone de Beauvoir in *The Mandarins* likens to the amoeba-
like nature of earthworms or lobsters: "We're like those earthworms
one vainly cuts in two, or those lobsters whose legs grow back
again" (196). Nonetheless, it is the anguish before the void which
often leads to attitudes of seriousness: "But the moment of false
agony, the moment you'd rather die than mend yourself still another
time—when I think of it, I lose heart" (196).

The awareness of self-regeneration had sustained Anne during
her depression over the broken affair with American author Lewis
Brogan. Unwilling to divorce herself from her life in France, Brogan had been unwilling likewise to accommodate himself to the
lifestyle of an expatriate. The two therefore had been at an impasse. The outcome was, on the part of Brogan, a refusal to love:
"But for a man such as he, there's very little distance between a
refusal to love and an absence of love. He had deliberately decided to
stop loving me. The result was that he no longer loved me" (548).

Anne's depression at the end of the novel stems as much from
her remorse over the broken affair as it does over her vanishing
youth, which the broken affair has come to represent:

> Dead is the child who believed in paradise, dead the girl
> who thought immortal the books, the ideas, and the man
> she loved, dead the young woman who walked overwhelmed
> through a world promised to happiness. . . . They're as
> dead . . . as Lewis's love. (608)

She is tempted to commit suicide, but the voices of the living, Henri, Nadine, and Robert, summon her back to life. Her refusal to subject them to the grief of her loss gives her the strength to go on living:

> I am here. They are living, they speak to me, I am alive.
> Once more, I've jumped feet first into life. Words are enter-
> ing my ears; little by little, they take on meaning. . . . I say to
> myself that, since they were strong enough to wrest me
> from death, perhaps they will know how to help me to live
> again. (610)

Likewise, the intellectuals Henri Perron and Robert Dubreuilh make a new beginning at the end of the novel. The leftist group S.R.L. has been disbanded, no longer deemed relevant, and Henri, having lost the controlling interest in *L'Espoir* (514), the newspaper that he had founded, has tendered his letter of resignation (512). The two nonetheless embark on a new venture, the joint editorship of a new leftist weekly (573) to serve as an independent voice to the Communist Party. Earlier, Dubreuilh had made the following argument to Henri for his participation: "Besides the Communist sheets, there isn't a single leftist weekly. If we could really have a magazine with a big circulation and pictures, articles, everything, it would be well worth-while" (573).

The novel *Nausea* by Jean-Paul Sartre dramatizes the philosophical concepts contained in *Being and Nothingness*, namely, the "rock like" nature of the in-itself in contrast to the fluid one of the for-itself that produces nausea and sensations of floating: "I [Roquentin] floated, dazed by luminous fogs dragging me in all directions at once" (18). Sartre in *Existential Psychoanalysis* considers water a symbol of the for-itself in its representation of perpetual change: "[W]ater is the symbol of consciousness—its movement, its fluidity, its deceptive appearance of being solid, its perpetual flight—everything in it recalls the For-itself" (140).

Demonstrative of the fluid nature of the for-itself is Roquentin of *Nausea*. The thirty-year-old Roquentin at the end of the novel decides to abandon his historical work on the Marquis de Rollebon, considering it superfluous: "[H]istory talks about what has existed—an existant can never justify the existence of another existant" (178). Inspired by the lyrics of the jazz tune "Some of these days," which immortalize the jazz artists, or the composer and the singer, Roquentin, on the day of his return to Paris from Bouville, decides to begin a new book, a novel, in order to make possible the re-creation of himself in the memory of others:

> A book. A novel. And there would be people who would read this book and say: "Antoine Roquentin wrote it, a red-haired man who hung around cafés" and they would think about my life as I think about the Negress's: as something precious and almost legendary. (178)

Similarly, a recurrent theme in Simone Schwarz-Bart's novel *The Bridge of Beyond* is that "a [black] has seven spleens and doesn't give up just like that at the first sign of trouble" (115). Significantly, each new beginning for the major protagonist Télumée is symbolized by the move of the cabin formerly occupied with her grandmother Toussine, first from Fond-Zombi (117) to La Folie (126) and, finally, to La Ramée, which she describes as "the whole hinterland of which it is the heart—Fond-Zombi, Dara, Valbadiane, La Roncière, La Foli—so that by settling here, with my back to the sea, I am still facing, even if only in the distance, my own great forest" (168).

Télumée's first move from Fond-Zombi to La Folie had been precipitated by the dissolution of her marriage to Elie, a sawyer, whose chronic unemployment had led to dissipation and abusiveness. Prior to her death, Toussine had counseled, "You musn't stay in Fond-Zombi. Your eyes musn't go on seeing that man and that house. If you go away perhaps your heart will recover, and the root of your luck will grow and bloom again" (117).

At the end of *The Bridge of Beyond*, Télumée has re-discovered happiness, but she has experienced loss as well many times over. She is widowed and alone. Her second marriage to Amboise had ended tragically. Delegated as part of an envoy of striking cane cutters to negotiate higher wages, the appeal of the emissaries, led by Amboise, was denied, and as the men prepared to rush the factory, boilers were turned on, subsequently killing Amboise and two others (154). The presence of Sonore, a young female brought to her by a mother of eleven seeking a cure for her skin abscesses, had enabled Télumée "to grow young again" (158). The wanderer from Côte-sous-le-vent, Angel Medard, whom the two had befriended, however, had alienated Télumée and her adopted daughter. Medard poisons Sonore's mind against Télumée, "I learned later that he'd talked to Sonore in secret about her foster mother Télumée who got up and lay down with spirits. I was a charmer of children" (163), and convinces her to part company with Télumée: "While I was slaving down in the valley he had got my child's clothes together and taken her to the main road, where they caught a bus to the commune of Vieux-Habitants. I never saw Sonore again" (163).

Despite her suffering, Télumée is without rancour. She considers that suffering has not been in vain. Conversely, she considers that man is made resplendent precisely as a result of his struggle against life's vicissitudes:

> I wonder if people can bear this uncertainty, the sparkling brightness of death. But despite their frivolity about death, and whatever they do, in whatever direction they bustle, whether they chop or cut, sweat in the canefields, hold firm or abandon, or are lost in the night of the senses, there is still a sort of air, a panache, about them. They come and go, make and unmake, in the heart of uncertainty, and out of it all comes their splendour. (172)

The Creole proverb likewise encapsulates the theme of survival. Toussine tells Télumée, "However heavy a woman's breasts, her chest is always strong enough to carry them" (12).

The shared theme in Beryl Gilroy's *Boy-Sandwich* and *Frangipani House*, in Simone Schwarz-Bart's *The Bridge of Beyond*, and in Simone de Beauvoir's *The Mandarins* is, similarly, that of survival, "to survive is, after all, perpetually to begin to live again" (*The Mandarins* 234).

The Graingers, confined to a nursing home, overcome their fear of change and return to Picktown to live out their remaining years. Their return to their cultural roots, the West Indies, has had the effect of imbuing them with new life: "I can see my grandparents living on and on into the future" (*Boy-Sandwich* 105). Similarly in *Frangipani House*, Mama King has reconstituted herself—"first as child, then as woman, wife, mother, grandmother, mad-head old woman, beggar, and finally old woman at peace at last" (104). She declines the offer of Cindy and her husband Chuck to live with them in America, noting that their newborn twin sons are deserving more of their time and affection. As for herself, she is content to live out the remaining years in her own home, having re-discovered independence: "I stayin' here in this house my brother Abel buy for me" (109).

Self-regeneration is also the theme of Alice Walker's *The Third Life of Grange Copeland*, Toni Morrison's *Beloved* and *Jazz*, and of Paule Marshall's *Brown Girl, Brownstones*. In his first life at age thirty-five (17), Grange Copeland had abandoned his son Brownfield, his wife Margaret, and her illegitimate daughter Star and had fled North. A Georgia sharecropper who was $1200 in debt to Shipley, Grange had considered flight his only escape from perpetual penury, since with Shipley, the scales were always unbalanced, "Shipley did not take kindly to people running off owing him money, no matter that they had paid off whatever debts they might have owed many times over" (30-31).

The defeat of Grange had been registered when he had surveyed his family's two-room cabin that "resembled a swaybacked animal turned out to pasture" (16). He is challenged by the very prospect of having to decide the order of the repairs and, hence, decides to do nothing. His resignation is communicated through body language; that is, he shrugs (17). Increasingly, this attitude of futility extends to all that surround him. Brownfield, for example, aged fifteen, is devastated by his father's indifference. Although accustomed to his father's silences, "His father almost never spoke to him unless they had company" (5), it was only after the discovery that Grange on the night of his flight North could not bring himself to touch him that Brownfield became aware of the extent of the void between them:

He saw his father's hand draw back, without touching him. He saw him turn sharply and leave the room. He heard him leave the house. And he knew, even before he realized his father would never be back, that he hated him for everything and always would. And he most hated him because even in private and in the dark and with Brownfield presumably asleep, Grange could not bear to touch his son with his hand. (28)

The net effect on Brownfield of Grange's desertion and his mother's subsequent suicide is entrapment, since Brownfield has been shackled to the land by Grange's unending debt; also, moral dispossession, since by the loss of both parents, Brownfield has been deprived of a foundation on which to construct his future. A contrast has been made by Robert Butler to the early childhoods of Brownfield and his daughter Ruth:

A crucial part of [Ruth's] liberation is contained in the fact that she does not grow up in the kind of spiritual and emotional vacuum which blighted Brownfield's life. Although she has had to face the physical poverty and racism which characterize her father's existence, she gains the benefit of the family life he was deprived of, and this puts her in contact with nourishing cultural and personal values. (197)

In Grange's third life, Grange seeks penance for the tragedies wrought in his first life. When Grange returns to Georgia ten years later to find Brownfield married to Mem, Josie's niece, in recompense for his neglect of Brownfield and his wife Margaret, who had killed both herself and her illegitimate child after Grange's abandonment, he bestows upon Mem and the grandchildren the warmth that his own family had craved (101).

The truest measure of Grange's re-birth, however, is his nurture of his granddaughter Ruth whom Grange had taken to live with him and Josie after Brownfield, in a fit of rage, had murdered Mem. The two had become inseparable, "Where Grange went, what he did, Ruth did" (181), and her innocence, or purity, had made it impossible for Grange to relate to her his past and, in so doing, foment the racial hatred that he had found so liberating in his second life, as he had discovered that enmity is a soul destroyer (223).

Mary Helen Washington speaks of "the process of cyclical movement in the lives of Walker's black women" and notes that Ruth of *The Third Life of Grange Copeland* is reflective of the third cycle of female—the emergent woman:

> Ruth emerges into a young woman at the same time as the civil rights movement, and there is just a glimpse at the end of the novel of how that movement will affect Ruth's life. We see her becoming aware, by watching the civil rights activists—both women and men—that it is possible to struggle against the abuses of oppression. Raised in the sixties, Ruth is the natural inheritor of the changes in a new order, struggling to be, this marking the transition of the women in her family from death to life. (47)

Among the female authors that Alice Walker has identified as influencing her vision is Simone de Beauvoir, precisely because of her optimism. In an interview with John O'Brien, Walker had acknowledged some of her literary progenitors:

> The white women writers that I admire: Chopin, the Brontës, Simone De Beauvoir, and Doris Lessing, are well aware of their own oppression and search incessantly for a kind of salvation. Their characters can always envision a solution, an evolution to higher consciousness on the part of society, even when society itself cannot. Even when society is in the process of killing them for their vision. (332)

The transcendent nature of the human spirit, or the soul, is affirmed as well in Toni Morrison's *Beloved*. At the end of the novel, the ghost of Beloved has been exorcised; Sethe has been rescued from the brink of insanity; Denver has escaped isolation; Paul D, after his symbolic death (conveyed imagistically in the underground 'coffins' where he and the forty-six other prisoners are housed) and rebirth, has returned to begin a new life with Sethe and to repair the damage to their wounded psyches. He tells her, "You your best thing, Sethe. You are" (273).

The re-invention of self, poignantly rendered in the image of the snake shedding its skin, is deemed by Toni Morrison in *Jazz* as instrumental to black survival: "I talk about being new seven times

..., but back then, back there, if you was or claimed to be colored, you had to be new and stay the same every day the sun rose and every night it dropped" (135). The fifty-three-year-old Joe Trace, whose words are quoted above, has re-invented himself seven times, and at the end of the novel, he and his wife Violet are on the precipice of a new beginning. Joe's murder of the eighteen-year-old Dorcas Manfred, with whom he has had an illicit affair, has served ironically as a catalyst for re-conciliation rather than division. Heretofore, the couple of a thirty-some year marriage had been at cross purposes. Violet had attempted to supplant the golden-haired Golden Gray whom True Belle had helped rear in the grandmother's affection, thus repressing her authentic self while Joe Trace in Faulknerian fashion had sought recognition from a phantom mother, Wild. His pursuit of recognition from the parent who has rejected him, similar to that of Charles Bon in *Absalom, Absalom!* who seeks recognition from his white father, the scion Thomas Sutpen, leads him to consort with the one with whom an amorous relationship is considered taboo: the eighteen-year-old Dorcas who Violet conceives of alternately as a whore and "the daughter who fled her womb" (109). The obvious link of the characters to those in William Faulkner's novel has been noted by Nancy J. Peterson: "The episode [Golden Gray] is . . . a stunning reworking of various Faulknerian motifs, such as long-kept secrets revealed and miscegenation (recall that Morrison's masters thesis at Cornell explored the theme of alienation in Faulkner and Woolf)" (211).

The epiphany of Violet, namely, that each has sought from the other precisely that which the other could not give, finally enables the two to achieve synthesis; rather than remaining instruments of one another, at the end of the novel, they have reconciled themselves with the past that they had buried deep within themselves and have embarked on a new life together constitutive of comradeship and intimacy: "Joe found work at Paydirt, a speakeasy night job that lets him see the City do its unbelievable sky and run around with Violet in afternoon daylight" (222).

The theme of re-generation recurs in Paule Marshall's *Brown Girl, Brownstones* as well. A year following Deighton's death, Selina of *Brown Girl, Brownstones* remains in mourning, wearing the signature black expressive of her grief; nonetheless, her visits to "the tomb" that is the tenant Miss Mary's room gradually restore to her a desire for life (204). In addition to this desire to live, she craves the license to live, which the "summer woman" Suggie Skeete provides her and which delivers her from her inertness. Suggie tells Selina that she must live, not despite the death of Deighton, who was the essence of life, but because of it:

> "Life is too strong out here, mahn. You think your father would want you walking 'bout like this? Not him. Not the way he did dress. Not the way he did love his sport! Take them off. You wun forget him if you do. Beside, you got to do the living for him." (209)

Not long after this tête à tête, Suggie is evicted as an undesirable tenant by Silla in a bid for her daughter's affection. The sixteen-year-old Selina vows, however, "to show her" (211) and becomes involved thereafter with the twenty-nine-year-old Clive Springer, a beat artist, whose "slack body" (228), "hooded eyes" (235), and silken textured skin (238) recall Deighton. Similarly, like Deighton, he has a penchant for starting projects that he never finishes: "A closed grand piano, scarred by cigarette burns, was near an old-fashioned coal stove; an easel with an unfinished painting stood beside the sink under the window, with the palette, brushes and oils on the drainboard" (241).

The sado-masochistic relationship of Clive with his mother is another reminder of Deighton and his sado-masochistic relationship with Silla that has begun its re-enactment in Selina's relationship with Silla. Selina's advice to Clive foretells her own departure at the end of the novel which seems necessary in order to avoid a repetition of the destructive cycle:

> "It would hurt her [Clive's mother] less, it would be far kinder of you if you did go away. Far away, and send her a postcard every once in a while telling how nice the weather is! That would be better than staying here—reminding her of what she's done to you, and with her reminding you of what you've done to her. . . ." (296)

Similarly, in Buchi Emecheta's *In the Ditch*, the new beginning comes when Adah accepts change, thus making it possible for her to begin her slow climb out of "the ditch." At first Adah had found reasons to reject the offers from the Council to move out of the Mansions. The first was the offer of a maisonette on the four-teenth and fifteenth floors of a high-rise building (120); the second, a shared house with an elderly woman who owned "an elephant" of a dog (123). When the third offer had come, Adah had accepted it, deciding that "The last place in which she was going to incarcer-ate herself was in the ditch" (127).

Finally, Rama's emergence at the end of *So Long a Letter* from seclusion after the traditional Islamic period of mourning—four months and ten days (8)—for her late husband Modou Fall repre-sents a new beginning. On the eve of Aïssatou's arrival, Rama eagerly awaits the reunion with her childhood friend. She acknowl-edges that their friendship has been strengthened by their mutual loss. Subsequently, it confirms the truth of her closing statement: "It is from the dirty and nauseating humus that the green plant sprouts into life" (89).

The grandeur of women that these works affirm is illuminated by the mythic character Sisyphus who, condemned by the gods to roll a boulder up a steep hill only to see it roll down again once it has reached the summit, is nonetheless wedded, or reconciled, to his fate. That is, with each descent, he is determined to make a new beginning, despite his recognition of the futility of his struggle. Albert Camus has written in *The Myth of Sisyphus*:

> As for this myth, one sees merely the whole effort of a body straining to raise the huge stone, to roll it and push it up a slope a hundred times over; one sees the face screwed up, the cheek tight against the stone, the shoulder bracing the clay-covered mass, the foot wedging it, *the fresh start* (my emphasis) with arms outstretched, the wholly human secu-rity of two-earth-clotted hands. At the very end of his long effort measured by skyless space and time without depth, the purpose is achieved. . . . He is stronger than his rock. (120-21)

A dramatization of struggle in perpetuity is contained in Albert Camus' novel *The Plague*. The town of Oran, "a large French port on the Algerian coast" (3), has been stricken by an outbreak of the plague that has resulted in the following "prophylactic measures": citizens who have displayed symptoms of the epidemic have been quarantined; the town's gates have been closed; and a curfew has been imposed to curb lawlessness (161). Dr. Rieux, the physician who narrates the events of the novel, has, before the wane of the plague, the hopeless task of diagnosis and evacuation of plague victims to the quarantine camps, where they eventually expire. Despite this grim reality, Dr. Rieux perseveres in his battle against the plague, refusing to admit defeat. Some perceive Dr. Rieux's resolve as "abstraction," yet it is his seeming mercilessness that enables him daily to "set [his] shoulders to the wheel [rock] again":

> "You haven't a heart!" a woman told him on one occasion. She was wrong; he had one. It saw him through his twenty-hour day, when he hourly watched men dying who were meant to live. It enabled him to start anew each morning. He had just enough heart for that, as things were now. (178)

The theme of persistent struggle in the face of defeat is also encapsulated in the journalist Rambert who, not native to the town, had been cut off from his loved one after the town's gates had been closed. Rambert, however, prior to becoming a member of the voluntary sanitary squads, never tired of seeking ways to smuggle himself out of Oran. After being put in contact by Cottard with the leader of a smuggling ring, Rambert's plot to smuggle himself out is foiled continuously. Not only must he make contact with the smuggler's third-hand contacts, "He [Gonzales] is going to put you in touch with two of our friends who will introduce you to some sentries whom we've squared" (139), but once the contact has been made, the third-hand contacts, the armed sentries, must await their turn at guard duty. The upshot is endless snafus and waiting. In light of the ceaseless effort demanded in the face of insuperable odds, Rambert likens his quest for liberty to the plague:

> "So you haven't understood yet?" Rambert shrugged his shoulders almost scornfully.
> "Understood what?"
> "The plague."

"Ah!" Rieux exclaimed.
"No, you haven't understood that it means exactly that—
the same thing over and over and over again." (152)

The Sisyphean rock, or "the plague," may be conceived as the burden of race, caste, gender, poverty, or age that inhibits individuals' capacity for free expression. The works by African-American, African, and Caribbean female authors, despite their specific emphasis on culture, nonetheless, have a universal appeal inasmuch as the limitations imposed by race, gender, poverty, and age invariably reflect the limitations, or the facticity, of the human condition and the ability of humankind to triumph over them.

Of the female authors examined in this study—Mariama Bâ, Buchi Emecheta, Toni Morrison, and Alice Walker—Bâ proposes, as a response to female oppression, sisterhood, as well as education and economic independence; Emecheta, education, and the African American writer Toni Morrison, reciprocal self-love. Terry Otten asserts in *The Crime of Innocence in the Fiction of Toni Morrison* that "In all Morrison's novels alienation from the community . . . invariably leads to dire consequences, and the reassertion of community is necessary for the recovery of order and wholeness" (93). Alice Walker and Paule Marshall, however, are unique in that they make a plea for psychic healing on the part of both males and females that would disrupt the circularity of oppression and would prohibit, in the words of the R & B artist Tevin Campbell, the playing of "the same old game."

Albert Camus in his creation of the Stranger, in the novel by the same title, identifies the absurd man as one who "will not play the game" (Barnes 177). That is, he is a man without pretension of his ineluctable fate, namely, that he is mortal and lives under a death sentence. Thus, the absurd man lives in the moment, aware that death circumscribes the quantity of his experiences. Camus writes in *The Myth of Sisyphus:* "The present and the succession of presents before a soul which is at every moment conscious—that is the ideal of the absurd man" (63-64).

The absorption in the moment is descriptive of Meursault in *The Stranger.* Therein Meursault presides at his mother's wake at the Home of Aged Persons where she was an inmate and makes decisions attuned to his physical state (80). He refuses to view the corpse of his mother and when asked by the doorkeeper to give a reason for his refusal, responds, "Well, really I couldn't say" (6). On trial later for the murder of an Arab that he knew only second-hand (the Arab was brother to the mistress of Raymond Sintès, a neighbor whom Meursault had befriended), Meursault's indictment rests on the Prosecutor's argument that Meursault's failure to weep at his mother's funeral is revelatory of his criminal nature. For his part, Camus has remarked that Meursault's crime is his refusal to "play the game," or to lie:

> Now, lying is not only saying what is not. It's also saying more than *is,* and in matters of the human heart, more than we feel. We all do this every day, in order to simplify life. Meursault, contrary to appearances, does not want to sim-plify life. He tells the truth, he refuses to exaggerate his feelings, and immediately society feels itself threatened. (qtd. in Barnes 177)

Juxtaposed to Meursault is the chaplain who visits Meursault in his prison cell while he awaits execution for murder. The "cocksure-ness" of the chaplain in an afterlife and his concomitant denial of his mortality make him demonstrative of Sartrean bad faith. Hence, he is described by Meursault as "living . . . like a corpse . . . [not] sure of being alive" (151). Meursault, on the other hand, in a mo-ment of epiphany, has recognized the absurd nature of the exist-ence of man, namely, his mortality that accords him his passion. Consequently, he understands for the first time his mother's desire to take a fiancé at sixty: "With death so near, Mother must have felt like someone on the brink of freedom, ready to start life all over again. No one, no one in the world had any right to weep for her. And I, too, felt ready to start life all over again" (154).

Morvan Lebesque, author of *Portrait of Camus: An Illustrated Biography,* has remarked the resemblance between the creator and his creations. More to the point, he has remarked Camus' journalistic integrity, or the author's refusal to "play the game" while employed from 1938 to 1940 at the newspaper *Alger Républicain,* rival to the powerful *Echo d'Alger* (21): "Camus wrote to be understood and avoided all unclarity and all base desire to please. And, we may be sure, he was understood only too well. By 1938 indignant voices were heard attacking *this journalist who was not playing the game"* (my emphasis). Those who "have invented pleasing rules of the game which make it easier for them to maintain an unperturbed balance even while they stand on the abyss" (Petersen 49) are the antithesis of those who prefer to live life consciously. In effect, those who prefer to live incognito, such as Deighton Boyce of Marshall's *Brown Girl, Brownstones*, who is a follower of the Divine movement, exist in bad faith.

Hazel E. Barnes identifies as a form of "masculine bad faith" the preconceptions that some hold of women that deny women as free subjectivities:

> Masculine bad faith consists in regarding women only as women instead of as human beings. It may take the form of contempt, in which case women serve to bolster the male ego in much the same way as the Jew helps to guarantee the position of the anti-Semite. It may also appear in the guise of exaggerated respect such as we find in knightly circles during the Age of Chivalry or in pre-Civil War Southern United States. In this case woman is supposedly put on a pedestal even above man. But she holds this position at the cost of allowing herself to be determined entirely by the ideal which man has of her. (137)

Emblematic of the "masculine bad faith" are the attitudes, respectively, of John Buddy of Zora Neale Hurston's *Jonah's Gourd Vine*, Brownfield of Alice Walker's *The Third Life of Grange Copeland*, Francis of Buchi Emecheta's *Second-Class Citizen*, and Ousmane of Mariama Bâ's *Scarlet Song* that devalue women. On the other hand, emblematic of egalitarian relationships are those existent between Hélène and Jean Blomart of *The Blood of Others*, by Simone de Beauvoir, and Congo Jane and Will Cudjoe of *Daughters*, by Paule Marshall. The coalescence of the respective couples is the outgrowth of their confraternity in defense of human liberty. For example, Hélène and Jean Blomart had worked alongside one another as part of the Resistance movement during the German Occupation, while Congo Jane and Will Cudjoe had fought side by side to rid the island of its colonialist divisions. The monument that has been erected in the latter's memory becomes not only representative of their nationalist spirit, but also their comradeship. As legend has it, "You can't call her name or his without calling or at least thinking of the other, they were so close" (377). Marshall considers their relationship in *Daughters* as a model for the future: "Whatever feminist note is struck in the novel is not meant to obscure what I hope will be seen as a major theme in *Daughters:* the need for black men and women to come together in *wholeness* and unity. It is this which informs the novel at its deepest level" (Dance 20).

Hence, it may be concluded that, collectively, the works in this study are endowed with the humanistic quality often associated with existentialist thought. Hazel Barnes describes humanistic existentialism as the literature of possibility because it delineates human potentiality, or the capacity for humankind to re-invent themselves. The following quote may also be applicable in part to the works contained in this study: "Because it presents to us a new picture of man [woman], and because this picture is one which includes the view that man [woman] is free to determine future portraits of himself [herself], the existentialist is concerned above all else with pointing out to us what are the possibilities of man [woman]" (*Humanistic Existentialism* 37).

WORKS CITED

Bâ, Mariama. *So Long a Letter.* Trans. Modupé Bodé-Thomas. London: Heinemann, 1981.

Barnes, Hazel E. *Humanistic Existentialism: The Literature of Possibility.* Lincoln: U of Nebraska P, 1959.

Beauvoir, Simone de. *The Mandarins.* Trans. Leonard M. Friedman. New York: Norton, 1991. Originally published in French as *Les mandarins* (Paris: Gallimard, 1954).

―――. *The Blood of Others.* Trans. Roger Senhouse and Yvonne Moyse. New York: Knopf, 1948. Originally published in French as *Le sang des autres* (Paris: Gallimard, 1945).

Butler, Robert James. "Alice Walker's Vision of the South in *The Third Life of Grange Copeland.*" *African American Review* 27, no. 2 (summer 1993): 195-204.

Camus, Albert. *The Myth of Sisyphus and Other Essays.* New York: Knopf, 1955. Originally published in French as *Le Mythe de Sisyphe* (Paris: Gallimard, 1942).

———. *The Plague.* Trans. Stuart Gilbert. New York: Knopf, 1948. First published by Gallimard, 1947.

———. *The Stranger.* New York: Knopf, 1946. Originally published in French as *L'Etranger* (Paris: Gallimard, 1942).

Emecheta, Buchi. *In the Ditch.* Oxford: Heinemann, 1994.

Gilroy, Beryl. *Boy-Sandwich.* Oxford: Heinemann, 1989.

———. *Frangipani House.* Oxford: Heinemann, 1986.

Lebesque, Morvan. *Portrait of Camus: An Illustrated Biography.* Trans. T.C. Sharman. New York: Herder and Herder, 1971. Originally published in French as *Camus par lui-même* (Paris: Editions du Seuil, 1963).

Marshall, Paule. *Brown Girl, Brownstones.* New York: Feminist Press, 1981.

———. *Daughters.* New York: Plume, 1992.

———. Interview by Daryl Cumber Dance. *The Southern Review* 28, no. 1 (winter 1992): 1-20.

Morrison, Toni. *Beloved.* New York: New American Library, 1987.

———. *Jazz.* New York: Knopf, 1992.

Otten, Terry. *The Crime of Innocence in the Fiction of Toni Morrison.* Columbia: U of Missouri P, 1989.

Petersen, Carol. *Albert Camus.* Trans. Alexander Gode. New York: Frederick Ungar, 1969.

Peterson, Nancy J. "'Say make me, remake me': Toni Morrison and the Reconstruction of African-American History." *Toni Morrison: Critical and Theoretical Approaches.* Ed. Nancy J. Peterson. Baltimore: John Hopkins UP, 1997. 201-21.

Sartre, Jean-Paul. *Existential Psychoanalysis.* Trans. Hazel E. Barnes. New York: Philosophical Library, 1953.

———. *Nausea.* Trans. Lloyd Alexander. New York: New Directions, 1964. Originally published in French as *La Nausée* (Paris: Gallimard, 1938).

Schwarz-Bart, Simone. *The Bridge of Beyond.* Trans. Barbara Bray. Oxford: Heinemann, 1982. First published in French as *Pluie et vent sur Télumée Miracle,* 1972.

Walker, Alice. *The Third Life of Grange Copeland.* New York: Simon & Schuster, 1970.

———. "An Interview with John O'Brien." *Alice Walker: Critical Perspectives Past and Present.* Eds. Henry Louis Gates, Jr., and K.A. Appiah. Amistad Literary Series. New York: Amistad, 1993. 326-46.

Washington, Mary Helen. "An Essay on Alice Walker." Gates and Appiah, 37-49.

Winchell, Donna Haisty. *Alice Walker.* Twayne's U.S. Authors Series 596. New York: Twayne, 1992.

BIBLIOGRAPHY

Abrahams, Cecil, ed. *The Tragic Life: Bessie Head and Literature in Southern Africa.* Trenton: Africa World Press, 1990.

Abruña de, Laura Niesen. "The Ambivalence of Mirroring and Female Bonding in Paule Marshall's *Brown Girl, Brownstones.*" *International Women's Writing: New Landscapes of Identity.* Contributions in Women's Studies 147, eds. Anne Brown, and Marjanne E. Goozé. Westport: Greenwood, 1995.

Aegerter, Lindsay Pentolfe. "A Dialectic of Autonomy and Community: Tsitsi Dangarembga's *Nervous Conditions.*" *Tulsa Studies in Women's Literature* 15 (1996): 231-40.

d'Almeida, Irène Assiba. "The Concept of Choice in Mariama Bâ's Fiction." *Ngambika: Studies of Women in African Literature.* Eds. Carol Boyce Davies and Anne Adams Graves. Trenton: Africa World Press, 1986.

Anthony, Barthelemy. "Western Time, African Lives: Time in the Novels of Buchi Emecheta." *Callaloo: A Journal of African American and African Arts and Letters* 12, no. 3 (summer 1989): 559-74.

Atwood, Margaret. "Haunted by Their Nightmares." Rev. of *Beloved,* by Toni Morrison. *New York Times Book Review,* 13 September 1987: 49-50.

Bâ, Mariama. *Scarlet Song.* Trans. Dorothy S. Blair. Essex: Longman, 1986.

———. *So Long a Letter.* Trans. Modupé Bodé-Thomas. London: Heinemann, 1981.

Baldwin, James. *Go Tell It on the Mountain.* New York: Dell, 1952.

Barksdale, Richard K. "Castration Symbolism in Recent Black American Fiction." *College Language Association Journal* 29, no. 4 (June 1986): 400-13.

Barnes, Hazel E. *Humanistic Existentialism: The Literature of Possibility.* Lincoln: U of Nebraska P, 1959.

Bazin, Nancy Topping. "Feminist Perspectives in African Fiction: Bessie Head and Buchi Emecheta." *Black Scholar* 17, no. 2 (March-April 1986): 34-40.

————. "Southern Africa and the Theme of Madness: Novels by Dorris Lessing, Bessie Head, and Nadine Gordimer." Brown and Goozé, 137-49.

————. "Venturing into Feminist Consciousness: Two Protagonists from the Fiction of Buchi Emecheta and Bessie Head." *The Tragic Life: Bessie Head and Literature in Southern Africa.* Ed. Cecil Abrahams. Trenton: Africa World Press, 1990. Originally published in *SAGE: A Scholarly Journal on Black Women* 2, no. 1 (spring 1985): 32-36.

————. "Weight of Custom, Signs of Change: Feminism in the Literature of African Women." *World Literature Written in English* 25, no. 2 (1985): 183-97.

Beauvoir, Simone de. *The Blood of Others.* Trans. Roger Senhouse and Yvonne Moyse. New York: Knopf, 1948. Originally published *Le sang des autres* (Paris: Gallimard, 1945).

————. *The Coming of Age.* Trans. Patrick O'Brian. New York: Norton, 1996. Originally published as *La Vieillesse* (Paris: Gallimard, 1970).

————. *The Mandarins.* Trans. Leonard M. Friedman. New York: Norton, 1991. Originally published in French as *Les mandarins* (Paris: Gallimard, 1954).

————. *The Second Sex.* Trans. H.M. Parshley. New York: Knopf, 1952. Originally published in French as *Le Deuxième Sexe* (Paris: Gallimard, 1949).

Benjamin, Jessica. *The Bonds of Love: Psychoanalysis, Feminism, and the Problem of Domination.* New York: Random, 1988.

Berger, Roger A. "The Politics of Madness in Bessie Head's *A Question of Power.*" Abrahams, 31-43.

Bloom, Harold, ed. *Modern Critical Views: Toni Morrison.* New York: Chelsea House, 1990.

Bone, Robert A. "James Baldwin." *James Baldwin: A Collection of Critical Essays.* Ed. Keneth Kinnamon. Englewood Cliffs: Prentice, 1974.

Brawley, Benjamin. *A Short History of the American Negro.* Rev. ed. New York: Macmillan, 1924.

Brice-Finch, Jacqueline. "Paule Marshall's Women Warriors." *Xavier Review* 13 (spring 1993): 77-84.

Brickell, Herschel. "A Woman Saved." Rev. of *Seraph on the Suwanee,* by Zora Neale Hurston. *Critical Essays on Zora Neale Hurston.* Ed. Gloria L. Cronin. New York: G.K. Hall, 1998. 195-96.

Brock, Sabine, and Anne Koenen. "Alice Walker in Search of Zora Neale Hurston: Rediscovering a Black Female Literary Tradition." Günter Lenz, ed. 167-77.

Brown, Alan. "'De Beast' Within: The Role of Nature in *Jonah's Gourd Vine.*" *Zora in Florida.* Eds. Steve Glassman and Kathryn Lee Seidel. Orlando: U of Central Florida P, 1991.

Brown, Anne., and Marjanne E. Goozé, eds. *International Women's Writing: New Landscapes of Identity.* Contributions in Women's Studies 147. Westport: Greenwood, 1995.

Brown, Ella. "Reactions to Western Values as Reflected in African Novels." *Phylon: A Review of Race and Culture* 48, no. 3 (fall 1987): 216-28.

Bruner, Charlotte, and David Bruner. "Buchi Emecheta and Maryse Conde: Contemporary Writing from Africa and the Caribbean." *World Literature Today* 51, no. 1 (winter 1985): 9-13.

Buncombe, Marie H. "Androgyny as Metaphor in Alice Walker's Novels." *College Language Association Journal* 30, no. 4 (June 1987): 419-27.

Busia, Abena P.B. "This Gift of Metaphor: Symbolic Strategies and the Triumph of Survival in Simone Schwarz-Bart's *The Bridge of Beyond. Out of the Kumbla: Caribbean Women and Literature.* Eds. Carole Boyce Davies and Elaine Savory Fido. Trenton: Africa World Press, 1990.

―――. "Words Whispered over Voids: A Context for Black Women's Rebellious Voices in the Novel of the African Diaspora." *Studies in Black Literature.* Vol. 3. Eds. Joe Weixlmann and Houston A. Baker, Jr. Greenwood, Florida: Penkeville Publishing Company, 1988.

Butler, Robert James. "Alice Walker's Vision of the South in '*The Third Life of Grange Copeland.*'" *African American Review* 27, no. 2 (summer 1993): 195-205.

―――. "Making a Way out of No Way: The Open Journey in Alice Walker's *The Third Life of Grange Copeland.*" *Black American Literature Forum* 22, no. 1 (spring 1988): 65-79.

Cairncross, John. *After Polygamy Was Made a Sin: The Social History of Christian Polygamy.* London: Routledge and Kegan Paul, 1974.

Campbell, Josie P. "To Sing the Song, To Tell the Tale: A Study of Toni Morrison and Simone Schwarz-Bart." *Comparative Literature Studies* 22, no. 3 (fall 1985): 394-412.

Camus, Albert. "Author's Preface." *Caligula and Three Other Plays.* By Camus. Trans. Justin O'Brien. New York: Knopf, 1958. v-x.

―――. *Caligula and Three Other Plays.* Trans. Stuart Gilbert. New York: Knopf, 1958.

―――. *The Myth of Sisyphus and Other Essays.* Trans. Justin O'Brien. New York: Knopf, 1955. Originally published in French as *Le Mythe de Sisyphe* (Paris: Gallimard, 1942).

―――. *The Plague.* Trans. Stuart Gilbert. New York: Random, 1948. First published by Gallimard, 1947.

————. *The Rebel: An Essay on Man in Revolt.* Trans. Anthony Bower. New York: Knopf, 1956. Originally published in French as *L'Homme Révolté* (Paris: Gallimard, 1951).

————. *The Stranger.* Trans. Stuart Gilbert. New York: Knopf, 1946. Originally published in French as *L'Etranger* (Paris: Gallimard, 1942).

Carpenter, Lynette, and Wendy K. Kolmar, eds. *Haunting the House of Fiction: Feminist Perspectives on Ghost Stories by American Women.* Knoxville: U of Tennessee P, 1991.

Cham, Mbye B. "Contemporary Society and the Female Imagination: A Study of the Novels of Mariama Bâ." *Women in African Literature* 15 (1987): 89-101.

Chambers, Jack. *Milestones 2: The Music and Times of Miles Davis Since 1960.* 2 vols. New York: Morrow, 1985.

Chancer, Lynn S. *Sadomasochism in Everyday Life: The Dynamics of Power and Powerlessness.* New Brunswick, New Jersey: Rutgers UP, 1992.

Christian, Barbara. *Black Women Novelists: The Development of a Tradition, 1892-1976.* Westport, CT: Greenwood, 1980.

Christian, Barbara, ed. *"Everyday Use": Women Writers, Texts and Contexts.* New Brunswick:Rutgers UP, 1994.

Ciolkowski, Laura E. "Navigating the *Wide Sargasso Sea:* Colonial History, English Fiction, and British Empire." *Twentieth Century Literature* 43 (fall 1997): 339-59.

Cobham, Rhonda. "Revisioning our Kumblas: Transforming Feminist and Nationalist Agendas in Three Caribbean Women's Texts." *Callaloo* 16, no. 1 (winter 1993): 44-64.

Coundouriotis, Eleni. "Authority and Invention in the Fiction of Bessie Head." *Research in African Literatures* 27 (1996): 17-32.

Cronin, Gloria L. "Introduction: Going to the Far Horizon." *Critical Essays on Zora Neale Hurston.* Critical Essays on American Literature. Ed. James Nagel. New York: G.K. Hall, 1998. 1-29.

Cudjoe, Selwyn R. *V.S. Naipaul: A Materialist Reading.* Amherst: U of Massachusetts P, 1988.

Cummings, Kate. "Reclaiming the Mother('s) Tongue: *Beloved, Ceremony, Mothers and Shadows.*" *College English* 52, no. 5 (1990): 552-69.

Dance, Daryl. "Daddy May Bring Home Some Bread, But He Don't Cut No Ice: The Economic Plight of the Father Figure in Black American Literature."*Journal of Afro-American Issues* 3 (summer/fall 1975): 297-308.

Dangarembga, Tsitsi. *Nervous Conditions.* Seattle: Seal Press, 1988.

Davies, Carole Boyce. *Black Women, Writing and Identity: Migrations of the Subject.* London and New York: Routledge, 1994.

————. "Mother Right/Write Revisited: *Beloved* and *Dessa Rose* and the Construction of Motherhood in Black Women's Fiction." *Narrating Mothers: Theorizing Maternal Subjectivities.* Eds. Brenda O. Daly and Maureen T. Reddy. Knoxville: U of Tennessee P, 1991.

Davies, Carole Boyce, and Elaine Savory Fido, eds. *Out of the Kumbla: Caribbean Women and Literature.* Trenton: Africa World Press, 1990.

Davies, Carole Boyce, and Anne Adams Graves, eds. *Ngambika: Studies of Women in African Literature.* Trenton: Africa World Press, 1986.

Davis, Christina. "Mother and Writer: Means of Empowerment in the Work of Buchi Emecheta." *Commonwealth: Essays and Studies* 13, no. 1 (autumn 1990): 13-21.

Davis, Cynthia A. "Self, Society, and Myth in Toni Morrison's Fiction." Bloom, 7-25.

Davis, George A., and O. Fred Donaldson. *Blacks in the United States: A Geographic Perspective.* Boston: Houghton, 1975.

Davison, Carol Margaret. "A Method in the Madness: Bessie Head's *A Question of Power.*" Abrahams, 19-29.

Delancey, Dayle. "Motherlove Is a Killer: *Sula, Beloved,* and the Deadly Trinity of Motherlove." *SAGE* 7, no. 2 (fall 1990): 15-18.

Denniston, Dorothy Hamner. *The Fiction of Paule Marshall: Reconstructions of History, Culture, and Gender.* Knoxville: U of Tennessee P, 1995.

Dickerson, Vannessa D. "The Property of Being in Paule Marshall's *Brown Girl, Brownstones.*" *Obsidian II: Black Literature in Review* 6, no. 3 (winter 1991): 1-13.

Dieke, Ikenna. "Toward a Monastic Idealism: The Thematics of Alice Walker's *The Temple of My Familiar.*" *African American Review* 26, no. 3 (fall 1992): 507-14.

Douglass, Frederick. *Narrative of the Life of Frederick Douglass: An American Slave.* 1845. Reprint. Cambridge: Harvard UP, 1960.

Dove, Rita. Foreword. *Jonah's Gourd Vine,* by Zora Neale Hurston. 1934. Reprint. New York: Harper, 1990. vii-xv.

"Drum." *Funk and Wagnalls Standard Dictionary of Folklore, Mythology and Legend.* New York: Funk and Wagnalls, 1972.

"Drum." *Larousse Dictionary of World Folklore.* Ed. Alison Jones. New York: Larousse, 1995.

Edson, Laura. "Mariama Bâ and the Politics of the Family." *Studies in Twentieth Century Literature* 17, no. 1 (winter 1993): 13-25.

Edwards, Thomas R. "Ghost Story." Rev. of *Beloved,* by Toni Morrison. *The New York Review of Books,* 5 November 1987: 18-19.

Eilersen, Gillian Stead. *Bessie Head, Thunder Behind Her Ears: Her Life and Writing.* Portsmouth, NH: Heinemann, 1995.

Eliade, Mircea, ed. *The Encyclopedia of Religion* 9. New York: Macmillan, 1987.

Emecheta, Buchi. *The Family*. New York: George Braziller, 1990.

———. *Head Above Water: An Autobiography*. London: Heinemann, 1986.

———. *In the Ditch*. Oxford: Heinemann, 1972.

———. Interview by Susheila Nasta. *Guardian Conversations* Videocassette. The Roland Collection of Films on Art, 1988.

———. *The Joys of Motherhood*. New York: George Braziller, 1979.

———. *Second Class Citizen*. New York: George Braziller, 1975.

Emenyonu, Ernest N. "Technique and Language in Buchi Emecheta's *The Bride Price, The Slave Girl* and *The Joys of Motherhood*." *The Journal of Commonwealth Literature* 23, no. 1 (1988): 130-41.

Ensslen, Klaus. "History and Fiction in Alice Walker's *The Third Life of Grange Copeland* and Ernest Gaines' *The Autobiography of Miss Jane Pittman*." *History and Tradition in Afro-American Culture*. Ed. Günter H. Lenz. Frankfurt: Campus Verlag, 1984.

Evans, Mari, ed. *Black Women Writers (1950-1980): A Critical Evaluation*. New York: Doubleday, 1984.

Fanon, Frantz. *Black Skin, White Masks*. Trans. Charles Lam Markmann. New York: Grove, 1967.

———. *The Wretched of the Earth*. Trans. Constance Farrington. New York: Grove, 1963.

Faulkner, William. *Absalom, Absalom!* New York: Random, 1936.

Felton, Estelle. "Jonah's Gourd Vine (1934)." Rev. of *Jonah's Gourd Vine*, by Zora Neale Hurston. *Zora Neale Hurston: Critical Perspectives Past and Present*. Eds. Henry Louis Gates, Jr. and K.A. Appiah. New York: Amistad, 1993. Originally published in *Opportunity*, August 1934.

Fetzer, Glenn W. "Women's Search for Voice and the Problem of Knowing in the Novels of Mariama Bâ." *College Language Association Journal* 35 (1991): 31-41.

Finkelman, Paul. *Dred Scott v. Sandford: A Brief History with Documents*. The Bedford Series in History and Culture. Boston: Bedford, 1997.

Fishburn, Katherine. *Reading Buchi Emecheta: Cross-Cultural Conversations*. Contributions to the Study of World Literature 61. Westport: Greenwood, 1995.

Fitzgerald, Jennifer. "Selfhood and Community: Psychoanalysis and Discourse in *Beloved*." *Modern Fiction Studies* 39, nos. 3 and 4 (fall/winter 1993): 669-87.

Frank, Katherine. "The Death of the Slave Girl: African Womanhood in the Novels of Buchi Emecheta." *World Literature Written in English* 21, no. 3 (autumn 1982): 476-97.

———. "Feminist Criticism and the African Novel." *African Literature Today* 14 (1984): 34-48.

Furman, Jane. *Toni Morrison's Fiction.* Columbia: U of South Carolina P, 1996.

Gaston, Karen C. "Women in the Lives of Grange Copeland." *College Language Association Journal* 24, no. 3 (March 1981): 276-86.

Gates, Henry Louis, Jr., and K.A. Appiah, eds. *Alice Walker: Critical Perspectives Past and Present.* New York: Amistad, 1993.

———. *The Classic Slave Narratives.* New York: Penguin, 1987.

———. *Zora Neale Hurston: Critical Perspectives Past and Present.* New York: Amistad, 1993.

Gérard, Albert, and Jeannine Laurent. "Sembene's Progeny: A New Trend in the Senegalese Novel." *Studies in Twentieth Century Literature* 4, no. 2 (spring 1980): 133-45.

Gibson, William. *Family Life and Morality: Studies in Black and White.* Washington, D.C.:UP of America, 1980.

Gilbert, Sandra M., and Susan Gubar. *The Madwoman in the Attic: The Woman Writer and the Nineteenth-Century Literary Imagination.* New Haven: Yale UP, 1979.

Gillespie, Marcia Ann. "Toni Morrison's *Beloved:* Out of Slavery's Inferno." *Ms.* (November 1987): 68.

Gilroy, Beryl. *Boy-Sandwich.* Oxford: Heinemann, 1989.

———. *Frangipani House.* Oxford: Heinemann, 1986.

Glassman, Steve, and Kathryn Lee Seidel, eds. *Zora in Florida.* Orlando: U of Central Florida P, 1991.

Gordon, Lewis R., ed. *Existence in Black: An Anthology of Black Existential Philosophy.* New York: Routledge, 1994.

Grimes, Dorothy. "Mariama Bâ's *So Long a Letter* and Alice Walker's *In Search of Our Mothers' Gardens:* A Senegalese and an African American Perspective on 'Womanism.'" *Global Perspectives on Teaching Literature.* Eds. Sandra Ward Lott, Maureen S.G. Hawkins, and Norman McMillan. Urbana: National Council of Teachers of English, 1993.

Gruening, Martha. "Jonah's Gourd Vine (1934)." Rev. of *Jonah's Gourd Vine,* by Zora Neale Hurston. *Zora Neale Hurston: Critical Perspectives Past and Present.* Eds. Henry Louis Gates, Jr. and K.A. Appiah. New York: Amistad, 1993. Originally published in *The New Republic,* 11 July 1934.

Hamner, Robert D. Ed. *Critical Perspectives on V.S. Naipaul.* Washington, D.C.: Three Continents Press, 1977.

Harding, Wendy, and Jacky Martin. "Reading at the Cultural Interface: The Corn Symbolism of *Beloved." MELUS: The Journal of the Soci-*

ety for the Study of the Multi-Ethnic Literature of the United States 19, no. 2 (summer 1994): 85-97.

———. *A World of Difference: An Inter-Cultural Study of Toni Morrison's Novels*. Contributions in Afro-American Studies 171. Westport: Greenwood, 1994.

Harris, Trudier. "Three Black Women Writers and Humanism: A Folk Perspective." *Black American Literature and Humanism*. Ed. R. Baxter Miller. Lexington: U of Kentucky P, 1981.

Head, Bessie. *Maru*. London: Heinemann, 1971.

———. *A Question of Power*. London: Heinemann, 1974.

Heller, Scott. "Africa Diaspora Studies: Reconceptualizing Experiences of Blacks Worldwide." *Chronicle of Higher Education*, 3 June 1992, sec. A: 7-8.

Hemenway, Robert E. *Zora Neale Hurston: A Literary Biography*. With a Foreword by Alice Walker. Urbana: U of Illinois P, 1977.

Hernton, Calvin C. *Sex and Racism in America*. New York: Anchor, 1965.

Heumann, Virginia Kearney. "Morrison's 'Beloved.'" *The Explicator* 54 (fall 1995): 46-50.

Higman, B.W. *Slave Populations of the British Caribbean 1807-1834*. Baltimore: John Hopkins UP, 1984.

Hill, Janice E. "Purging a Plate Full of Colonial History: The 'Nervous Conditions' of Silent Girls." *College Literature* 22 (1995): 78-91.

Hillman, Eugene. *Polygamy Reconsidered: African Plural Marriage and the Christian Churches*. Maryknoll, NY: Orbis, 1975.

Hirsch, Marianne. "Maternity and Rememory: Toni Morrison's *Beloved*." *Representations of Motherhood*. Eds. Donna Bassin, Margaret Honey, and Meryle Mahrer Kaplan. New Haven: Yale UP, 1944.

Holloway, Karla F.C., and Stephanie A. Demetrakopoulos. *New Dimensions of Spirituality: A Biracial and Bicultural Reading of the Novels of Toni Morrison*. New York: Greenwood, 1987.

———. *Moorings & Metaphors: Figures of Culture and Gender in Black Women's Literature*. New Brunswick, N.J.: Rutgers UP, 1992.

hooks, bell. *Sisters of the Yam: Black Women and Self-Recovery*. New York: South End Press, 1993.

Horvitz, Deborah, "Nameless Ghosts: Possession and Dispossession in *Beloved*." *Studies in American Fiction* 17, no. 2 (fall 1989): 157-67.

House, Elizabeth. "Toni Morrison's Ghost: The Beloved Who Is Not Beloved." *Studies in American Fiction* 18, no. 1 (spring 1990): 17-26.

Howard, Lillie P. *Alice Walker and Zora Neale Hurston: The Common Bond*. Contributions in Afro-American and African Studies 163. Westport: Greenwood, 1993.

Hurston, Zora Neale. *Dust Tracks on a Road: An Autobiography.* 1942. Reprint, edited and introduced by Robert E. Hemenway. 2nd ed. Urbana: U of Illinois P, 1984.

———. "High John De Conquer." *American Mercury* 57 (October 1943): 450-58.

———. "Hoodoo in America." *American Folklore* 44 (October-December 1931): 317-417.

———. *Jonah's Gourd Vine.* 1934. Reprint, with a foreword by Rita Dove. New York: Harper, 1990.

———. *Mules and Men.* 1935. Reprint, comp. Cheryl A. Wall. *Zora Neale Hurston: Folklore, Memoirs, and Other Writings.* New York: Library of America, 1995. 1-267.

———. *Seraph on the Suwanee.* 1948. Reprint, with a Foreword by Hazel V. Carby. New York: Harper, 1991.

Iannone, Carol. "A Turning of the Critical Tide?" Rev. of *The Temple of My Familiar,* by Alice Walker. *Commentary* (November 1989): 57-59.

Jablon, Madelyn. "Rememory, Dream History, and Revision in Toni Morrison's *Beloved* and Alice Walker's *The Temple of My Familiar.*" *College Language Association Journal* 37, No. 2 (December 1993): 136-44.

Jackson, Kathy Dunn. "The Epistolary Text: A Voice of Affirmation and Liberation in *So Long a Letter* and *The Color Purple.*" *The Griot* 12, no. 2 (fall 1993): 13-20.

Jacobs, Harriet A. *Incidents in the Life of a Slave Girl.* Written by Herself. 1861. Reprint, edited and introduced by Jean Fagan Yellin. Cambridge: Harvard UP, 1987.

James, Stanlie M. "Mothering: A Possible Black Feminist Link to Social Transformation?" *Theorizing Black Feminisms: The Visionary Pragmatism of Black Women.* Eds. Stanlie M. James and Abena P.A. Busia. New York: Routledge, 1993. 44-53.

Jaynes, Gerald David. *Branches Without Roots: Genesis of the Black Working Class in the American South, 1862-1882.* New York: Oxford UP, 1986.

Jessee, Sharon. "'Tell me your earrings': Time and the Marvelous in Toni Morrison's *Beloved.*" Singh, Skerrett and Hogan, 198-211.

Jones, Kirland. "Folk Humor as Comic Relief in Hurston's *Jonah's Gourd Vine.*" *The Zora Neale Hurston Forum* 1, no. 1 (fall 1986): 26-31.

Jordan, Elaine. "'Not My People': Toni Morrison and Identity." *Black Women's Writing.* Wisker, 111-26.

Kapai, Leela. "Dominant Themes and Technique in Paule Marshall's Fiction." *College Language Association Journal* 16 (September 1972): 49-59.

Kardiner, Abram, M.D., and Lionel Ovesey, M.D. *The Mark of Oppression: Explorations in the Personality of the American Negro.* Cleveland: World Publishing, 1962.

Katrak, Ketu H. "Womanhood/Motherhood: Variations on a Theme in Selected Novels of Buchi Emecheta." *The Journal of Commonwealth Literature* 22, no. 1 (1987): 159-70.

Keizs, Marcia. "Themes and Style in the Works of Paule Marshall." *Negro American Literature Forum* 9 (fall 1975): 67, 71 *passim.*

Kemp, Yakini. "Romantic Love and the Individual in Novels by Mariama Bâ, Buchi Emecheta and Bessie Head." *Obsidian II: Black Literature in Review* 3, no. 3 (winter 1988): 1-16.

Kenyon, Olga. "Alice Walker and Buchi Emecheta Rewrite the Myth of Motherhood." *Forked Tongues? Comparing Twentieth Century British and American Literature.* Eds. Ann Massa, and Alistair Stead. London: Longman, 1994.

Killinger, John. *Hemingway and the Dead Gods: A Study in Existentialism.* Lexington: U of Kentucky P, 1960.

King, Adele. "The Personal and the Political in the Work of Mariama Bâ." *Studies in Twentieth Century Literature* 18, no. 2 (summer 1994): 177-88.

King, Bruce. *V.S. Naipaul.* New York: St. Martin's, 1993.

Klein, Reva. "No Grey Areas." *Times Educational Supplement,* 29 July 1994: 15.

Krist, Gary. "Other Voices, Other Rooms." *The Hudson Review* 45 (spring 1992): 141-48.

Kubitschek, Missy Dehn. *Toni Morrison.* Critical Companions to Popular Contemporary Writers. Ed. Kathleen Gregory Klein. Westport: Greenwood, 1998.

Lamming, George. *In the Castle of My Skin.* With an introduction by the author. New York: Schocken, 1983.

Leake, Katherine. "Morrison's *Beloved.*" *Explicator* 53, no. 2 (winter 1995): 120-23.

Lebesque, Morvan. *Portrait of Camus: An Illustrated Biography.* Trans. T.C. Sharman. New York: Herder and Herder, 1971. Originally published in French as *Camus par lui-même* (Paris: Editions du Seuil, 1963).

Lenz, Günter H., ed. *History and Tradition in Afro-American Culture.* Frankfurt: Campus Verlag, 1984.

Le Seur, Geta. "Janie as Sisyphus: Existential Heroism in *Their Eyes Were Watching God.*" *The Zora Neale Hurston Forum* 4, no. 2 (spring 1990): 33-40.

Levy, Andrew. "Telling *Beloved.*" *Texas Studies in Literature and Language* 33, no. 1 (spring 1991): 114-23.

Litvinskii, B.A. "Mirrors." *The Encyclopedia of Religion 9.* Ed. Mircea Eliade. New York: Macmillan, 1987.

Lowe, John. *Jump at the Sun: Zora Neale Hurston's Cosmic Comedy.* Urbana: U of Illinois P, 1994.

Marshall, Paule. *Brown Girl, Brownstones.* New York: Feminist Press, 1981.

———. *Daughters.* New York: Plume, 1992.

———. Interview by Kay Bonetti. Columbia, Mo.: Audio Prose Library, 1984.

———. Interview by Daryl Dance. *The Southern Review* 28, no. 1 (winter 1992): 1-20.

———. "A *MELUS* Interview" by Joyce Pettis. *MELUS* 17, no. 4 (winter 1991-92): 117-29.

———. *Praisesong for the Widow.* New York: Penguin, 1983.

———. "Talk as a Form of Action." Interview by Sabine Bröck. Ed. Gunter H. Lenz, 194-206.

Mason, Theodore O., Jr. "Alice Walker's *The Third Life of Grange Copeland:* The Dynamics of Enclosure." *Callaloo: A Journal of African American and African Arts and Letters* 12, no. 2 (spring 1989): 297-309.

Mathabane, Mark. *Kaffir Boy: The True Story of a Black Youth's Coming of Age in Apartheid South Africa.* New York: New American Library, 1986.

———. *Kaffir Boy in America.* New York: Macmillan, 1989.

Mathieson, Barbara Offutt. "Memory and Mother Love: Toni Morrison's Dyad." Singh, Skerrett, and Hogan, 212-32.

Matus, Jill. *Toni Morrison.* Contemporary World Writers. Ed. John Thieme. Manchester and New York: Manchester UP, 1998.

Mbalia, Doreatha Drummond. *Toni Morrison's Developing Class Consciousness.* Selinsgrove: Susquehanna UP, 1991.

Mbiti, John S. *African Religions and Philosophy.* New York: Doubleday, 1969.

McKay, Nellie Y., and Kathryn Earl, eds. *Approaches to Teaching the Novels of Toni Morrison.* New York: The Modern Language Association of America, 1997.

McKinney, Kitzie. "Memory, Voice, and Metaphor in the Works of Simone Schwarz-Bart." *Postcolonial Subjects: Francophone Women Writers.* Eds. Mary Jean Green *et al.* Minneapolis: U of Minnesota P, 1996.

―――. "Second Vision: Antillean Versions of the Quest in Two Novels by Simone Schwarz-Bart." *The French Review* 62, no. 4 (March 1989): 650-60.

―――. "Télumée's Miracle: The Language of the Other and the Composition of the Self in Simone Schwarz-Bart's *Pluie et vent sur Télumée Miracle." Modern Language Studies* 19, no. 4 (1989): 58-65.

Meisenhelder, Susan Edwards. *Hitting a Straight Lick with a Crooked Stick: Race and Gender in the Work of Zora Neale Hurston.* Tuscaloosa and London: U of Alabama P, 1999.

Memmi, Albert. *The Colonizer and the Colonized.* New York: Orion, 1965.

Meyer, Adam. "Memory and Identity for Black, White, and Jew in Paule Marshall's *The Chosen Place: The Timeless People." MELUS; The Journal of the Society for the Study of the Multi-Ethnic Literature of the United States* 20, no. 3 (fall 1995): 99-120.

Mezu, Rose U. "Buchi Emecheta: The Enslaved African Woman and the Creative Process." *The Zora Neale Hurston Forum* 8 (fall 1993): 61-85.

Miller, Adam David. "Women and Power, The Confounding of Gender, Race and Class." *The Black Scholar* 22, no. 4 (fall 1992): 48-51.

Moore, Wilbert E. *American Negro Slavery and Abolition: A Sociological Study.* New York: The Third Press, 1971.

Morrison, Toni. *Beloved.* New York: New American Library, 1987.

―――. *The Bluest Eye.* New York: Washington Square Press, 1970.

―――. Interview by Jane Bakerman. Taylor-Guthrie, 30-42.

―――. Interview by Kay Bonetti. Columbia, Mo.: American Audio Prose Library, 1983.

―――. Interview by Gail Caldwell. Taylor-Guthrie, 239-45.

―――. Interview by Marsha Darling. Taylor-Guthrie, 246-54.

―――. Interview by Thomas Le Clair. Taylor-Guthrie, 119-28.

―――. Interview by Amanda Smith. *Publishers Weekly* 21 August 1987: 50-51.

―――. Interview by Claudia Tate. Taylor-Guthrie, 156-70.

―――. *Jazz.* New York: Knopf, 1992.

―――. "The One Out of Sequence." Interview by Anne Koenen. Ed. Gunter H. Lenz, 207-21.

―――. *Paradise.* New York: Knopf, 1998.

―――. "Rootedness: The Ancestor as Foundation." Evans, 339-45.

―――. *Sula.* New York: New American Library, 1973.

Naipaul, V.S. *A House for Mr. Biswas.* New York: Penguin, 1961.

Nair, Supriya. "Melancholic Women: The Intellectual Hysteric(s) in *Nervous Conditions." Research in African Literatures* 26 (1995): 130-39.

Nigel, Thomas. "Alice Walker's Grange Copeland as a Trickster Figure." *Obsidian II: Black Literature in Review* 6, no. 1 (spring 1991): 60-72.

Nwachukwu-Agbada, J.O.J. "'One Wife Be For One Man': Mariama Bâ's Doctrine for Matrimony." *Modern Fiction Studies* 37, no. 3 (autumn 1991): 561-73.

Ojo-Ade, Femi. "Still a Victim? Mariama Bâ's *Une si Longue Lettre.*" *African Literature Today* 12 (1982): 71-87.

Olagun, Modupe O. "Irony and Schizophrenia in Bessie Head's *Maru.*" *Research in African Literatures* 25 (1994): 69-87.

Opie, Iona, and Moira Tatem, eds. *A Dictionary of Superstitions.* Oxford: Oxford UP, 1992.

Ormerod, Beverley. *An Introduction to the French Caribbean Novel.* Portsmouth: Heinemann, 1985.

Otten, Terry. *The Crime of Innocence in the Fiction of Toni Morrison.* Columbia: U of Missouri P, 1989.

Page, Philip. *Dangerous Freedom: Fusion and Fragmentation in Toni Morrison's Novels.* Jackson: UP of Mississippi, 1995.

Peters, Pearlie Mae Fisher. *The Assertive Woman in Zora Neale Hurston's Fiction, Folklore, and Drama.* Garland Series, ed. Graham Russell Hodges. New York: Garland, 1998.

Petersen, Carol. *Albert Camus.* Trans. Alexander Gode. New York: Frederick Ungar, 1969.

Peterson, Nancy J. "'Say make me, remake me': Toni Morrison and the Reconstruction of African-American History." *Toni Morrison: Critical and Theoretical Approaches.* Ed. Nancy J. Peterson. Baltimore: John Hopkins UP, 1997. 201-21.

Pettis, Joyce. "Legacies of Community and History in Paule Marshall's *Daughters.*" *Studies in the Literary Imagination* 25, no. 2 (fall 1993): 89-99.

————. "Talk as Defensive Artifice: Merle Kibona in *The Chosen Place, The Timeless People.*" *African American Review* 26 (spring 1992): 109-18.

Phillips, Maggi. "Engaging Dreams: Alternative Perspectives in Flora Nwapa, Buchi Emecheta, Ama Ata Aidoo, Bessie Head, and Tsitsi Dangarembga's Writing." *Research in African Literatures* 25, no. 4 (winter 1994): 89-103.

Pollard, Velma. "Cultural Connections in Paule Marshall's *Praisesong for the Widow.*" *World Literature Written in English* 25, no. 2 (1985): 285-98.

Porter, Abioseh Michael. *"Second Class Citizen:* The Point of Departure for Understanding Buchi Emecheta's Major Fiction." *International Fiction Review* 15, no. 2 (summer 1988): 123-29.

Powell, Betty Jane. "'Will the Parts Hold?': The Journey Toward a Coherent Self in *Beloved.*" *Colby Quarterly* 31, no. 2 (June 1995): 105-13.

Rahming, Melvin. "Towards a Caribbean Mythology: The Function of Africa in Paule Marshall's *The Chosen Place, The Timeless People.*" *Studies in the Literary Imagination* 26, no. 2 (fall 1993): 77-87.

Rainwater, Catherine, and William J. Scheick, eds. *Contemporary American Women Writers: Narrative Strategies.* Lexington: U of Kentucky P, 1985.

Rhys, Jean. *Wide Sargasso Sea.* New York: Norton, 1966.

Rich, Adrienne. *Of Woman Born: Motherhood as Experience and Institution.* New York: Norton, 1976.

Rigney, Barbara Hill. *Madness and Sexual Politics in the Feminist Novel: Studies in Brontë, Woolf, Lessing, and Atwood.* Madison: U of Wisconsin P, 1978.

————. "'A Story to Pass On': Ghosts and the Significance of History in Toni Morrison's *Beloved.*" Carpenter and Kolmar, 229-35.

Rodrigues, Eusebio L. "Experiencing Jazz." *Toni Morrison: Critical and Theoretical Approaches.* Ed. Nancy J. Peterson. Baltimore: John Hopkins UP, 1997. 245-66.

Rose, Jacqueline. "On the 'Universality' of Madness: Bessie Head's *A Question of Power.*" *Critical Inquiry* 20 (1994): 401-18.

Rueschmann, Eva. "Female Self-Definition and the African Community in Mariama Bâ's Epistolary Novel *So Long a Letter.*" Brown and Goozé, 3-18.

Sale, Roger. "Toni Morrison's *Beloved.*" Bloom, 165-70.

Samuels, Wilfred D., and Clenora Hudson-Weems. *Toni Morrison.* New York: Twayne, 1990.

Sartre, Jean-Paul. *Being and Nothingness: An Essay in Phenomenological Ontology.* Trans. Hazel E. Barnes. Secaucus: Philosophical Library, 1956.

————. "Childhood of a Leader." *Intimacy and Other Stories.* Trans. Lloyd Alexander. New York: New Directions, 1948.

————. *Existentialism and Humanism.* Translated and introduced by Philip Mairet. London: Methuen, 1948.

————. *Existential Psychoanalysis.* Trans. Hazel E. Barnes. New York: Philosophical Library, 1953.

————. *Nausea.* Trans. Lloyd Alexander. New York: New Directions, 1964. Originally published in French as *La Nausée* (Paris: Gallimard, 1938).

————. *No Exit and Three Other Plays.* Trans. Stuart Gilbert. New York: Knopf, 1948. Originally published as *Huis Clos* (Paris: Gallimard, 1945).

————. "Preface." *The Wretched of the Earth.* Trans. Constance Farrington. New York: Grove, 1967.

Sarvan, Charles Ponnuthurai. "Feminism and African Fiction: The Novels of Mariama Bâ." *Modern Fiction Studies* 34 (autumn 1988): 453-64.

Schapiro, Barbara. "The Bonds of Love and the Boundaries of Self in Toni Morrison's *Beloved." Contemporary Literature* 32, no. 2 (1991): 194-210.

Scharfmann, Ronnie. "Mirroring and Mothering in Simone Schwarz-Bart's *Pluie et vent sur Télumée Miracle* and Jean Rhys' *Wide Sargasso Sea." Yale French Studies* 62 (1981): 88-106.

Schmidt, Rita Terezinha. *"With My Sword in My Hand": The Politics of Race and Sex in the Fiction of Zora Neale Hurston.* Ph.D. diss., Univ. of Pittsburgh, 1983. Ann Arbor, MI: University Microfilms, 1988. 8411770

Schmudde, Carol. "The Haunting of 124." *African American Review* 26, no. 3 (fall 1992): 409-16.

Schwarz-Bart, Simone. *The Bridge of Beyond.* Trans. Barbara Bray. Oxford: Heinemann, 1974.

Segal, Carolyn Foster. "Morrison's *Beloved." Explicator* 51, no. 1 (fall 1992): 59-61.

Singh, Amritjit, Joseph T. Skerrett, Jr. and Robert E. Hogan. *Memory, Narrative, and Identity: New Essays in Ethnic American Literatures.* Boston: Northeastern UP, 1994.

Smith, Amanda. "Toni Morrison." *Publishers Weekly,* 21 August 1987: 50-51.

Smith-Wright, Geraldine. "In Spite of the Klan: Ghosts in the Fiction of Black Women Writers." *Haunting the House of Fiction: Feminist Perspectives on Ghost Stories by American Women.* Eds. Lynette Carpenter and Wendy K. Kolmar. Knoxville: U of Tennessee P, 1991.

Solberg, Rolf. "The Woman of Black Africa, Buchi Emecheta: The Woman's Voice in the New Nigerian Novel." *English Studies: A Journal of English Language and Literature* 64, no. 3 (June 1983): 247-62.

Speisman, Barbara. "Voodoo as Symbol in *Jonah's Gourd Vine." Zora in Florida.* Eds. Steve Glassman, and Kathryn Lee Seidel. Orlando: U of Central Florida P, 1991.

Staples, Robert. "The Dyad–Part II." *The Black Family.* Ed. Robert Staples. Belmont, CA: Wadsworth, 1971.

Staunton, Cheryl Wall. "Mariama Bâ: Pioneer Senegalese Woman Novelist." *College Language Association Journal* 37, no. 3 (1994): 328-35.

Stern, Alfred. *Sartre: His Philosophy and Existential Psychoanalysis.* 2nd rev. and enlarged ed. New York: Delacorte, 1967.

Stratton, Florence. "The Shallow Grave: Archetypes of Female Experience in African Fiction." *Emerging Perspectives on Buchi Emecheta.* Ed. Marie Umeh. Trenton: Africa World Press, 1996. Originally published in *Research in African Literatures* 19, no. 1 (summer 1988): 143-69.

Stringer, Susan. "Cultural Conflict in the Novels of Two African Writers, Mariama Bâ and Aminata Sow Fall." *SAGE: A Scholarly Journal on Black Women* (1988): 36-41.

Taiwo, Oladele. *Female Novelists of Modern Africa.* New York: St. Martin's, 1984.

Tate, Claudia. *Psychoanalysis and Black Novels: Desire and the Protocols of Race.* New York: Oxford UP, 1998.

Tate, J.O. "Smiley Face with Dreadlocks." Rev. of *The Temple of My Familiar,* by Alice Walker. *National Review,* 30 June 1989: 48, 50 *passim.*

Taylor-Guthrie, Danielle, ed. *Conversations with Toni Morrison.* Jackson: UP of Mississippi, 1994.

Thurer, Shari L. *The Myths of Motherhood: How Culture Reinvents the Good Mother.* Boston: Houghton, 1994.

Thurman, Judith. "A House Divided." Rev. of *Beloved,* by Toni Morrison. *The New Yorker,* 2 November 1987: 175-80.

Toffler, Alvin. *Future Shock.* New York: Random, 1970.

Topouzis, Daphne. "Women of Substance." *Africa Report,* (May-June 1988): 70-72.

Umeh, Marie. "African Women in Transition in the Novels of Buchi Emecheta." *Présence Africaine* 116 (1980): 190-99.

————. "A Comparative Study of the Idea of Motherhood in Two Third World Novels." *College Language Association Journal* 31, no. 1 (September 1987): 31-43.

————. *"The Joys of Motherhood:* Myth or Reality?" *Colby Library Quarterly* 18, no. 1 (March 1982): 39-46.

————, ed. *Emerging Perspectives on Buchi Emecheta.* Trenton: Africa World Press, 1996.

Uwakweh, Pauline Ada. "Debunking Patriarchy: The Liberational Quality of Voicing in Tsitsi Dangarembga's *Nervous Conditions." Research in African Literatures* 26 (1995): 75-84.

Vassa, Gustavus. *The Life of Olaudah Equiano.* Written by Himself. 1814. Reprinted in *The Classic Slave Narratives.* Ed. Henry Louis Gates, Jr. New York: Mentor, 1987. 1-182.

Walker, Alice. *Meridian.* New York: Washington Square P, 1976.

————. *In Search of Our Mothers' Gardens: Womanist Prose.* New York: Harcourt Brace Jovanovich, 1983.

————. *The Temple of My Familiar.* New York: Simon, 1989.

————. *The Third Life of Grange Copeland.* New York: Washington Square P, 1970.

Walker, Keith L. "Postscripts: Mariama Bâ, Epistolarity, Menopause, and Postcoloniality." *Postcolonial Subjects: Francophone Women Writers.* Eds. Mary Jean Green et al. Minneapolis: U of Minnesota P, 1996.

Wall, Cheryl A., ed. *Changing Our Own Words: Essays on Criticism, Theory, and Writing by Black Women.* New Brunswick: Rutgers UP, 1989.

————, comp. *Zora Neale Hurston: Folklore, Memoirs, and Other Writings.* New York: Library of America, 1995.

Washington, Mary Helen. "An Essay on Alice Walker." Gates and Appiah, 37-49.

Watts, Jill. *God, Harlem U.S.A.: The Father Divine Story.* Berkeley: U of California P, 1992.

Waxman, Barbara Frey. "Dancing out of Form, Dancing into Self: Genre and Metaphor in Marshall, Shange, and Walker." *MELUS* 19, no. 3 (fall 1994): 91-106.

————. "The Widow's Journey to Self and Roots: Aging and Society in Paule Marshall's *Praisesong for the Widow.*" *Frontiers* 9, no. 3 (1987): 94-99.

Weever de, Jacqueline. *Mythmaking and Metaphor in Black Women's Fiction.* New York: St. Martin's, 1991.

Weisbrot, Robert. *Father Divine and the Struggle for Racial Equality.* Urbana: U of Illinois P, 1983.

Wilentz, Gay Alden. *Binding Cultures: Black Women Writers in Africa and the Diaspora.* Bloomington: Indiana UP, 1992.

Williams, Eric. *History of the People of Trinidad and Tobago.* New York: Frederick A. Praeger, 1962.

Willis, Susan. "Alice Walker's Women." *New Orleans Review* 12, no. 1 (spring 1985): 33-41.

Wilson, Lucy. "Aging and Ageism in Paule Marshall's *Praisesong for the Widow* and Beryl Gilroy's *Frangipani House.*" *Journal of Caribbean Studies* 7, nos. 2-3 (winter 1989/spring 1990): 189-99.

Winchell, Donna Haisty. *Alice Walker.* Twayne's US Authors Series 596. New York: Twayne, 1992.

Wisker, Gina. "'Disremembered and Unaccounted For': Reading Toni Morrison's *Beloved* and Alice Walker's *The Temple of My Familiar.*" *Black Women's Writing.* Ed. Gina Wisker. New York: St. Martin's, 1993. 78-95.

Wolcott, James. "Party of Animals." Rev. of *The Temple of My Familiar,* by Alice Walker. *The New Republic* 29 (May 1989): 28-30.

Wright, Richard. "How 'Bigger' Was Born." In *Native Son*. New York: Harper, 1940. vii-xxxiv.

————. *Native Son*. New York: Harper, 1940.

Zimra, Clarisse. "Négritude in the Feminine Mode: The Case of Martinique and Guadeloupe." *Journal of Ethnic Studies* 12, no. 1 (spring 1984): 53-77.

INDEX